ROBERT W. GREGG is Dean of the School of International Service, the American University. At the time this book was in preparation he was Chairman of the Department of Political Science and Director of the International Relations Program, Maxwell School of Citizenship and Public Affairs, Syracuse University. He is editor of *International Organization in the Western Hemisphere*, coeditor of *The United Nations Systems and Its Functions*, and has contributed chapters to several books on international organizations.

CHARLES W. KEGLEY, JR., is an Assistant Professor of International Politics at the School of Foreign Service, Georgetown University. He has coedited *A Multi-Method Introduction to International Politics: Observation, Explanation, and Prescription*, and has contributed to the *Maxwell Review* and *World Affairs*.

AFTER VIETNAM

The Future of
American Foreign Policy

edited by
Robert W. Gregg
and
Charles W. Kegley, Jr.

Anchor Books
Doubleday & Company, Inc.
Garden City, New York
1971

Contents

Preface

This book had its origin in a symposium held in February of 1970 at the Maxwell Graduate School of Citizenship and Public Affairs, Syracuse University, on the topic of the future of American foreign policy after Vietnam. The symposium was one of several events which marked the occasion of Syracuse University's centennial year. It was sponsored jointly by five research and teaching programs of the Maxwell School: the International Relations Program, the South Asia Program, the Eastern African Studies Program, the Soviet and East European Studies Program, and the Program of Latin American Studies.

Six of the contributors to this volume,[1] all distinguished scholars in their respective fields of study in international politics and foreign policy, were invited to deliver original papers on aspects of American foreign policy in which they are recognized specialists. Four of these papers focused on American policy with respect to geographically defined regions in which the Maxwell School has area programs; two were devoted to the important issues and problems of post-Vietnam American policy in international relations broadly defined. The working assumption of the symposium was that these areas and issues had been, to one degree or another, overshadowed by the national preoccupation with Vietnam, and that the foreign policy of the United States with respect to these areas and issues was in need of a probing review. The

[1] Richard J. Barnet, Kenneth E. Boulding, Martin C. Needler, Richard L. Park, Marshall D. Shulman, Immanuel Wallerstein.

papers delivered at the symposium may be viewed as a call for such a review and a contribution to it.

In order that such a review of American foreign policy might be more balanced and comprehensive, the six symposium papers have been augmented in this volume with essays which address themselves in the same spirit of constructive criticism to other geographical and issue areas. Two of the additional essays were commissioned specifically for inclusion in this collection,[2] and were written by members of the Syracuse University faculty who had participated as panelists in the symposium. The other essays are recently published works of students of international politics,[3] each of which contributes a different perspective to the common theme.

By bringing together under one cover some of the most informed and provocative opinion about future American policy, the editors hope to provide the reader with an overview of some of the salient foreign policy issues which will confront the United States in the 1970s. Analysis of the future is a hazardous undertaking; even the most thoughtful of scholarship may be overtaken by events. The highly volatile situation in the Middle East is evidence of the thesis that today's diagnosis and prescription are vulnerable to tomorrow's headlines. A cease-fire between Israel and the UAR and Jordan was announced as these words were being written, and the commentary in this volume on the place of the Middle East in American foreign policy may appear to be out of focus when the book comes into print. Nor is this the only region in which events could make the scholar look less than prescient. But it is precisely this condition of ferment and uncertainty that compels our close attention to the future of American foreign policy and the global environment in which it must evolve. Errors of judgment may still be made, but a policy review which sheds new light in dark corners should

---

[2] William D. Coplin, Michael K. O'Leary.

[3] John S. Badeau, George W. Ball, Inis L. Claude, Jr., Richard A. Falk, Morton A. Kaplan, Leslie M. Lipson, Joseph S. Nye, Jr.; an article jointly authored by Max Singer and Aaron Wildavsky; and one written jointly by Graham T. Allison, Ernest R. May, and Adam Yarmolinsky.

reduce the number of errors and minimize the damage of those that are made.

Every book is dependent upon contributions by a number of people. This book is no exception. The editors would like to extend their special appreciation to Alan K. Campbell, Dean of the Maxwell School, for his support and encouragement of both the symposium and the book which emanates from it. They would also like to acknowledge the invaluable help in the preparation of the manuscript of Mrs. Juanita Hazell and Miss Gloria Andryszczyk. Finally, were it not for the deft pencil wielded by Mrs. Alice Trattner of Anchor Books, this would have been a considerably less polished volume.

Robert W. Gregg

Charles W. Kegley, Jr.

July, 1970

AFTER VIETNAM

The Future of American Foreign Policy

I An Introduction to Future Directions
in American Foreign Policy

ROBERT W. GREGG AND CHARLES W. KEGLEY, JR.

George Kennan, writing a number of years ago on the subject of United States foreign policy, questioned whether a democracy was

> . . . not uncomfortably similar to one of those prehistoric monsters with a body as long as this room and a brain the size of a pin: he lies there in his comfortable primeval mud and pays little attention to his environment; he is slow to wrath—in fact, you practically have to whack his tail off to make him aware that his interests are being disturbed; but, once he grasps this, he lays about him with such blind determination that he not only destroys his adversary but largely wrecks his native habitat. You wonder whether it would not have been wiser for him to have taken a little more interest in what was going on at an earlier date and to have seen whether he could not have prevented some of these situations from arising instead of proceeding from an undiscriminating indifference to a holy wrath equally undiscriminating.[1]

Twenty years later, there are those among the chroniclers and critics of contemporary American foreign policy who would contend that American actions in Vietnam dramatically illustrate the relevance and validity of Kennan's thesis. Many are convinced that American behavior is currently despoiling more than the environment external to the United States; un-

[1] George F. Kennan, *American Diplomacy 1900–1950* (New York: Mentor Books, 1951), p. 59.

like other periods of American awakening and involvement, the current one appears to have reached proportions which threaten to damage severely the nation within as well as the world without. The question today may thus be whether, in an age in which technology is expanding exponentially, a great power with a correspondingly great sense of mission and obligation can be tolerated by the states comprising the international system. To those states, the question of how the world is to be made safe for democracy may be of secondary importance to the question of how the world is to be made safe from democracy.

But these are apocalyptic thoughts. The Kennan thesis and some of its more popular contemporary corollaries deserve our attention because they provide a sobering frame of reference for the discussion of the very difficult but compelling question: After the war in Vietnam has ended, what will United States foreign policy be like? That general question, in turn, is made up of a whole series of more modest, more specific questions. But the shadow of Kennan's imagery rests upon all of these questions. It invests them with urgency.

The Vietnam experience is the catalytic agent that produced this volume. Vietnam has been an epochal event in the history of American foreign policy; it has generated a reassessment both of the conceptual foundations of that policy and of America's image of the world in which that policy has been based. It has forced the United States to re-evaluate its national priorities and to probe the probable consequences which any redefinition of the national interest would engender. It is the war in Vietnam, therefore, which has prompted the authors in this volume to address themselves to the prospects for a new orientation for the United States in world affairs.

Although the war in Vietnam serves as a point of departure for the analysis of the future course of American foreign policy, the concern of this volume is not with the war in Vietnam *per se*, its origins, its conduct, or when or how it will be concluded. These are all critically important subjects of inquiry and have properly received much attention. The question at issue here is not whether the United States should be castigated for its involvement in Southeast Asia, or whether American policy will be vindicated. Nor is it whether the withdrawal of the United States will be accomplished quickly or in years hence, or whether such a withdrawal should be regarded as triumph or sellout. Rather it is whether, in the midst of a divisive war, the end of which cannot be clearly foreseen, the future of American foreign policy can be charted or at least seriously considered.

Describing the future course of American foreign policy after Vietnam, before that war has been ended, is a hazardous undertaking. Indeed, one might question the wisdom of discussing the future of American foreign policy in a volume such as this until all the returns are in from Vietnam. None of the authors represented in this book has denied that American foreign policy will be inextricably linked to and affected by the Vietnam legacy and the lessons which are drawn from that experience. However, these essays are less an assessment of the immediate impact of the Vietnam conflict on future policy than they are a general evaluation of many diverse and interacting factors, including Vietnam, which will shape the contours of the world role of the United States in the years to come.

There are several reasons why such an approach is in order. The traumatic fact of Vietnam has hypnotized the United States; policy makers and public alike have been affected. It is as if the nation had a badly aching tooth, and all attention were focused on that one point of pain. Not only is it a matter of whether national policy is right or wrong, withdrawal too fast or too slow, and the costs extravagant or reasonable. It is also worthwhile to inquire whether the nation should get involved again under similar circumstances, and if so on what scale. Thus Vietnam not only colors current policy; it affects future policy as well. It has literally preempted attention, crowding other areas and other issues aside and shaping our image of those that do intrude. An obsessive concern with the Vietnam case may diminish our ability to assess the future accurately. Many are fearful that we shall not learn well enough the lessons of Vietnam. But it is just as conceivable that our fascination with the Vietnam experience may cause us to learn those lessons "too well," or to apply them inappropriately to situations where they are not relevant. Preoccupation with this particular involvement may encourage the development of an either/or attitude toward involvement in general.

The problem, therefore, is to disengage our minds from Vietnam, or at least a part of our minds. Our premise ought to be that the conclusion of that war or the prospect of its conclusion should generate a major rethinking of the foreign policy of the United States, not only with respect to Southeast Asia but also with respect to other issues and areas of the world which have heretofore been neglected during our "Vietnam period" or "interlude" or "fixation" or whatever it is that historians will label American policy in this troubled era.

To assert that American foreign policy has been obsessed with Vietnam and inattentive to other threads in the fabric of world politics is, of course, hyperbole. But if the assertion that Vietnam has driven all other areas and issues from the stage is a caricature of American policy and an affront to conscientious policy planners in Washington, then it might be recalled that good caricature often captures important truth. Fundamental review of major patterns of policy, foreign and domestic, is not as a rule conducted *in camera*, unattended by press and public. The changing of gears is usually noisy and the process open and frequently awkward, whether by design or otherwise. Some rumblings of review have been heard, but they have tended to emanate from the Vietnam war and collateral issues given shape by the war. There has simply been no comprehensive discussion of the future of American foreign policy.

Much attention has been devoted to the opportunity and even the necessity for a postwar reallocation of concern and resources to the domestic problems of city, race, education, pollution, and the like. Consensus as to particular policies may be elusive, but a review of priorities is widely acknowledged to be essential. This, it may be argued, is a prescription for the primacy of domestic over foreign politics. An equally strong case can be made for a review of priorities beyond the water's edge. It would be a tragedy if the legacy of Vietnam were a generation of mindless, reflexive isolationism or a wave of indifference to and rejection of the world beyond our shores. The alternative to neglect of foreign problems, or a ritual response to them, need not be a Hobson's choice between comprehensive interventionism and comprehensive isolationism. It can be, rather, a flexible policy, evolving from a thoughtful and searching review of those areas and issues of world politics which have been perforce neglected during our preoccupation with Saigon and Hanoi, pacification and Vietnamization, body counts, strategic hamlets, and domino theories. Such a policy would hopefully be rooted in a more profound understanding of those areas and issues, and not merely in conventional wisdom or time-honored but unexamined assumptions about what the world is like and how the United States ought to behave as a great power.

Although on the whole the essays in this volume look forward in hope, not backward in anger, it is difficult to discuss the future of American foreign policy without reference to some of the principal contours of recent American experiences with foreign policy. Even if the temptation to excoriate the Kennedy, Johnson, and Nixon administrations for the failures of their Southeast Asian policies is resisted on the ground that the future is more important than the past—if only because we may still be able to exercise some control over it —the past cannot be totally banished from our inquiry. It will be present in the form of national heritage and prevailing tradition, predisposing the nation and its officials to act in a manner consistent with socially sanctioned customs; it will be present as national style, unconsciously affecting the way we respond to events and to peoples beyond our shores; and it will be present as a legacy of commitments entered into, opportunities missed, and mistakes made. Hence inevitably the past, or at least our images of the past, will have a significant impact on how the United States behaves as a nation in the future. And therefore we must take cognizance of the past in discussing the future; we cannot escape it.

Moreover, from an analytic standpoint, it would be imprudent to ignore the immediate past in our desire to free the future from its paralyzing grip. We must study what has already happened if we are to discover what will happen, for it is only from history that we can extract some of the clues necessary to predict the probable conditions of the years ahead.

As George Savile (Lord Halifax) aptly phrased it, "The best qualification of a prophet is to have a good memory." And indeed, in their efforts to project and prescribe the future course of American foreign policy, the contributors to this volume have followed this advice, whether implicitly or explicitly. By looking at the past in order to foresee the future, they are asserting their acceptance of one of the methodological canons of social science expressed by Leibniz in the eighteenth century: "The present is big with the future, the future might be read in the past, the distant is expressed in the near."

It is possible to discern several trends in recent international politics, and more specifically in the foreign policy of the United States, which are salient for policy prescription and prognosis. The Vietnam "era" has stimulated the growth of these trends, all of which might conceivably be expected to persist and affect the nature of future policy. Thus the remainder of this essay will be devoted to brief commentary on some of these trends, hopefully clarifying the relationship of past, present, and future in American foreign policy.

If there are any real lessons to be derived from the Vietnam experience for policy makers in the United States, then surely one that is inescapable is that in the current international system the efficacy of military power as a bargaining tool is declining. Indeed, if Vietnam is to teach us anything, it should be the diminishing capacity of military means to shape the behavior of others. Vietnam has demonstrated in a vivid and deeply disturbing manner that superior firepower will no longer necessarily enable us to "get the other fellow to do what he would not otherwise do." Vietnam may have been the final test of the thesis that force yields influence; hereafter, American policy will have to be constructed in full consciousness of the inadequacies of military might in molding behavior. To attentive observers, Vietnam has dramatically illustrated the impracticality of seeking military solutions to political problems in the contemporary international system. Future American foreign policy will undoubtedly be affected by this fact.

A corollary lesson may be stated as follows: Military superiority or parity may no longer be safely regarded as a guarantee of security. It is one of the great paradoxes of the nuclear age that our development of such a vast destructive potential has rendered us less, rather than more, secure. Inasmuch as no increase in military capacity is likely to be sufficient to render us invulnerable, our escalating military build-up can only be judged by its effects on others; many responsible critics of American foreign policy subscribe to the view that military spending has tended to create incentives for reciprocal armament by our adversaries, to induce a psychological state of mutual fear and suspicion, and to increase the probability that those arms will ultimately be used. Thus some have contended that the continuation of the arms race is likely to produce results diametrically opposed to what was intended. If this proposition is valid, then it would seem to have crucial pertinence to future United States policy. It suggests that in the future security can be obtained only by preventing and resolving conflicts, not by winning them; that the possession of military power may be a liability and certainly has prudential limits; and that our safety may be diminished rather than enhanced by nuclear weapons. Whether in fact our nuclear capacity is inimical to our security interests is questionable, but for better or worse, those weapons will certainly affect the future course of American policy. Unfortunately we will not, as in the Vietnam situation, be able to afford the luxury of learning from experience the utility of those weapons. Miscalculation would be cataclysmic. Hence if it took as costly an event as Vietnam to demonstrate the inability of a great power to enforce its will on a small country, we should shudder at the costs we might have to pay to demonstrate the inability of arms to provide us with security.

Another trend which will have a bearing on the future course of American foreign policy is the apparent decline of ideology as a significant factor in international politics. The present age has been characterized by many as a transitional one in which "the end of ideology" is in sight. Polycentric tendencies within the Communist "bloc" and the decline of cohesion within the Atlantic alliance are symptoms of the decreasing extent to which ideology serves to explain international political behavior; indeed, today the Soviet Union may share more interests with the United States than with her ideological brother, China, and some would even argue that the furtherance of capitalist economies and democratic institutions throughout the world ranks low in the hierarchy of American goals if those goals are to be inferred from the actions of the United States in the world arena. Ideology thus appears to be an unreliable predictor of how nations will act in the latter third of the twentieth century.

However, it is evident that one of the paradoxical effects of American intervention in Vietnam has been to generate greater unity and solidarity within the "Communist camp," thereby stalling, although perhaps not reversing, the long-run tendency toward ideological fragmentation. Perceived belligerence from an habitual ideological enemy has caused the Communist states to moderate their differences and work more cooperatively for a common cause. Thus Vietnam has served to strengthen the Communist world rather than weaken it, and a bipolar world has thereby been perpetuated. What this suggests for American policy makers is that in the immediate future the United States will have to reckon with a Communist world that has been temporarily, if superficially, unified as a result of American actions, however much the long-term trend may point to the weakening of ideological commitments and bonds. The war in Vietnam has not only deferred "the end of ideology," it has obscured it. American preoccupation with Vietnam and the symbolism of that war has helped to perpetuate an ideological bias in this country's foreign policy posture and has simultaneously distracted attention from the permutations of the Sino-Soviet quarrel. The latter phenomenon, so fraught with danger for world peace, must be included prominently in any catalogue of trends in international politics that are to shape the future of American foreign policy.

Numerous other trends and conditions in the international system can be noted that will have a bearing on the United States and its future relationships with the rest of the world. Undoubtedly, for example, future American foreign policy will be affected by such systemic conditions as the growing gap between rich nations and poor, with the latter unable to make rapid or substantial gains in either absolute or relative terms; the unabated revolution in technology and its companion field, communication; the burgeoning world population, increasing at a rate which calls into question the future habitability of the planet; the dramatic increase in the number of international organizations, especially at the regional level and in the functionalist mold; the continuing transformation of alliance systems; the pervasive and volatile problem of racial animosity and confrontation in many forms and many places; the further growth of international trade and travel and the increasing permeability of national boundaries; and a host of others. The consequences of these developments are not easy to predict, but we can be certain that they will be dramatic.

If we recall Kennan's simile, above, we are prompted to consider not only the features of the international system within which the United States will have to operate in the future, but also those characteristics and conditions of the domestic system which will be instrumental in determining the nature of the American response to the world beyond its borders. It is clear that the war in Vietnam, probably the biggest "whack on the tail" that monster, the United States, ever received, will have wrought internal changes that affect both the kind of nation it is and the kind of foreign policy it is likely to pursue. Among the more vocal critics of the Vietnam experience, concern has been voiced for the effects of that war upon our democratic institutions at home. It is frequently observed that there is a tendency for foreign involvement to invite a concomitant restriction of civil liberties at home, particularly when such involvement is unpopular. Unfortunately, this proposition seems to be borne out by the facts in the Vietnam controversy. Dissent has frequently been equated with disloyalty, and patriotically motivated critics of the government's Vietnam policy have been accused of implicitly supporting the enemy. Thus current events seem to bear out Kennan's suggestion that democracies, when attempting to shape the destiny of others, have a proclivity to destroy themselves in the process.

In the long run, the Vietnam war has generated changes in our internal structure which may have an even greater and more direct bearing on the future of American foreign policy. It has been suggested that our involvement in Vietnam has encouraged the dominance of the military in our foreign and domestic policy making machinery; that it has enhanced the power and authority of the President in foreign affairs and accelerated the already considerable erosion of congressional prerogatives in that domain; and that it has led to the continued enlargement of a diffuse foreign policy bureaucracy whose growth has contributed to inertia and drift, and even to an ungovernable momentum in foreign policy making. These were trends already under way which Vietnam may merely have intensified. But it seems clear that they are likely to have a profound effect on the kind of foreign policy the United States pursues in the 1970s and beyond, and that their consequences are potentially even more serious than they have been to date.

Another domestic determinant of future American foreign policy will be the role of public opinion, although its impact is equally difficult to predict. Students of public opinion tell us that in recent years there has been a growth in that portion of the public that is attentive to foreign affairs, accompanied by a proportionate decrease in the number of people who remain apathetic to and uninformed about foreign policy. Vietnam and the domestic conflict it has generated have obviously stimulated this increased awareness. The war has also produced in the public a mood of skepticism of the government; the "credibility gap" and loss of faith in military opinions are symptomatic of this distrust. But more important for the immediate future has been the popular revolt against the Vietnam involvement and the reaction of the "silent majority" to that revolt. The result has been a division, even a polarization, of the public mood. What this portends is difficult to predict, but it does suggest that the coming period may be a volatile one for American foreign policy.

This brief survey of external and internal conditions and trends, certain to play some part in influencing the future course of American foreign policy, is intended to be suggestive rather than exhaustive. Some of the salient factors which could shape the posture of the United States in world affairs in the years ahead have been identified. Hopefully, they will provide a framework within which the more specifically oriented essays which follow may be placed.

The future is not easy to discern. Prognosis is a risky endeavor; astrologers are more at home with the future than social scientists, although it is the latter, not the former, whose advice and counsel we must seek. However, the difficulties inherent in charting the future of American foreign policy should not dissuade us from making the effort. It is the considered judgment of the authors whose essays appear in this volume that what is probable and what is desirable in the foreign policy of the United States after Vietnam may be and must be discussed intelligently now. While our contributors are all concerned with the future of American policy, they bring to that concern different specializations, different assumptions, and even different methodological persuasions. Although most of the authors draw on their knowledge and experience as experts in particular aspects of international relations to describe the *probable* future of American foreign policy, there is a normative quality to the essays as a whole.

The first pair of essays may properly be described as contributions to an overview of American foreign policy. William Coplin addresses himself to the hold which the folklore of power politics has upon the United States, and after analyzing the relationship between the Vietnam experience and the folklore, suggests that it may not, after all, be such a bad basis for American foreign policy. Richard Barnet discusses the future of "the American Empire," and in particular concerns himself with the future of the foreign policy bureaucracy which the war in Vietnam and a generation of containment policy have produced.

The next two essays are both concerned with a question that the war in Vietnam has brought so sharply into focus: When, if ever, should the United States intervene militarily? Graham Allison, Ernest May and Adam Yarmolinsky conclude their consideration of this crucial question by analyzing the case of Thailand, a country generally believed to be a leading candidate for precisely this kind of decision by Washington. Max Singer and Aaron Wildavsky undertake to develop a rationale for a policy of selective intervention according to what they term a "third-world averaging strategy."

Leslie Lipson's essay provides a useful introduction to an area by area preview of future American policy; he tours the globe and finds that the interests of the United States are vital in only three areas (not surprisingly, Southeast Asia is not one of them). The next essay, by Marshall Shulman, is of special importance because it concerns itself with the future of American-Soviet relations, and as such discusses issues that permeate all areas of the globe and influence all other American policies.

In the six essays that follow, the future of American relations with particular sections of the world is considered. Morton Kaplan looks at the future of the North Atlantic nations, Martin Needler at relations between the United States and Latin America, Richard Park at South Asia, Immanuel Wallerstein at Africa, and John Badeau and George Ball at the Middle East. By common consent, the Middle East is the most volatile region in the world today, and the one where the danger of a confrontation between the United States and the Soviet Union is most acute. This explains the inclusion of two essays on that area; moreover, the Badeau and Ball essays complement each other: The latter was written after the Soviet missile build-up in the UAR and reflects more urgency, whereas the former, more sanguine about Soviet intentions, speaks more comprehensively on the subject of a review of American policy in the region.

Following these area-oriented essays, Inis Claude and Joseph Nye address themselves to the future policy of the United States vis-à-vis the United Nations on the one hand and a variety of regional organizations on the other. These essays serve the dual purpose of reminding us of the alternative of multilateral approaches to persistent problems *and* of permitting us to revisit each of the several areas discussed earlier in the book through the vehicle of American relationships with such regional bodies as the European Common Market, the Organization of American States, and the Organization of African Unity.

The concluding essays are by Michael O'Leary, Kenneth Boulding and Richard Falk. The first of these analyzes the foreign-aid policy of the United States and is particularly concerned with the internal politics of foreign aid and the relationship between successful political leadership in domestic and foreign policy. The second focuses primarily on the internal situation, especially the American economy after the Vietnam war. It seems entirely appropriate, after surveying the future of American foreign policy, to return home and examine the impact of changed conditions upon the "war industry."

It might be noted that Southeast Asia has not been the subject of any essay in this anthology. It might be said with as much justification that it is the subject of all the essays. However, it seems appropriate to conclude the book with Richard Falk's summary statement of the lessons various American policy makers and influentials are drawing from the Vietnam experience, thereby bringing our readers full circle and focusing once more on the cause of all this malaise and self-scrutiny. For Vietnam, the Chinese giant that stands to the north, the alleged dominoes that stand to the south and west—they occur and recur as points of departure, as frames of reference, as object lessons, as counterpoints, as *idées fixes* in all that is written about the foreign policy of the United States. This book constructs scenarios for the future. But the inescapable fact is that Vietnam is the watershed which delineates past and future.

II The Folklore of Power Politics and American Foreign Policy in the 1970s

WILLIAM D. COPLIN

"Folklore" refers to traditional beliefs, preserved unreflectively among a people. Frequently the term is employed polemically to discredit ideas, to cast doubt upon their validity, to pin upon them the label "Myth". But the term may also be used in a more neutral fashion to identify a set of beliefs which orient persons, institutions, or societies to the world or environment in which they exist. It is the thesis of this essay that the American people and their leaders possess a set of assumptions about the world which may be characterized as the folklore of power politics. An attempt will be made to examine this folklore dispassionately, and in the process, hopefully to shed some light on its impact on future American foreign policy.

The folklore of power politics has to do with the set of views held by nation-states as they compete and cooperate in the international system. It is characterized by three basic assumptions. First, the state must be the absolute institutional value and its security the one immutable imperative for state action. If there is one thing that policy makers can always be certain of in the very uncertain world of international politics, it is that their actions must be designed to preserve their state. Second, the folklore of power politics implies that international politics is a struggle for power and that all states seek to increase their power. Although the forms of power have altered during the evolution of the state system, it has been generally thought that states are motivated by a drive for power, no matter what the stakes. The third basic assumption of the folklore of power politics is that the international system must be preserved in the face of threats of world-wide empire; hegemonial powers are to be resisted. Symbolized in the maxim "preserve the balance of power," this assumption is often accepted even by those states that threaten the system most.

While these three generic assumptions constitute the basis for the folklore of power politics and therefore provide an orientation for states in their foreign policies, the folklore also prescribes a number of more specific rules of state behavior: (1) Vigilance is always necessary if states are to safeguard their national security. (2) States should be moderate and flexible in their actions. (3) Ideology and other forms of absolute creed should not determine foreign policy actions. (4) States should always negotiate from strength, never from weakness. (5) International law is useful in regulating areas of agreement among states, but not where there is no coincidence of political wills. (6) The principle of the *quid pro quo* should underlie any international agreement. (7) A power vacuum will create instability. (8) Alliances are formed to counter threats to national security and increase or decrease in cohesiveness as a function of the intensity of the threat. (9) Great powers have worldwide interests and establish spheres of influence to protect those interests. (10) Powerful states have a special responsibility for preserving peace and stability in the international system. Although there are some inherent inconsistencies in these rules, they may all be derived from one or more of the three basic assumptions underlying the folklore of power politics.

This essay will attempt to assess the ways in which the folklore of power politics affects American foreign policy. After briefly discussing how the folklore became firmly entrenched as the basic orientation of American foreign policy and more particularly how it led to the involvement of the United States in Vietnam, we will turn to an analysis of the projected role of the folklore for American foreign policy in the 1970s. We will discuss the impact of the Vietnam war on the folklore and assess its implications for American foreign policy in the near future.

THE FOLKLORE OF POWER POLITICS FROM
CONTAINMENT TO VIETNAM

To understand the role of the folklore of power politics in
American foreign policy in the 1960s, it is necessary to go
back to the late 1940s. Following the Second World War,
American policy makers and public opinion leaders were convinced that something had to be done about the naiveté which
they were convinced had dominated American foreign policy
up to that time. Metaphors such as "ugly duckling" and "pre-
historic monster" (see the quote from George Kennan in
Chapter I) were employed in the general attack upon the
course of American foreign policy in the century. The Stim-
son Doctrine of nonrecognition and the Kellogg-Briand Pact
became, for the critics of American foreign policy, symbols
of how not to conduct foreign policy. Although the attack
continued throughout the 1950s and to a somewhat lesser
extent into the 1960s, it was in the late 1940s that the United
States was most consciously searching for a new orientation
to world politics.

The search ended with the discovery and implicit acceptance of the folklore of power politics. Many of the most influential Americans felt that the inadequacies of American
foreign policy in the past had been a product of the lack of
appreciation of the role of power in international politics.
Prior to World War II, the United States had failed to pursue
actively its security interests; had been immoderate and inflexible; had allowed absolutist ideals to dominate its actions;
had failed to be prepared militarily; had considered law to
be an adequate replacement for political action; had ignored
the role of self-interest in international agreements; had allowed power vacuums to develop; had looked at alliances
with disdain; had not recognized that it had worldwide interests; and had avoided its responsibilities in maintaining international peace and security. Even though one can argue, as
William Appleman Williams and others have argued, that the
failure of American foreign policy did not lie in ignoring the
realities of power, and in fact could be attributed to a preoc-

cupation with power, the climate of influential opinion after the Second World War bespoke an urgent need for a power politics orientation to foreign affairs.

The doctrine of containment represented the incorporation of the assumptions of power politics into American foreign policy. Although there was something of an ideological element in the doctrine, given its anti-Communist orientation, containment was as close an approximation of the power politics assumptions as could have been expected. It evoked concern for international peace and stability generally as the only path to national security. It counseled military and political strength simultaneously with the need for moderation and flexibility. It eschewed legalism and suggested that calculation of self-interest should be the basis for dealing with other states. Finally, it suggested that power vacuums in the system represented the greatest threats to international peace and security.

The behavior of the United States in the 1940s, '50s and '60s can most easily be interpreted as a product of the folklore of power politics. Although couched in the ideological rhetoric of fighting communism, the policy was not unlike that pursued by major *status quo* powers in other eras. The serious and intense concern for national security was matched by a mammoth commitment to an increase in military presence, then by alliance. The United States accepted the power politics guidelines with alacrity.

Even what might be considered departures from the folklore of power politics could be interpreted as variations on the theme. The most ostensible departure appeared to be John Foster Dulles' policy of massive retaliation because of its apparent lack of moderation and flexibility. However, the inflexibility in the rhetoric of massive retaliation could not hide the fact that Dulles could be extremely flexible, as in fact he was in Hungary, Suez, and Geneva.

Vietnam policy could also be viewed not as a departure from the folklore of power politics, but as a natural outgrowth of many of the assumptions inherent in the folklore. Indochina represented a power vacuum that would be vulnerable to expansionist powers. To preserve international peace and security, it was necessary to fill the power vacuum. In addition, for the United States to turn its back on Indochina would be a reversion to policies of the pre-World War II era, when the United States had turned its back on Europe. Two particular aspects associated with the folklore of power politics, however, played a crucial role in America's involvement in Vietnam.

The first was the problem of defining national security. Although the folklore of power politics places a great deal of emphasis on national security as an organizing concept in the formulation of foreign policy, it provides almost no guidelines for distinguishing security from nonsecurity interests. In the classical state system, the problem was not so serious because geographical proximity and the relative lack of international interdependence created a physical measure of national security. The further from one's border an event took place, the less importance that event assumed in terms of national security. However, in the contemporary world, physical proximity has become a less reliable measure of the degree of security interest associated with a set of events. The definition of national security appears to have become a more subjective exercise.

In the pre-World War II period, American foreign policy had clearly distinguished between security and non-security interests on the basis of geographical location. The Monroe Doctrine identified the Western Hemisphere as the arena of events affecting American national security while the rest of the world involved nonsecurity, although not necessarily unimportant, interests for the United States. However, part of the critique of American foreign policy before World War II had been that it failed to understand the worldwide scope of American security interests. Containment at the doctrinal level and the Berlin Blockade at the event level confirmed the lesson; the Monroe Doctrine became universalized and geographical restrictions were removed from the definition of what affected American national security.

This stretching of the national security concept was compatible with the folklore of power politics, but it probably would not have led to Vietnam if it had not been for a second important problem posed by the folklore, the need for a re-definition of the role of military force. By the middle 1950s it had become obvious that the use of unlimited force to win wars was no longer acceptable. Nuclear weapons had provided at least the United States and the Soviet Union with the capacity to create virtually unlimited and certainly unimaginable damage, even while going down in defeat. Dulles' response to this situation was to create a highly tense nuclear threat system, at least at the rhetorical level, but his critics argued that this was an inadequate military doctrine, for who would believe that rational policy makers in Washington would really commit nuclear suicide? The question of how to make the system credible and keep it that way was raised again and again.

Credibility thus tended to become a goal of foreign policy, rather than the merely instrumental objective it had been previously. The folklore had suggested that American credibility—that is, the willingness of the United States to use force —once raised became central. This preoccupation with credibility led American military doctrine, and ultimately the foreign policy orientation of the United States, away from Dulles and massive retaliation and toward a policy of graduated deterrence, all within the framework of the folklore of power politics.

Presidents Kennedy, Johnson, and Nixon have all attempted to tie the national security issue to Vietnam through the concern for credibility. Invocation of Munich (a historical demonstration—or is it myth—that failure of will increases the appetites of aggressors) and the domino theory (an analogy which implies that one's allies will collapse under the pressure of one's enemies if one's credibility is questioned) reveal the extent to which national security has been universalized geographically and expanded conceptually. They express symbolically the American commitment to meet aggression anywhere. To maintain credibility is to maintain everyone's territorial integrity. These are mutations of the folklore of power politics which are characteristic of the contemporary period. Vietnam was the natural product of this elasticity in the application of the folklore.

THE IMPACT OF VIETNAM ON THE FOLKLORE

There is no question that a large portion of influential American opinion considers the involvement of the United States in the Vietnam war to have been a failure. It is not so much the costs in human life and financial resources, although both are quite substantial for a symbolic enterprise, as it is an awareness across a large segment of influential American opinion that both the objectives and the conduct of the war have been colossal mistakes. Although the critics of the war—including President Nixon, who has himself implied on a number of occasions that involvement in the war was a mistake—have not agreed on where the mistake lies, the consensus on the failure of American foreign policy is as large and powerful as was the consensus on the need for a new approach to foreign policy following World War II.

If the origins of American acceptance of the folklore of power politics are instructive, we may conclude that when a large body of opinion feels that foreign policy has failed, basic attitudes and beliefs are liable to be changed. This suggests that we must confront the question of how the Vietnam experience will affect the relationship between the folklore of power politics and American foreign policy. We will do this by looking at the lessons which the influential public have drawn from the American involvement in Vietnam.

The majority of Americans who are likely to influence politics within the United States consider the Vietnam war to be a mistake resulting not from the folklore itself but rather from the faulty application of the folklore. Academics like Hans Morgenthau, the original academic spokesman for the folklore, and political figures like J. William Fulbright continue to affirm the basic ideas and assumptions of the folklore of power politics while bitterly criticizing American leaders for misapplying those ideas. Some critics have even alleged that Vietnam represents a return to the old idealistic, legalistic, moralistic, and naive approach which characterized the foreign policy of the United States in pre-power days. Blaming American leaders for ignoring the maxims of the folklore, these critics argue that Vietnam does not affect American security interests and that there is no need to prevent and/or counter aggression anywhere—in any form that it may occur. Nixon's Guam Doctrine seems merely to confirm the Morgenthau-Fulbright criticism.

A much smaller though quite vocal group of critics has drawn a radically different lesson from American involvement in Vietnam. This group, which encompasses revisionist historians of the Cold War and advocates of unilateral disarmament, sees Vietnam as only one in a series of excesses caused, in part at least, by the folklore of power politics itself. It is not only convinced that American policy has been inflexible, immoderate, and ideological in its obsession with the Communist challenge; it takes issue with virtually all of the assumptions of the folklore. Vigilance, it is argued, is a euphemism for paranoia. Strength in negotiation is seen not as prudent counsel but as an invitation to the development of counter-strength. Similarly, the admonition to fill power vacuums is viewed as a prescription for the clash of forces, the admonition to demand the *quid pro quo* in bargaining as a prescription for the clash of wills. In effect, the folklore of power politics, with its emphasis on the thesis that great powers have great interests and great responsibilities, is viewed by the radical critique as a blueprint for the escalation of conflict. The rallying cry of these critics seems to be "First of all, let's try peace." Often tied to criticisms of other facets of American society such as repression of dissidents, the radical critique seeks a genuine revolution in the minds of men.

This motivation clearly explains the behavior of the more extreme portion of the peace movement. A number of scholars have shown us that marches, demonstrations, and protests contribute to rather than detract from Nixon's political support throughout the nation. Moreover, there seems to be substantial evidence of a negative correlation between the length of a war and domestic support for it—domestic support diminishes over time. We might assume that in the case of a limited war in which the political leaders try not to generate too much moral fervor, the negative correlation would be even stronger. If the extreme wing of the peace movement were as concerned with ending the war as many of the moderates seem to be, their best strategy would presumably be to stay out of the streets. However, if their aim is to destroy a set of beliefs about the proper role of the United States in world affairs and to replace the folklore of power politics with a thoroughly new set of assumptions, then increasing the awareness of the American people of the Vietnam mistake through protests, demonstrations, and even violence are understandable strategies.

Beneath the rhetoric of the debate on Vietnam and cutting across different groups of opponents to the war, therefore, exists an increasingly tense dialogue between those who continue to accept the folklore of power politics and those who do not. Although the former are a clear majority, not only in terms of numbers but also of influence, the latter are not without support. Moreover, as the costs of the Vietnam enterprise continue to mount, we can assume that support for the radical critique of the folklore will not diminish and may in fact grow.

The defenders of the folklore have a number of factors on their side in addition to more and stronger political support. The most important is that men do not like to abandon their basic beliefs. The very concept of folklore implies the organic growth of a set of ideas, subject to constant shifts but relatively invulnerable to frontal assaults. Inertia alone will provide a certain amount of protection for the folklore. In addition, international events will continue to occur that will send most men scurrying back to a traditional reliance upon the folklore. For example, ever-present developments in the Middle East crisis that appear to be a permanent feature of the international system will continue to re-enforce those aspects of the folklore which assert the importance of military strength and the need to maintain a balance of power. Finally, the defenders of the folklore are aided by the lack of a serious alternative. While those opposed to the folklore have a large number of well-articulated criticisms, they have yet to settle on a set of symbols, assumptions, and attitudes that could orient the United States to a different role in world affairs, or, in effect, a new, workable folklore.

However, those who have attacked the folklore have something more than rhetoric and general disgust for the war on their side. They benefit from a generalized frustration, shared by persons of all persuasions, with the inability of the United

States to exercise a controlling influence in world affairs commensurate with its size, power, and wealth. They also benefit from what has been variously termed the "generation gap," the "youth revolution," the "revolt against authority," etc. A large number of highly educated youth have become thoroughly dissatisfied with many of the institutions and norms of American society; this disillusionment necessarily includes opposition to what the folklore stands for. Rejection of the folklore of power politics appears to be inherent in the rejection of many of the folkways and mores of American society. The success of those criticizing the role of the folklore of power politics in American foreign policy, therefore, might depend on a number of factors not directly related to questions of foreign affairs. Were a social revolution or even a political revolution to occur in the United States, peacefully or otherwise, it would probably change the basic orientations of American foreign policy.

However, barring social and political revolution and barring an increase in American involvement in Indochina and other trouble spots in Asia and Africa, it appears that the folklore of power politics will continue to shape American foreign policy throughout the 1970s. Vietnam has not convinced the majority of influential Americans that the folklore is inadequate; in fact, the Vietnam mistake has led many to an increased commitment to the folklore, albeit in a somewhat refined form.

AMERICAN FOREIGN POLICY IN THE 1970s:
A FLEXIBLE FOLKLORE OF POWER POLITICS

Given the folklore of power politics as the framework for American foreign policy in the 1970s, we should attempt to assess its implications for the United States and for the rest of the world. This task can best be performed by dealing with the following four questions that are suggested by the interrelationship between the folklore of power politics and American foreign policy: (1) Will the folklore lead to another Vietnam? (2) Will the folklore continue to create excessive economic and psychic costs? (3) Is the folklore really necessary, inasmuch as it appears to contribute to a highly competitive and tense international system? (4) Will the folklore prevent the cooperation among states necessary to meet the mutual social, economic, and political problems facing all nations throughout the world? Although other questions might be asked, these four seem to focus most clearly on the future role of power politics in American foreign policy.

(1) Will the folklore lead to another Vietnam?

It was argued earlier in this essay that the adaptation of the folklore to contemporary conditions in the international system has contributed greatly to American involvement in Vietnam. Although it is by no means impossible that this will happen again, certain developments among influential opinion leaders seem to suggest that it will not. Vietnam itself has already become a symbol, much as the appeasement in Munich has become a symbol, greatly affecting American behavior. Although meaning somewhat different things to different people, Vietnam carries at least two very clear meanings for the application of the folklore of power politics to American foreign policy in the future.

First, Vietnam has forced influential American opinion to realize that some geographical limitations must be placed on the national security concept. Implicitly, there has developed a general agreement that events in Africa and Asia do not directly affect American national security as much as events in Latin America and Europe. Although there continues to be active involvement in the Middle East and in the Far East, and although there remains a national security orientation to American activities in those two areas, Vietnam has driven home the fact that security interests have to be delimited geographically.

Secondly, there has been an increasing recognition among a wide spectrum of American opinion that involvement in internal subversive warfare is extremely costly. The blind faith that the Kennedy administration placed in the capability of the military to deal with guerrilla warfare has been replaced by a hardheaded realization that the cost-benefit ratio for involvement in internal war between incumbent regimes and insurgent guerrillas is extremely unbalanced. Moreover, no American political leader will ignore the domestic political costs of long-term limited warfare.

If Vietnam has compelled a refinement in the application of the national security concept to American interests and a reassessment of American military capabilities, it has not removed the danger of involvement in Vietnam-type situations entirely. By connecting the question of credibility to the Vietnam issue, American Presidents have succeeded in generalizing the country's security interests to a point where there is a risk that any defeat for the United States will be construed as damaging to American security. At a level of unimaginable paranoia, this might theoretically apply even to the willingness of the United States to accept a defeat within the United Nations on some type of anti-American resolution. Allowing the credibility question to be so generalized could have dire consequences for future American foreign policy, and there is nothing in the folklore of power politics to prevent its application to almost every situation.

However, on balance it appears that the Vietnam experience will lead to a refinement of the folklore of power politics sufficient to prevent one-sided intervention in indigenous civil war situations. Although there will always be the temptation to fill a power vacuum and to meet perceived aggression with strength, Vietnam appears to have driven home the point that one's national security is not directly affected by every change of government in the world or even by every transfer of sovereign authority.

(2) Will the folklore continue to create excessive economic and psychic costs?

The folklore of power politics places certain demands on American society in the form of a large commitment to military expenditures and a concern for national survival that can lead to high stress and anxiety. The question that must be faced is whether or not these demands need be as excessive as they have been through the 1950s and 1960s. The answer to the question requires the establishment of criteria by which to judge excessiveness. How responsible has the folklore been for the enormous military costs and anxiety-stress toll we have suffered through in the past twenty years?

From a long-range perspective, it appears that the folklore of power politics, with its emphasis on military strength and its assumption about the competitiveness of the state system, does generate a large demand for military expenditure and does stimulate high levels of tension. Military arms races are characteristic of the international system, as are real and imagined threats to national survival, and the folklore of power politics serves to symbolize and communicate both. However, if the folklore provides the framework for huge military expenses and preoccupation with national survival, it does not make excesses in either area inevitable. Power politics requires constant vigilance, not megalomania, military capability, not a gigantic military-industrial complex. The excesses that we have seen in the American response are encouraged but not predetermined by the folklore of power politics. They can probably be attributed to internal social, economic, and political factors, together with the folklore of power politics, rather than by the folklore itself.

An excessively large military establishment seems to have grown from the interlocking politics and economics of the military-industrial complex. The crosscutting social and economic links between the military and industry have generated a great deal of political power for those interests which would benefit from a large military establishment. But did not the folklore of power politics provide the opportunity for such political links to develop? Although the answer is affirmative, the point is neither more nor less telling than to argue that the need for a better road system in the United States has produced a Department of Transportation-road builder complex. The important point is whether or not the military establishment, now grown excessive, can be restrained within the frame of reference of the folklore of power politics. If the senators and congressmen who have been fighting military expenditures in the early years of the Nixon administration are representative, it would appear that reducing military expenditures is compatible with the folklore, since those legislators are also proponents of the folklore.

However, what of the psychic costs of the folklore? Is it necessary that roads, school buildings, space activities, and foreign aid programs be funded on the ground that they serve national security needs? Must the question of security be raised symbolically if not literally in thousands of governmental activities and political conditions?

Political leaders in the United States have learned in the post-World War II period that the folklore can provide a useful rationale for their programs. Taking the path of least resistance, they found that it was possible to build a coalition based upon support for social welfare and an activist foreign policy. Although the Democrats appear to have exploited the coalition most fully, the Republicans have not ignored it. Consequently, an obsessive concern for national security became the hallmark of American foreign policy and a political strategy for mobilizing a rather cumbersome political system.

In the case of both military and psychic excesses, therefore, the folklore of power politics has been facilitative; it has not been determinative. If these excesses are to be curbed, changes will have to take place within the socio-economic-political sphere of American society rather than within the realm of this country's orientation to the outside world. Whether such changes will in fact occur remains an open question.

(3) Is the folklore really necessary, inasmuch as it appears to contribute to a highly competitive and tense international system?

A number of writers have argued that the assumptions of power politics contribute to a world of highly competitive states and that this competitiveness endangers world peace. Since the United States is a major power, it is sometimes asserted that her adherence to the folklore contributes disproportionately to a highly insecure world. The problem with this assertion is that even if the United States were willing to reject the folklore of power politics, there is no evidence that other states would reject it. Indeed, recent history provides substantial evidence that the leaders of most states throughout the world subscribe as fully as has the United States to some version of the folklore of power politics. The Communist states approach international law and organization as if they were living in the nineteenth century, protecting themselves from supranational enemies. The developing states act as if nationalism were worth more than a healthy infusion of foreign capital. Even the states of Western Europe continue to play nationalistic games at the symbolic level, while moving gingerly toward certain highly limited forms of international cooperation.

Therefore, even if the United States were somehow to abandon its obsession for national security and its disposition to use force to protect what it perceives to be its national security interests, it is highly unlikely that the rest of the states of the world would follow suit. The United States would be acting as Woodrow Wilson is alleged to have acted at Versailles when he allowed the British, French, and Italians to rape Europe in return for an ambiguous commitment to an unborn international institution.

If the folklore of power politics contributes to a competitive and dangerous international system, it is submitted that the way to handle the situation is not to reject the folklore while the other states in the system continue to accept it. It would appear that the proper strategy is to attempt to operate within the folklore in order to ensure that global competitiveness does not lead to global conflagration. It is not an easy task, but it is one that has a much better chance of success than a strategy of playing the international hippie.

(4) Will the folklore prevent the cooperation among states necessary to meet the mutual social, economic, and political problems facing all nations throughout the world?

The following question has been frequently posed: How can a group of states, jealously guarding their own selfish interests, handle such mutual problems as economic stability, environmental pollution, conservation, and overpopulation? This question is based on the assumption that the folklore of power politics inhibits and may even prohibit the kind of cooperation among nations necessary to cope with these problems. Ultimately, it is based on the unproven proposition that a highly decentralized international system is inherently incapable of coping with such problems. Such a viewpoint is open to more rigorous questioning than it has received. One conspicuous exception to this proposition is the progress made in the post-World War II world in controlling extreme vacillations in domestic and international business cycles. The destructive cycles of the 1920s and 1930s have been replaced by the more moderate vibrations of the 1950s and 1960s. Building on the technical know-how of the economist, states have been able to cooperate sufficiently to have created a relatively stable international economic environment.

The tremendous growth of international institutions at both the governmental and nongovernmental levels is a significant response to mutually perceived problems across national borders. Although progress has been slow, the international record is not very much worse than the national record of many states in dealing with social, economic, political, and environmental problems. At least in terms of institutional growth, therefore, the folklore of power politics does not seem to be incompatible with the need to coordinate public policy more effectively at the international level.

A further point might be raised with respect to the ability of the international system, as pictured in the folklore, to cope with mutual problems. There is increasing evidence in the domestic realm that the highly centralized administration of public policy is not always efficient. The need to localize control over education and pollution, for example, is becoming increasingly apparent in some cases. If centralization is not always the key to effective public policy, it seems somewhat nearsighted to maintain that the international system must be more highly centralized to deal with contemporary problems. It just might be that an increasingly interdependent world is best administered through the decentralized political organization of the international system, provided that a forum for the coordination and rationalization of state policies at the international level can be maintained simultaneously within a system of competing states.

Finally, the folklore of power politics has not prevented meaningful international cooperation in Soviet-American relations since the Korean war. Within the context of the worldwide power struggle between these two giants, there have been many instances of cooperation along a wide spectrum of issue areas. From Antarctica and outer space to the Suez Crisis and the dispute between India and Pakistan over Kashmir, power politics has not prevented at least a modicum of cooperation.

In fact, one could argue that it is precisely because a general consensus exists on the folklore of power politics that states are able to cooperate in a large number of issues. If mutual distrust at the security level can be kept within symbolic and moderate limits, cooperation at other levels is not only possible but may also be facilitated. The reasons for this lie not only in the capacity of the human being to become involved in highly complex and ambivalent relationships but also in the nature of political systems within states. Domestic political groups that are prone to feed on distrust and fear of national survival are occupied with issues of national security, leaving more specialized interest and bureaucratic groups the flexibility necessary to handle transnational problems. One should not confuse the xenophobia and intransigence that frequently color the rhetoric of national security with the general capacity of the state as a political institution to cooperate effectively within the international system.

There seems to be some evidence, then, that the folklore of power politics does not prevent international cooperation and in fact allows it to exist across a wide variety of non-security issue areas. The danger of the national security issue overtaking the entire foreign policy of a state is real, but the history of the last twenty years indicates that it is remote. Whether more or less cooperation would result if the folklore of power politics were replaced by a folklore which avoids or minimizes the issue of national security is open to question, since such a folklore would presumably unleash many groups and vested interests that could then work more singlemindedly against joint international action. More importantly, it appears to be an irrelevant question, since the folklore of power politics seems to be here to stay.

CONCLUSION

Not only is it possible to explain past American foreign policy by examining the set of assumptions underlying it; it is also possible to project the future impact of those assumptions on American foreign policy. It has been the purpose of this essay to suggest that while it is natural for men to criticize ideas that have been around for a long time and have contributed to much of mankind's suffering, it is both inaccurate and unwise to blame the ideas alone. The folklore of power politics represents a loose set of guidelines through which states have oriented their behavior to the outside world. To blame that folklore for the mistakes of the past is to ignore the large role human failings and the pressures of domestic politics have played in those mistakes. To search for a radically different folklore may be the worst form of escapism, especially if it allows men to avoid accepting responsibility for what they do. The folklore of power politics provides a workable framework within which men can establish relations among states. Although the nature of those relations will necessarily be competitive in some areas, the folklore neither determines nor prevents the costly mistakes of the kind made in the past. It allows a substantial latitude within which the political leader may operate, assuming that the leader is capable of controlling himself and the interests around him.

This essay, then, has attempted to show that the folklore of power politics need not lead to international adventurism and domestic excesses. Nor should it prohibit the kind of concerted international action that will be necessary in the 1970s to meet common social, economic, and political problems. If we fail to avoid foreign policy mistakes and domestic turmoil on the one hand, or to cope with common international problems on the other, the explanation for that failure will not lie in the fact that men have a set of archaic, atavistic, and irrelevant beliefs. Rather, it will be attributable to the weakness of political leaders who do not appreciate the symbolic nature of the folklore and the need for constraint and moderation, as well as to the failure of their followers to accept the costs of the folklore and the burdens of patience that an imperfect world places on the human drive for success.

III   The Security of Empire

RICHARD J. BARNET

It is safe to say that there is no one in the United States who is *for* the Vietnam war. Even those who demand "victory" admit that they are seeking the vindication of an error: "We never should have gone in, but now that we're there, let's really give it to them." According to the authoritative analysis of public opinion polls published in *Scientific American,* a majority of Americans want to get out of Vietnam and support the President only on the assumption that that is what he is doing. Most of the officials of the Johnson administration responsible for the major escalations of the conflict now concede that the costs far outweigh any benefits—benefits gained from postponing the day of reckoning when the United States must admit to the world that it cannot achieve its goal of maintaining an independent non-Communist South Vietnam close to the periphery of China.

The Vietnam commitment has been rejected because it did not work. Whether there will be more Vietnams depends critically upon the analysis of that failure. Although the war is far from over, the "lessons" of Vietnam are filling volumes. The whole direction of American foreign policy for the next generation will depend upon which lessons are accepted as the new orthodoxy.

The untroubled advocates of mass bombardment believe that the Vietnam catastrophe is the product of a failure of will, a sentimental unwillingness to kill enough people fast enough. For Hanson Baldwin, for example, the lesson of Vietnam is that "We must learn to fight limited wars without limiting our power so greatly that we exhaust ourselves and defeat our objective." For the disappointed military, the decision not to "close" the port of Haiphong may well achieve the status of a "stab in the back" myth despite the fact that, as Townsend Hoopes has shown, photographic evidence obtained by United States Intelligence indicated that the port was not crucial to the supply of the Vietcong.

More sophisticated critics of the Vietnam war can be found in the Counterinsurgency Division of the Joint Chiefs of Staff. They favor a liquidation of the Vietnam war on the best available terms, recognizing that they are none too good; but they reject neither the analysis of the world that brought 600,000 troops to Vietnam in the first place nor the essential contours of the strategy under which they fought there. Interviews with such officers conducted by members of the Institute for Policy Studies revealed that the Vietnam failure has been effectively rationalized in that bureaucracy as an accident of history and geography. Thailand is quite another matter; unlike South Vietnam, neither the country nor the government was invented by the United States. "The historical circumstances of Thailand," one officer explained, "make it a good bet. It has experienced centuries of stable governments, has religious and social cohesion, has a secure economic base, and is included under treaty arrangements with the United States." The Philippines, too, are a good place to try counterinsurgency warfare because "the country is surrounded by water, so it would be impossible for an insurgent movement to receive outside aid."

Some of the civilian managers who lived through the escalation of the Vietnam war have had a somewhat more radical learning experience. They question the old Cold War myths about "monolithic communism". They appear to have learned that the Soviet Union is not engaged in an ideological crusade but is developing into an impressive, though still moderately cautious, imperial power. For some this belated discovery is unaccountably a source of comfort. From this new perspective they conclude that one need not intervene everywhere—some dominoes are more important than others. A war with guerrillas in, say, Thailand need not necessarily be equated with a war with the Soviet Union or China. There is a greater willingness to accept the existence of local politics and local issues and less readiness to see the Kremlin's hand in every revolutionary movement. This analysis leads to injunctions of caution to avoid "overcommitments" and at the same time some agonizing self-doubt about "neo-isolationism." The advocates of a policy of more careful interventionism appear to assume that Lyndon Johnson intended to send 600,000 troops into a quagmire, divide his country, and slink out of office. They may be unaware that two years earlier, according to a high official who was present, when the chairman of the Joint Chiefs of Staff told President Johnson that we would need 700,000 troops for five years more, the President rose from his chair, told the general he must be crazy, and walked out of the room. The officials who made the crucial Vietnam decisions trapped each other and in some cases trapped themselves. Is there any reason to believe that the admonition not to get trapped again is an adequate guide to policy?

The official lessons of the war are revealed in President Nixon's foreign policy statement for the 1970s in which he attempts to apply the principles of Vietnamization on a global scale. The Nixon defense budget gives a more concrete expression of these ideas. The United States will "lower its profile" by encouraging "indigenous" troops to fight each other with American weapons or where possible by resorting to automated war through the technology of the "electronic battlefield." The point of the Nixon policy statement is to show how the original objectives of American foreign policy can be achieved at lower cost and lower risk. According to the Nixon analysis of the American dilemma in foreign policy, which has been repeatedly revealed in presidential statements on Vietnam itself, the problem is how to maintain present American commitments through military power without involving the American people in an interminable, ambiguous war in which large numbers of Americans continue to get killed week after week. President Nixon has made one thing very clear: He does not intend to preside over liquidation of the system of military pacts, commitments, and bases the United States has developed around the world, nor does he intend to redefine the standard Cold War concept of the American national interest. Unless the United States is able to work its will where it chooses through the adroit management of its military power, the nation will be revealed as a "pitiful helpless giant."

The "Nixon Doctrine" is really an exercise in nostalgia. It is a throwback to the calmer days of the Eisenhower era when John Foster Dulles suggested that we "let Asians fight Asians" and "back them up" with nuclear weapons. The effect of the Nixon Doctrine, if it is taken seriously, is to increase the reliance on nuclear weapons around the world, for if military costs and large scale troop deployments are to be cut while foreign policy commitments and objectives remain the same, there is no alternative but to make the nuclear threat more credible to all potential enemies. There is increasing evidence that in NATO planning nuclear weapons are coming to play a more important role. The Nixon administration's interest in the technology of the "electronic battlefield," in which a few skilled technicians at a comfortable distance from the hostilities play out the game of war, is another attempt to keep down the financial and human cost of a policy of permanent military involvement. The increased reliance on non-Americans to do the fighting reflects the political judgment of the Administration that the American people want the fruits of military success but are not willing to pay for it with the lives of their sons. After more than 50,000 have died in Vietnam it has finally become irrelevant that many more have died on the nation's highways.

These lessons share certain characteristics. They all deal with issues of technique and management and do not touch fundamental questions of national interest or foreign policy objective. They assume that the role the United States has defined for itself in the last generation is correct, that the analysis of the Cold War is sound, and that whatever changes are needed are primarily matters of style. We should continue to do what we have been doing, but without quite so much zeal and with greater selectivity.

But it is impossible to act judiciously or to avoid more mistakes if the intellectual framework within which objectives are defined and policies pursued is itself wrong. If the Vietnam catastrophe is not seen as a symptom of a far more fundamental disorder of American foreign policy, it is doomed to be repeated. A straw in the wind was the Cambodian invasion which violated most of the cautious precepts of the "Nixon Doctrine" a scant three months after it was published. A serious re-examination of American foreign policy must start with some basic questions about who we are and what we are doing in the world.

Critical introspection that avoids the twin dangers of self-deception and self-hatred is an incredibly difficult process for human beings as individuals. For organizations it is harder still, and for nations it may be impossible. But the road to true security will be blocked for Americans until we come to see that this nation—rather than the problem solver of the world—is itself a major problem of world order. Indeed, the role the United States has chosen to play makes it the world's most dangerous nation. This does not mean that other nations are necessarily more peace-loving or morally superior to the United States or that they might not have used their power in similar destructive ways had they fallen into the same historical circumstances. It is an ironic accident of history that the concentration of power and riches that have come our way now poses our greatest national problem. The United States had the misfortune to reach its imperial heights after the age of empires had passed.

By any historical definition the United States is a global empire. The United States is the only country in the world whose soldiers are on every continent. The United States is the only country in the world that stations thousands of nuclear weapons around the world, far from its shores. The United States is the only country that regularly flies aircraft on hostile missions over countries like China and Cuba with which we are not at war. The United States is the only country that reserves the right to drop more than a megaton of bombs in a year on an ally like South Vietnam. The United States is unique in its abilities to manipulate the internal politics of other countries through a variety of techniques ranging from advertising to assassination. The jurisdiction of American law and the protection of American power have a sweep that exceeds most of the empires of the past. In addition to the millions of square miles that have been annexed by the United

States in the past century, the American government exercises reasonably effective control over much vaster territories as a result of the financial dependence of other governments and their reliance upon our military aid to protect them from foreign attack and domestic revolution. American citizens own more than $100 billion in foreign assets. Each year they consume two thirds of the world's oil, more than half the world's copper and rubber—in short about 60 per cent of all the world's consumable resources.

These facts used to be cause for uncritical self-congratulation. We basked in our power, unaware that the objectives, the techniques, and even the rhetoric fell into an imperial tradition. A few American statesmen and State Department bureaucrats self-consciously adopted the imperial role. Writing about the American intervention in Greece in 1947, a State Department official could scarcely conceal the personal excitement of being a minor Disraeli. "Great Britain had within the hour handed the job of world leadership, with all its burdens and all its glory to the United States." That rhetoric was to recur many times and was included in more than one presidential inaugural. But the official stance was to deny that we were an empire even while we were exulting in our imperial power. Former Ambassador Charles Bohlen, writing in 1969, concluded with a typically generous judgment of our national motives: "We had no sinister design, no hidden purpose, certainly no imperialist ambitions. Our policy was not dictated by an American material need and certainly not in response to any American ambition." The United States could not be imperialist since we gave back the Philippines and had an aid program. Moreover, we did not drop the atomic bomb on the Soviet Union when we had a nuclear monopoly. Although the proposition is unprovable, the decision not to follow the vocal proponents of "preventive war" in the military establishment in the early postwar years is thought to be a unique act of self-restraint and an unparalleled example of civic virtue. "Burdens" and "responsibilities," according to the official view of recent history, were continually being "thrust" upon us. It was never very clear in many cases who was doing the thrusting. In others, such as Greece and Vietnam, it was a matter of self-propulsion.

Through aimless altruism the United States continued to grow richer and more powerful, thus proving beyond all doubt that God was for free enterprise.

In recent years the United States has become more outspoken in claiming the right to determine whether a conflict anywhere in the world constitutes a threat to its national security or international order and what should be done about it. In the Johnson administration there was increasingly less reticence about proclaiming the "national interest" as the guide to policy, and apologists for American foreign policy began to talk about the United States as an empire. Only those states "with enough will and enough resources to see to it that others do not violate" the rules of international law, Secretary of State Rusk declared, are the ones to be entrusted with enforcing the peace. When he was Undersecretary of State, George Ball suggested that such responsibility "may in today's world be possible . . . only for nations such as the United States which command resources on a scale adequate to the requirements of leadership in the twentieth century." In other words, power is the basis of legitimacy. There is nothing exceptional about powerful countries asserting the imperial prerogative of using force and coercion on the territory of another without its consent. The Athenian Empire minced no words about this. "The strong do what they can and the weak do what they must," the Athenian general reminded the Melians. Empire is its own justification, the fifteenth-century Italian humanist Lorenzo Valla advised his prince. The expansion of a nation's power comes through "mere violence," but this should not dismay a conscientious leader, his contemporary Poggio Bracciolini observed, for has it not always been "the most powerful empires, such as Athens, which promoted letters and learning?" Most empires have claimed the right to control the politics of other peoples in the name of a great idea. Athens offered protection and civilization, Rome the blessings of the law, Britain enlightenment of savages, and so on.

There are modern defenders of American imperialism who resemble disappointed lovers. Through the pain of Vietnam they have discovered that the rulers of America, despite Boy Scout rhetoric, have been men of average principles and in-

telligence with standard ambitions and prejudices who, by
having at their disposal more military and economic might
than any collection of rulers in history, have been in a position
to do more damage than most. Having made this discovery,
they fear, as Pericles once did, that it is too late for America
to play "the peace lover and the honest man." The fate of
empires is to be feared and hated. Once imperial responsibilities are acquired, it is not safe to let them go. There is no
middle way. Either the United States must be feared throughout the world—that is the meaning of the euphemism "credibility"—or we will end up a pitiful helpless giant. There is
profound self-contempt and despair reflected in this view of
the world. The United States lacks the resources, the skills,
and the imagination to find a national identity other than
Top Dog or Loser. There is no room in the world for America
except as a steadily expanding power. There is no security
except as an empire.

Most Americans, however, do not feel comfortable thinking of themselves as imperialists. There is a long tradition of
anti-colonialism. There have been anti-imperialist movements
in American history, although not in the postwar era. It was
not until the Vietnam war that the foreign policy consensus
of a generation fell apart. Because suspicion of militarism
and belief in democratic idealism has always coexisted in
America, along with the weakness for the heroic ethic and
the rampant chauvinism characteristic of all big nations,
American policy makers have ingeniously constructed a system of absolution within which to pursue an imperialist policy
with easy conscience. The system of absolution is more than
rhetorical camouflage. All nations including Nazi Germany
are invariably "peace-loving" according to their own official
documents. Hitler talked about the Jews as a "threat" whose
evil justified their extermination, but we know from his re-
corded private conversations that he recognized his own words
as propaganda.

For American policy makers the system of absolution is a
fundamental way of looking at the world. It is a set of deeply
held beliefs that enable men to rationalize the will to dominate, and in turn to destroy what they cannot dominate. These
beliefs are taken very seriously and are a part of the con-

sciousness of a generation. They color every official act and the public explanation of every official act taken in the name of the United States.

The system of absolution rests on the assumption of an identity of interests. There is no conflict between the "national interest" of the United States as it is defined by those in power at any given moment and the legitimate security interests of mankind. What is good for the United States is by definition good for the "forces of freedom," the "free world," or the decent people of the planet. Whoever opposes the will of the United States is by definition dangerous or subversive. The United States—the exceptional nation—apparently stands above the international system, not within it. She is the setter of standards, the bearer of the law, and the judge of ends and means. Therefore, when she destroys other countries like Vietnam, she is saving them from a fate considered worse than death.

A system of absolution makes it possible to explain away the suffering and hatred a policy may cause by noting that despite its tragic cost the policy eventually will bring the greatest good to the greatest number. That is one reason it is termed "pragmatic." A victory in Vietnam, even if purchased at the cost of millions of lives of Vietnamese, is defended by asserting that it will prevent World War III or a future pitched battle in San Francisco.

In the system of absolution within which American policy makers operate it is heresy to point out that there may be real conflicts of interest between the people who live in the United States and inhabitants of the rest of the world. It is possible to talk about conflicts which are invented or exploited by the forces of international communism to harass us, but it is rarely possible to talk about conflicts which inhere in the nature of the international system and in the present pattern of distribution of resources on the planet. Sometimes in flashes of candor the existence of the obvious conflict of interest between people who inhabit the richest country in the world and consume most of its resources and people who make less than $100 a year is noted. When he talked to the troops in Vietnam, Lyndon Johnson voiced some of the elemental fears Americans seldom dare express: "There are 3 billion people in the world and we have only 200 million of them. If might did make right, they would sweep over the United States and take what we have. We have what they want." According to official ideology, the claims on resources by the poor of the world are not legitimate. Their poverty is a consequence of their bad luck, laziness, racial inferiority, or some combination of all of them. There is only one way for them to make progress, and that is by accepting the American definition of "development" and how to achieve it. The fact that the American theory of promoting "stability" and "growth" through limited capital grants and loans, private investment, and military aid has done nothing to prevent the widening of the gap between the rich and the poor is not permitted to disturb the theory.

Thus when Secretary of State James Byrnes stated shortly after World War II that the goal of American foreign policy was to make the world safe for the United States, he undoubtedly considered his slogan an almost altruistic formulation, for it rested on the assumption that in such a world everybody else, except for the troublemakers, would be safe and happy too. But the meaning of a "world safe for the United States" has been interpreted so broadly by a generation of American leaders as to be almost indistinguishable from a world run by the United States.

What has the United States meant by a "safe" world? First, we have meant the physical protection of the United States. The fundamental fact of the nuclear age is that no government, however powerful, can defend its people. There is no physical defense against nuclear weapons adequate to *prevent* an attacker from destroying American society if he is prepared to risk destruction himself. That being so, American military planners have sought safety by continually raising the level of threat and intimidation to *deter* attack. American security has also been thought to depend on presenting a believable possibility that the United States might be the first to use nuclear weapons to protect some political or economic interest considered "vital." To convey the psychological impact of our overwhelming power to friend and foe alike the United States maintains a worldwide military apparatus which, in traditional strategic terms, is as obsolete as the Maginot

Line. The Air Force maintains a string of bases around the world acquired in the days before transcontinental jets and rockets, which do not make the territory of the United States any less vulnerable. The Navy keeps a vast fleet afloat in the belief, as self-serving as it is implausible, that the next war will be like the last one. Forces deployed overseas cannot protect the American poeple from nuclear attack, and no other kind of attack on the United States is likely. Even the highly imaginative contingency planners in the Pentagon have difficulty envisaging a land or amphibious invasion of the United States.

Overseas forces are maintained at a cost of more than $50 billion a year partly because of the pressures of the military bureaucracies themselves and partly because of a general strategic notion shared by the top civilian leadership that a "show of force" around the world and a "military presence" in areas of tension can be translated into American political power. The Vietnam war is an example of the limitations of this theory. After spending more than $200,000,000,000 and more than 40,000 lives, the United States is not able to turn its capacity for doing violence into effective political power over what it considers to be a primitive society. America can destroy Vietnam but it cannot shape it to its will. But at the same time, in other areas of the world, the presence of American forces does have the effect of inhibiting the forces of revolutionary change.

The counterrevolutionary impulse has been a cornerstone of American policy since the end of the Second World War. On an average of once every eighteen months the United States has sent its military or para-military forces into other countries either to crush a local revolution or to arrange a coup against a government which failed to acquire the State Department seal of approval.

Why has this been thought necessary to make the world safe for the United States? There have been essentially two theories about the connection between indigenous revolutionary change and American security. In the early days of the Cold War it was assumed that any Communist revolutionary was a Kremlin agent. Ho Chi Minh's independence movement, Ambassador William C. Bullitt explained in 1947, was designed to "add another finger to the hand that Stalin is closing around China." Mao Tse-tung was on a short tether from Moscow, according to Dean Rusk in a speech made two years after the Chinese revolution. Mao's regime was "a colonial Russian government."

It is now accepted by almost everybody that communism is no longer "monolithic." Of course it never was in the Rusk-Bullitt sense; far from being planned and initiated by the Soviet Union, the revolutionary movements in China, Indochina, Greece, Cuba, and many other places were often opposed and discouraged by the Kremlin as embarrassments to the diplomatic relationships the Soviet Union was pursuing as a Great Power. The Soviet Union has barely disguised its reluctance at being sucked into the Vietnam war to counter the American intervention. For years after the Geneva settlement of 1954 the Soviet Union acquiesced in the maintenance of a United States protected anti-Communist South Vietnam which was contrary to the spirit of the settlement. The Soviets proposed the admission of South Vietnam as a separate member of the United Nations as late as 1960.

As long as the myth of "indirect aggression"—the transformation of local revolutions into Soviet invasions by a Trojan horse—was credible, a counterrevolutionary policy could be defended as the traditional balance of power politics. Every revolution was part of a pattern of world conquest emanating from a rival center of power. Thus the situation was sufficiently similar to Hitler's expansionism to justify a similar military response.

It is true that the Soviet Union sought to dominate every nation into which its troops marched in the Second World War and to establish subservient "revolutionary" governments. But every revolutionary government that has come to power without the Red Army has turned out to be ambivalent, cool, or even hostile to the Soviet Union—Yugoslavia, Albania, North Vietnam, China, and Cuba. In each case the relationship is complex, but in none of them can it be said that the existence of the Communist regime clearly adds to the power of the Soviet Union.

The second theory about the relationship between internal change in other countries and the security of the United

States concerns the impact of such changes on the American economic system. A world safe for the United States, according to American strategists, requires more than physical safety and the containment of potential Great Power rivals. It is a world safe for capitalism, and since an essential idea of modern capitalism is growth, it is also a world in which the opportunity for economic expansion is not foreclosed.

The rise of socialist revolutionary regimes, particularly in the newly independent nations of Asia and Africa and in Latin America, is seen as threatening for several reasons. First, American prosperity is dependent upon maintaining trade under the favorable conditions which the commanding position of the United States in the world economy now makes possible. During the Second World War, American planners such as William L. Clayton argued that the only alternative to the expansion of foreign trade was "to turn our country into an armed camp, police the seven seas, tighten our belts, and live by ration books for the next century or so." In testifying for free trade before Congress, Dean Acheson spoke in a similar vein. Unless the United States was free to expand foreign markets, he warned, that would "completely change our Constitution, our relations to property, human liberty, our very conception of law." According to a 1940 *Fortune* magazine poll, postwar planners thought the crucial question was how "to organize the economic resources of the world so as to make possible a return to the system of free enterprise in every country." The belief has persisted that when revolutionary governments come to power their countries are "lost" as sources of raw materials, investment opportunities, and potential markets. To an extent these fears are accurate. Revolutionary socialist societies are likely to be hostile to the establishment of Coca-Cola plants, Hilton hotels, the circulation of *Readers Digest,* and many other familiar by-products of American foreign investment. They are also likely to be tough bargainers on terms and conditions of trade; but it is not true that they oppose, as a matter of principle, trade with the capitalist world including the United States. In virtually every case where trade relations have ceased, it has been at the initiative of the United States, not the revolutionary government. The State Department has sought to use trade restriction as a political weapon to hasten the downfall of socialist governments, notably Cuba.

When revolutionary governments come to power in countries possessing strategic raw materials needed by the United States, another potential security problem arises, since such governments might cut off the supply for ideological reasons. Ian McGregor, chairman of American Metal Climax, Inc., points out that the United States uses an average of twenty pounds of copper a year per person while the rest of the world gets along on three pounds per person. Hanson Baldwin, the former military analyst for the New York *Times,* writes that United States military strategy must be designed to ensure continued American "access to raw materials, overseas trade, and overseas investment" which "are essential to the viability of the United States economic system and to our prosperity." The standard of living in the United States, the managers of the American empire have concluded, cannot be maintained unless Americans continue to have access to strategic materials in sufficient quantities and on favorable terms. There can be no national security unless American power is wielded in such a way as to guarantee a world environment compatible with America's present and projected consumption rates. As McGregor's analysis makes clear, there is no way to obtain security without convincing the rest of the world through the projection of American power that they have no alternative but to continue to subsist on a fraction of what they would need in serious programs of industrial development. The only other solution to this fundamental and growing conflict of interest is to reduce America's claim on the total resources of the planet. But every official assumption about national security excludes that possibility.

There is a third connection between revolutionary change in other countries and American national security which is neither military nor economic; it is psychological. The United States has consciously sought to expand its system so that other countries will not only buy its products but also accept its values. We have wanted to be accepted as the world's definition of the good society. To a considerable extent this has happened. Only a few revolutionary societies have held out a vision of the future different from the American model—what Walt Rostow called "the high mass consumption society." Even the Soviet Union has adopted as its goal the American model of the highly industrialized consumer society. Their brand of socialism is a means for "overtaking and surpassing the United States" on the way to the same utopia.

For almost fifty years, however, America has been experiencing a national identity crisis. In the thirties, amidst depression, seemingly permanent unemployment, and great social unrest there was a serious loss of faith in the American system as it then existed. In the thirties and early forties the pretensions of the foreign "isms"—state capitalism, communism, fascism and others—that they, rather than free-enterprise America, represented "the wave of the future" caused shudders of doubt in the United States. Victory in the Second World War brought new confidence; yet there was enough awareness that the war had transcended but not solved the domestic crises of the thirties to make both decision makers and the public uneasy about the future at the very moment of America's supreme power. Thus the rhetorical claims of Communist ideologists that they were the new "wave of the future" struck a terror out of all proportion to the real strength of what the State Department called "international communism." The pursuit of national security through empire was a policy designed to prove to the world but especially to ourselves that America was a winner. As long as our criteria of "development" and "progress"—such as the ratio of cars to bicycles on the main street of the capital—was accepted by other nations, this provided a kind of validation for the American system at home. If we were the envy of the world, this made it easier to conclude, as a prominent American social scientist wrote somewhat prematurely in 1960, that the United States had solved the "major problems of industrial society." By the same token, a few American policy makers worried openly about what many more intuitively feared, that if the "wave of the future" should take the world toward a goal other than the high mass-consumption society based largely on free enterprise, how long could that system survive in America? Men of power in America have feared noncapitalist "encirclement" almost as much as Stalin feared capitalist "encirclement." The difference was that the Americans had a much less modest view of what they could do about it.

These concepts of security, these visions of a world safe for the United States determine the character of America's global commitments. To talk about restricting commitments without examining and coming to terms with the fears and dreams out of which the commitments grow is unrealistic. A bureaucracy which has developed an imperial world view is not easily controlled. Bureaucratic momentum continually traps and pushes statesmen into making decisions they might wish to avoid. The rhetoric of security creates political pressures which promote policies of domination. If the real lessons of Vietnam are to be learned, the imperial definitions of security must be rejected. The world cannot be shaped to an American vision. We cannot "organize the peace," to use Dean Rusk's expression. We cannot find safety by trying to bend the world to our will. To exert constructive influence over a world in great danger will first require educating ourselves in the reality that we cannot make the world safe for the United States as it is today. To help change the world in the direction of peace and justice the United States must itself experience important changes and develop a much more modest definition of national security.

In a nonimperial definition of national security the criterion of success is not "winning the game," as Miles Copeland in his book *The Game of Nations* accurately describes the objectives of Great Power "diplomacy," but in bringing about concrete changes in the international environment that improve the human condition. The United States will not achieve security until United States foreign policy makers come to see that the "game of nations" is substantially irrelevant to the real security interests of the American people. Americans will not sleep better if the CIA installs the next king of Saudi Arabia. Nor should they. The United States will not collapse if poor countries like Cuba are permitted to experiment with revolution without constant American harassment. There is no objective reason why a Communist South Vietnam poses a security problem for the United States other than the fact that we have made ourselves look ridiculous and evil trying to prevent it. General MacArthur once said that there is no security, and that of course is doubly true today. To set as a "national security" goal the concept of "stability" in a world in convulsion, in which radical change is as inevitable as it is necessary, is as practical as King Canute's attempt to command the tides.

To be able to roll with the tides and still keep intact the essentials of our own political experiment and our own identity is the real security task. To do that will require less arrogance about having the answers to world development when we do not have the answers to our own problems of development. Americans must be prepared to change their style and standard of living, and perhaps even the way their economic system works; to the extent necessary to make this possible. Such a policy against the rampant waste which we have come to call progress is not altruism but the politics of survival.

IV Limits to Intervention

GRAHAM T. ALLISON, ERNEST R. MAY AND ADAM YARMOLINSKY

Not since World War II have Americans been so uncertain about the proper role of the United States in the world. The broad bipartisan consensus that characterized American foreign policy for two decades after the war has been overcome by widespread, bipartisan confusion about the nature of the world, the character of the challenges that policy makers confront, and the proper employment of nonnuclear forces. Vietnam is not the only cause of this confusion. Changes in American perceptions were evident earlier: As the fear of monolithic communism waned, hope grew that the United States and the Soviet Union could coexist peacefully; and the public showed diminishing interest in providing aid to less developed countries. But the expenditure of blood and treasure in Vietnam has deepened fundamental doubts throughout our society—from the highest levels of government to college campuses and Midwestern farms—as to whether the United States should in any circumstances become involved again in a limited war. A *Time*–Louis Harris poll in May indicated that only a minority of Americans are willing to see United States troops used to resist over Communist aggression against our allies: in Berlin, 26 per cent; in Thailand, 25 per cent; and in Japan, 27 per cent.

This pervasive uncertainty, confusion, and discontent create an opportunity to reformulate the guidelines of American foreign policy and to educate the larger public about the responsibilities of the United States—their extent and their limits. The burden of this job falls primarily on the Nixon administration, and it is clear that the President and his National Security Council have considered these problems and surveyed various alternative postures. President Nixon's July speech at Guam suggests at least the outline of a tentative doctrine. What remains is to make that doctrine more precise —a task that has apparently been begun within the councils of government. Our purpose here is to suggest ways in which it should be carried forward and considerations which should be taken into account in the process.

Four general observations can be made about the character of the problem. First is the ubiquity of the visceral reaction: "No more Vietnams!" This simplistic formula seems to guide the prescriptions even of some past participants in government. The impulse to avoid a future Vietnam is as powerful today as was the impulse in the 1930s to avoid another World War I or the impulse after 1945 to avoid another Munich. The temptation to leap from the flagging horse we have been riding to any horse headed in the opposite direction seems compelling.

Second is the difficulty of the problem itself: Much of the traditional rationale for the size and shape of non-nuclear forces proves on examination to be highly questionable. It is not clear that such forces contribute to deterring major non-nuclear conflicts or that such conflicts are sufficiently likely to justify their standing by in readiness. Only military planners, professionally committed to belief in the worst contingencies, today assign significant probability to a sudden Soviet march across the north German plain, a surprise attack by the Red Army on the Mediterranean flank of NATO, or even an unheralded descent by Communist China on Burma or Thailand. Equally, it is unclear what role American nonnuclear forces can play in the kinds of minor wars that do seem probable. Vietnam hardly encourages the conviction that they are suitable instruments for coping with insurgency in a foreign state. But the obvious alternatives to the traditional rationale do not pass muster either. One cannot say that there are no politico-military reasons for an American military presence of some sort in Europe or the Mediterranean. The ready availability of some United States force serves as a deterrent and therefore necessarily as a significant element in defense against possible overt attack on, say, Venezuela or South Korea. It is essential to recognize not only that no simple doctrines are readily to be discovered but that the questions themselves are not easy to understand.

Third is the impossibility of specifying any geographical area where developments are certain to be of such limited interest as never to raise the possibility that the United States should use nonnuclear force. If one could simply write off the less developed countries of Southeast Asia or Africa, the problem might be more manageable. But a reasonably thorough and unblinkered survey of the globe discloses conceivable situations in every area in which any responsible administration might have to consider introducing American forces.

Finally, there is no evidence that any set of principles can be identified which unambiguously distinguishes cases in which United States nonnuclear forces should and should not be used.

In attempting to design desirable, feasible guidelines for future uses of nonnuclear forces one must acknowledge that this issue is highly sensitive to the outcome of Vietnam and the interpretation given that outcome in the United States. The argument here proceeds on the assumption that the likely settlement will be sufficiently adverse to American interests to assure disagreement both among decision makers and among informed citizens about the degree to which we have achieved our initial objectives.

Even though there are no unambiguous guidelines, there is a fairly clear checklist of factors that would determine how any President or presidential adviser or even any responsible observer would judge a case of possible intervention. These factors include:

The American sense of commitment. Commitment can be based on formal treaties, letters exchanged between chiefs of state or high government officials, historical ties, past blood shed in defense of common goals, and the like.

The American sense of interest. Since this interest is no longer a function primarily of trading opportunities, territorial ambitions or imperialist pretensions, it is to be measured largely in terms of the sense of danger to the delicate equilibrium between the major world powers. Some situations will inevitably seem more dangerous than others, either because of possible immediate results or because of possible effects on expectations of leaders in either hostile or friendly states. National interest is also a function of substantive domestic concerns, as with the fate of Israel, or the possibility of a black-white confrontation in southern Africa.

The estimated probability of success, at various levels of cost and risk. The most attractive situation to decision makers—and to the American public—will be one that seems to offer a high probability of success at relatively low risk.

Each of these factors involves judgment on the basis of uncertain estimates. Differences among reasonable men, especially over future dangers in acting or failing to act, are inevitable. Because of these uncertainties, there are large numbers of cases in which it is difficult to predict whether the United States would decide for or against intervention.

The uncertainties surrounding calculations about intervention are overshadowed by a second cluster of factors: the context in which the specific decision is made. This context includes:

The immediate background. A sudden event like the North Korean attack on South Korea or the collapse of the Dominican government in 1965 poses one kind of problem. A more slowly developing event like the Berlin Blockade or the North Vietnamese intervention in South Vietnam poses another. A gradually festering situation such as that on the Israeli-Syrian frontier or in present-day Guatemala poses still another.

Comparative perspectives. Situations will vary also in similarity to past situations. The Dominican Republic in 1965 looked like Cuba in 1959. Reactions to, say, a coup in Guatemala could vary, depending on whether the situation was read as another Cuba or another Dominican Republic.

A crucial question over the next few years will certainly be whether a situation does or does not look like another Vietnam.

The historical trend. President Kennedy's decision to increase American advisers in Vietnam seems inseparable from the sequence of events leading from the Bay of Pigs through Vienna, Laos and Berlin. There was a strong feeling that the line had to be drawn somewhere, even if that meant "the wrong war. . . ."

Congressional and public moods. Congress and the public might take one attitude toward North Korea and another toward, say, Bulgaria—not recently guilty of provocative behavior. Similarly, attitudes toward a situation in Africa could be affected by attitudes of and toward Blacks at home.

II

Conceding all the surrounding uncertainties, one can still distinguish three categories of cases: (1) overt aggression by a major Communist power against a United States ally; (2) overt aggression by any state against a nation not a United States ally (e.g. Russia against Finland, China against India, a combination of Arab states against Israel or Jordan); (3) internal violence jeopardizing a friendly state, perhaps aided from outside but not involving significant overt action by foreign ground, air or naval units. (In the first two categories, overt aggression should be understood as comprehending any cases in which organized units of the armed forces of one nation move in significant numbers across the established frontiers of another nation; the term thus includes large-scale infiltration into insurgent-held territory and other situations sometimes described as "proxy war.")

Each category comprehends many kinds of cases. Even with regard to nations covered by the same alliance treaty, the United States does not have identical commitments. Within NATO, for example, we feel a greater sense of national commitment to Britain than to, say, Greece or even to Norway, despite our equal obligation to all. Some nonallies may have stronger moral claims than some allies. Israel, for example, certainly stands higher with the American public than Portugal or Paraguay. Persistent internal violence in South Korea would pose policy problems quite different from those presented by similar violence in Pakistan, and violence in Pakistan would wear a different appearance depending on whether outsiders numbered thousands or tens of thousands and whether they were Chinese or Russians. Even so, these categories are not only distinguishable but sufficiently different to admit differing policy guidelines.

The First Category: Overt Aggression Against an Ally. Today the Rio Treaty, the North Atlantic Treaty, the Southeast Asia Treaty, the ANZUS Pact and mutual defense pacts with Japan, Korea, Taiwan, and the Philippines commit the United States to the defense of 42 nations. Auxiliary arrangements, such as United States patronage of CENTO, have created a number of additional commitments. None of these commitments is in perpetuity. The obligations of the United States under these arrangements are of differing degrees and kinds. Thus the Rio and NATO treaties assert that "an armed attack against any [contracting] State shall be considered an attack against all and, consequently, each of the said contracting Parties undertakes to assist in meeting the attack," while the Southeast Asia Treaty provides that "aggression by means of armed attack against any of the Parties would endanger [each Party's] own peace and safety" and each Party agrees "to meet the common danger in accordance with [its] constitutional processes." In addition, some have been amplified by unilateral Executive or Congressional declarations. The Southeast Asia Treaty obligation to Thailand was markedly strengthened, for example, by a joint communiqué issued in 1962 by Secretary Rusk and Thai Foreign Minister Thanat Khoman which stated that the United States regarded Thailand's independence and integrity as "vital to the national interest of the United States;" it held that the American commitment to Thailand under the Southeast Asia Treaty was binding, regardless of whether other signers concurred or not. Statements by Secretary Dulles and a congressional resolution of January 29, 1955, suggested that our obligation to the Republic of China included the defense of Quemoy and Matsu.

All such commitments deserve thoughtful re-examination. Given the history of executive-legislative controversy over Vietnam, some should be reviewed and either reaffirmed or revised in consultation with the Senate. With respect to all treaty commitments which the Government chooses to reaffirm, however, it seems appropriate that the President establish and announce a *presumption that the United States will intervene on behalf of an ally which is a victim of overt aggression.* Only by clearly reaffirming those commitments which are judged genuinely vital can the United States make clear that the aftermath of Vietnam is not to be a withdrawal into a fortress America.

The Second Category: Aggression Against a Non-Ally. The issue becomes more complex in cases of overt aggression against a nation not linked to the United States by a treaty of alliance. There is clearly a very considerable range of such cases in which the United States would not be prepared to intervene. If other governments judge the likelihood of American action by the three criteria of commitment, interest, and risk of escalation, none will launch an overt attack on a nation friendly with the United States unless it judges the American commitment weak or the risk to the United States high. The critical question is likely to be one of United States interest, and that is likely to turn on whether other major powers are involved, on either side. In cases where no other major power is involved, there should be *a presumption against United States intervention.* Where the American response could be undertaken jointly with another major power, the risk of escalation might be reduced. This presumption, as stated, would not prejudice our responding to a United Nations Security Council decision to impose sanctions against an aggressor, up to and including military force.

The Third Category: Internal Disorder. Here, more than elsewhere, there may be some ambiguity about what constitutes American military intervention. Various forms of intervention—e.g. diplomatic, economic, covert, and military —are obviously related. Indeed, in the most visible cases— Laos and Vietnam—military involvement has occurred in stages—from military aid missions, to arms, to advisers, to helicopters, and finally to combat operations. But it is essential to draw a sharp line between official combat operations and the rest. For the admitted expenditure of American blood changes the character of subsequent choices about further investments of men and money. The term "military intervention" is therefore restricted here to cases involving either (1) the presence of American military personnel in sufficient numbers to cast doubt upon their claim to be traditional advisers, or (2) combat operations involving United States air or naval forces.

Before a decision on such intervention confronts the President, other government officials will have made many decisions and taken many actions that will critically affect his decision to intervene or not. Here, therefore, we must consider not only what presumptions should govern the expectations and behavior of officials, but also what procedures should be followed to place choices before the President.

Though Vietnam provides no satisfactory and simple rules, it does suggest a number of relevant lessons. First, the effects of intervention are uncertain. Vietnam suggests how hard it is to judge what makes for stability and instability in the developing world. Second, American power is more limited than many people have assumed. The massive application of our military power has not been able to achieve a military victory. Our best efforts have not been able to establish a stable popular government in Saigon. Third, any nonnuclear intervention in a nuclear world is likely to be a limited commitment; but once blood has been shed, it is extraordinarily difficult, especially as a matter of domestic policy, to cut losses.

These "lessons" seem all the more persuasive because the United States has no commitment to preserve any national regime. In few cases can one find a vital American interest that would be affected by a change of internal regimes. Our forces have a difficult time defeating national guerrillas that a government cannot overcome by itself. The belief that our troops and technology can be relied upon to cope with insurgency problems that national governments are unable to deal with encourages flabbiness in some existing regimes. It is highly uncertain what effect external military intervention will have on subversion, and what effect external efforts to control subversion will have on modernization. Indeed, nothing seems surer than that in some societies internal violence will be necessary for modernization.

These factors complement the overwhelming preference of the American public. Therefore, the Administration should make a serious effort to establish *a strong presumption against intervention in cases of internal disorder and/or subversion, even when there is outside encouragement and aid.* Such a presumption need not be inconsistent with a willingness to supply economic aid, military equipment and even, in some cases, advisers.

Difficulties present themselves in connection with all three of the proposed presumptions. It is arguable, for example, that renewed evidence of United States fidelity to treaty obligations could dissuade NATO allies from contributing a "fair share" to their own defense. It could also be argued that the second presumption would encourage the Arabs to attack Israel. The most persuasive counterarguments, however, are those against a presumption of nonintervention in cases of internal disorder. It can be contended that to establish such a presumption will encourage disgruntled groups in less developed countries to attempt insurgency, and will announce to nations bent on aggression that low-level aggression pays. These objections have bite. But they ignore two further considerations.

First, expectations about American willingness to intervene will be but one factor in the decision of disaffected citizens to rebel, of revolutionaries to fight on, and of regimes like those in Peking or Hanoi to support aggression beyond their frontiers. The factors that determine a choice to pursue revolution and insurgency are overwhelmingly local, and the factors that bear on a government's decision to support insurgency beyond its borders turn on a large number of considerations other than likely United States reactions. Indeed, it seems very uncertain what the effect will be on potential aggressors of statements by the United States about its intentions regarding intervention. Second, reduced expectation of United States intervenion would create incentives for national governments to set their own houses in order, to be more responsive to citizens' interests, and to shore up their own counterinsurgency capabilities. Too often American support of rightist status quo regimes has resulted in restraints upon discontented religious and ethnic minorities, thus making the country more, rather than less, vulnerable to subversion. Although much uncertainty surrounds this entire set of calculations, it seems likely that a presumption against United States intervention will encourage insurgency by some small amount. On the other hand, this price is small in comparison with the cost of any alternative.

A different kind of objection focuses on the likely reactions of those within the American bureaucracy who are responsible for national security. If the President attempts to establish a presumption against military intervention, will his advisers and agents cooperate? Or will they instead permit or encourage developments which might lead the President to conclude that our vital interests *are* involved? This is not to question the loyalty or responsibility of the national security bureaucracy, but merely to assert that their perspectives and priorities inevitably differ from those of the President. Particularly in the aftermath of Vietnam, the concern of our foreign-policy establishment that this country do more to enhance its deterrent posture will conflict with the presumptions suggested above. The departments must, of necessity, focus on separate and therefore parochial pieces of problems, while the President must think about the whole. The departments concentrate on their jobs; it is elected officials who must strike the balance between foreign and domestic priorities.

This objection cuts deeply—but less deeply than might at first appear. If a President wanted to create a presumption for or against United States military intervention in certain kinds of cases, he could not accomplish it by fiat. But it should not be impossible for him to have his way. Several procedures—largely extensions of those recently put into effect —could help accomplish this objective.

Recognizing the inevitable differences between the perspectives and priorities of the President and his agents, the

President's staff could supplement the supervision of cabinet officers over their own bureaucracies by carefully monitoring the work of desk officers, the cables, ambassadors' statements, military advisory activities, etc. Though this effort would meet with strong resistance and objections about undue political interference, behavior will not change without such monitoring and penalties for action contrary to national policy.

A related but distinct requirement is for competitive information, estimates and evaluations. Any single source of information, whether Foreign Service, CIA, military or whatever, is likely to present data biased toward a particular policy outcome. The odds are that multiple sources will offset rather than reinforce one another.

Efforts must also be made to find institutional ways to guarantee competition. A specific instance of this general requirement concerns military analyses, estimates and budgets. No one familiar with the development of United States choices in Vietnam can underestimate the importance of more systematic analysis of proposed uses of American forces, more careful projection of enemy reactions, and an attempt to consider the consequences if less favorable projections turn out to be right. While the analytic difficulties are substantial, powerful evidence suggests that the application of techniques such as systems analysis could markedly improve both estimates and sensitivities to the consequences if favorable estimates fail. The military services should be pressed to present their proposals and projections in more systematic form, and the President should also have available independent, competing analyses. Program budgets of projected military operations, produced outside the military establishment, could provide the President with a competing angle from which to view alternative uses of military forces.

In cases where the question of nonnuclear military intervention arises, procedures should give the President an adequate map of alternative courses and arguments, as well as an understanding of the troop requirements and budgetary demands that will result in the event of various possible outcomes of a given action. They should chart the hard choices that lie ahead if the outcome is not the preferred one. They should facilitate more independent consideration of each stage of escalation or de-escalation, making the decision makers aware of new perspectives and new arguments.

What is proposed here is clearly only an extension of procedures already in effect. Existing practices may be adequate to support a policy of absolute noninvolvement in the military problems of other nations. They are probably adequate to support an activist policy of intervention—although perhaps not to deal with its consequences. But they are wholly inadequate to control all the relatively low-level actions that may embroil the United States in a foreign conflict and to provide the information necessary for presidential judgments.

III

How these three presumptions might be applied can be illustrated by a sensitive current case—that of Thailand. The Southeast Asia Treaty, as interpreted in the Rusk-Thanat communiqué, obligates the United States to come to Thailand's defense in the event of overt attack. The Administration should adhere to this position, pending a review of the commitment by the President in concert with the Senate Foreign Relations Committee.

Such a review might well result in revocation of the Rusk-Thanat communiqué. Not all nations in SEATO agree that members can act in the absence of unanimity, and the President and the Senate might conclude that this more restrictive interpretation accords with the text of the treaty and the intentions of its negotiators. (When recommending Senate ratification in 1954, several members of the Foreign Relations Committee made explicit their understanding that any action under the treaty would be collective.) Indeed, considering the fact that the treaty was designed to safeguard arrangements in Southeast Asia which subsequent developments have long since altered, serious review might conceivably result in revision or even renunciation of the treaty.

Even in the former case, Thailand would cease to be assured of protection by the United States, for it seems unlikely that either France or Britain would support SEATO action in Thailand's defense. Thailand would therefore revert to the status of a friendly state not safeguarded by alliance with the United States. The second presumption would then come into play. The President would indicate to the Thais, to the world, and to his own bureaucracy that, while Thailand can probably count on United States support in the event of overt Chinese attack, the Thai government should assume that American forces would not take part in combating an overt North Vietnamese attack so long as neither Chinese nor Soviet troops participated in significant numbers. Fighting North Vietnamese alone, the Thais should expect supplies and equipment; they might receive uniformed advisers; but they would be aided by United States combat units only if a combination of European powers or the U.S.S.R. or perhaps Japan indicated willingness to join in genuine collective action.

The foregoing paragraph should make clear the extent to which the presumptions suggested here differ from those now controlling, for at present the organs and agents of the Executive Branch assume United States military action to be probable in any case in which Communist forces cross the frontier of a non-Communist state. What is said above should also illuminate the need for measures to strengthen presidential direction and control of the bureaucracy. For there can be no question that adoption of a presumption against automatic defense of Thailand would arouse anguished and determined resistance. The diplomatic, AID, USIA, and CIA missions in Bangkok and other parts of Southeast Asia, the Military Assistance Command in Thailand, the Commander in Chief, Pacific, and virtually all Asian hands in Washington would not only attempt to prevent such a change but would, for a long time afterward, make every effort to bring before the President evidence arguing for a return to previous policy. Some might even seek to contrive situations showing him the error of his way.

The same might be true, though not to the same extent, if the third presumption were applied to Thailand. The starting point is different, for the Southeast Asia Treaty does not explicitly commit the United States to defend the Thai government against internal violence. In case of threats "other than armed attack," says Article IV (2) of the treaty, the signatories are obligated only "to consult." Implicitly, any SEATO action must be a result of unanimous agreement. After asserting that American commitments relating to direct aggression do not depend on accord with other SEATO members, the Rusk-Thanat communiqué spoke of "indirect aggression" and implied that America's duty to Thailand resembled its duty to Vietnam. But, as early as 1966, the Defense Department took steps to limit American involvement in Thailand's counterinsurgency effort. The Nixon administration has said it will not be bound by American-Thai military contingency plans for dealing with cases short of armed attack. Washington has thus made the first moves toward establishing a presumption that it will not intervene in event of internal violence. It remains only for the Administration to issue further public statements and give unambiguous directives to missions in Bangkok and Vientiane, making clear that American military personnel and equipment will not be employed for counterinsurgency purposes unless and until the President issues contrary instructions.

Obviously, the introduction of these new presumptions would increase by some margin the risks to Thailand's integrity and independence. Reinterpretation, revision or abrogation of the Southeast Asia Treaty could lead some planners in Peking to view as less serious the danger that an effort to conquer Thailand would result in war with the United States. On the other hand, the presumption as we have stated it would not cause them to view the danger as negligible. In any case, we would assume that estimates of the efficacy of SEATO constitute only one among many factors influencing Chinese policy and that a change in such estimates would not in itself lead the Chinese government to choose a complex, costly, and uncharacteristic course of action. Indeed, one can argue that, since China's military moves thus far have been, or at least seemed, defensive in character, we could advantageously reduce the appearance of threat to China by closing down American air bases in Thailand and withdrawing United States military personnel now stationed there.

More worrisome, because more likely, is the possibility that adoption of the second presumption would encourage North

Vietnamese aggression against Thailand. One cannot consider this contingency without taking account of how the third presumption would affect events in Laos. At present, the United States is intervening in Laos, albeit under some camouflage, for American military personnel are performing combat missions. If the presumptions recommended here were to be put in force, American aid to the non-Communist Laotians would be limited to money, matériel and, at most, provision of advice at government and army headquarters level. Since the Communist Pathet Lao receive support from organized units of the North Vietnamese army, and since the ebb or cessation of fighting in South Vietnam will free still more North Vietnamese units, it is predictable that the result of a reduction in United States involvement would be a relatively early triumph by the Pathet Lao. The Kingdom of Laos would become a North Vietnamese satellite. Given kinships among tribes on both sides of the Laos-Thailand border and the presence already of Communist insurgents in northern and northeastern Thailand, it is at least possible that events would so develop as to bring a North Vietnamese invasion of Thailand comparable to earlier North Vietnamese invasions of Laos and South Vietnam.

Thailand would be at a serious disadvantage. Although its population is almost twice that of North Vietnam, the disparity will narrow if Hanoi controls Laos and parts of South Vietnam. More important, the Thai army is less than one fourth the size of North Vietnam's, and, except for one division that has served in South Vietnam, it has no comparable combat experience. In open warfare, the Thais would probably lose, leaving the way open for a North Vietnamese march to Bangkok. Reasoning thus, one could argue that the recommended presumptions should not apply in this case and that the President should indicate his readiness to commit United States forces in order at least to even the odds.

There are, however, good reasons for not doing so. In the first place, the sequence of events just described is only one among many that might develop. It is by no means inevitable that large numbers of North Vietnamese would remain in Laos after Communists came to power in Vientiane; certainly it seems likely that the victorious Pathet Lao would wish their allies to depart. Though judgments about the Hanoi government are notoriously susceptible to error, one can at least imagine arguments that might be used within that government to oppose any courses of action that might lead to war with Thailand—police responsibilities at home and in "liberated" Laos and South Vietnam; lengthy and vulnerable lines of communication; relative weakness in the indigenous Communist movement in Thailand; the relative absence in Thailand of any resources that would contribute to fulfilling North Vietnam's long-delayed industrial development plans; the possibility that to attack Thailand would be to walk into an American trap (as, Communists now say, the North Koreans walked into such a trap in 1950); and the danger that, in such event, North Vietnam would lose its ability to remain relatively independent of Moscow and particularly of Peking.

At present the Thai armed forces are instruments of government, not instruments of war. They receive a relatively small share of the total budget (12 per cent, as compared with 20 per cent in North Vietnam, 33.5 per cent in India and 45 per cent in Pakistan). The Thais might decide on a serious defense effort. At the same time, or perhaps as an alternative, they might seek some accommodation with the Pathet Lao and North Vietnamese. Historically, the Thais have displayed great flexibility and skill in diplomacy. They have preserved their independence for more than seven hundred years, and there is no reason to suppose that they would show want of resource in doing so now.

Nor is there reason for believing that the Thais could not adapt to the presumption that American forces would not be available to help them combat internal violence. In fact, Thai leaders take pride in the fact that, unlike the Vietnamese, they have not become dependent on American personnel for the maintenance of internal order. Their view thus far has been that, with American funds and supplies, they can cope with any foreseeable level of domestic insurgency.

Adoption of the three proposed presumptions would obviously increase by some margin the possibility of Chinese aggression. It would increase still more the risks for Thailand of a North Vietnamese attack and of mounting insurgency, supported from outside by Chinese and/or North

Vietnamese. It would make not at all unlikely a shift on the part of Thailand either to a more neutral status or to outright alignment with Communist states.

Even with full recognition of these risks, and of lesser risks in other areas, adoption of the three presumptions set forth earlier appears desirable. In regard to the specific case of Thailand, these presumptions would reflect the broadest definition of American national interest that is likely to be accepted by the American people and Congress in the foreseeable future. It is improbable that the public and Congress would approve a long-term commitment of American forces to meet any contingency except perhaps an overt Chinese attack. There is no way in which a commitment of forces to combat North Vietnamese or to offset Chinese or North Vietnamese support of Thai insurgents could avoid becoming a long-term commitment unless—and perhaps not even then— the United States were to resort to forms and levels of violence never employed even in Vietnam. If these estimates are correct, it follows that, in the Thai case as in others of less sensitivity, the President should not only adopt the recommended presumptions but make his adoption of them unmistakably clear to those who work for him.

Even if the suggested presumptions were in effect, the United States would still have obligations requiring substantial nonnuclear forces. Their adequacy could well determine the extent to which the margins of the presumptions might be tested. But the size of nonnuclear standing forces— and thus of the budget for what is identified as "general-purpose forces"—is primarily related to commitments to resist major overt aggression, and choices about the number of such contingencies. Forces that can be used to meet major contingencies can also be used in smaller contingencies. It has become as fashionable as it is obvious to assert that American nonnuclear forces can be reduced only as American commitments shrink. But this prescription neglects two further factors: contingency planning and force mixture. The Nixon administration is reported to have examined the problem of contingency planning and to have reduced the preparedness requirement from a capability for simultaneously fighting two major wars and one minor war, to a capability for one major and one minor war at the same time. The question of the quantity and mix of forces required to deal with particular kinds of crises should be subjected to similar scrutiny.

The time is ripe for such re-evaluation for a number of reasons. First is the cost squeeze within the military budget, primarily the result of increasing unit costs and domestic needs and pressures. Second is the increasing mobility of general-purpose forces, which makes the same units available for a wide range of secondary contingencies; hence the requirements for these contingencies are not additive. Third is the fact that the chief determinant of force requirements is a psychological rather than a military variable, i.e. the conception in Russian minds of a credible American commitment to nonnuclear defense of Europe, and the conception in West European minds of a credible American deterrent, not only against attacks by the Soviet Union but against independent action by either of the two Germanys. This dual credibility at the nonnuclear level is important, both because of the political danger of unraveling NATO and the military danger of encouraging nuclear proliferation through European loss of confidence in nonnuclear defense. Recalculation of the forces necessary to meet the United States commitment in Europe may or may not produce a different result, but it should make the commitment more credible to the extent that the rationale is more realistic. The same sort of re-evaluation could produce similarly useful results with respect to United States forces in Japan and Korea.

The Administration should be able to establish as a target the reduction of general-purpose forces to levels that characterized the Eisenhower period. Those levels—fourteen Army and Marine divisions, sixteen tactical air wings, the traditional fifteen attack carrier task forces, and nine anti-submarine carrier task forces—would entail no significant reduction in the American capability to meet a major European contingency, and would leave a small force for dealing with a minor contingency. If actually established, such force levels would cost approximately $30 billion per year less than present general-purpose forces (including those deployed in Viet-

V   A Third-World Averaging Strategy

MAX SINGER AND AARON WILDAVSKY

WASHINGTON (AP)—United States policy makers privately voiced unhappiness Thursday over the coup in Peru, but they expect the new military leadership to be pro-West and anti-Communist. And eventual recognition of the new regime seems likely. [Later dispatches reveal that the United States has suspended diplomatic relations and is reconsidering its foreign aid program in Peru.]

On the record, the State Department held to a strict no comment on judging the predawn Army overthrow of President Fernando Belaunde Terry.

Press officer Robert J. McCloskey indicated the United States would consult with its hemisphere allies on what posture to adopt toward the new regime—but would like Latin Americans to make the first move.

Off the record, United States authorities acknowledged the military takeover came as a setback to the goal of United States policy and of the United States-supported Alliance for Progress hemisphere development program.

Covey T. Oliver, assistant secretary of state for inter-American affairs, had been citing the absence of a coup in Latin America since the June 1966 Argentine military takeover as a sign of growing democratic stability in the area.

Just what Washington will do next depends on developments.

After the latest previous coup in Peru, in 1962, the Kennedy administration tried to show United States disapproval by breaking off United States relations and aid. Berkeley *Daily Gazette*, Friday, October 4, 1968.

This routine press dispatch epitomizes everything that is wrong with American foreign policy toward developing nations. Why should American foreign policy makers be unhappy about a coup in Peru? Why should a normal, regular, and all too predictable event be interpreted by American officials as a setback in foreign policy? Why should the success of American policy be predicated upon stability in areas characterized by turmoil? Why should the United States consult with anyone on what posture to take when there is no apparent reason for being anything other than correct in its behavior toward Peru? Why should the United States government be going through the old routine of considering whether or not to maintain diplomatic relations and foreign-aid programs in a nation that has done nothing to it? Why should the democratic character of a weak and strife-torn country be of greater concern to State Department officials than apparently it is to many of its citizens?

Our purpose is to suggest new ways of thinking about and implementing American foreign policy toward developing nations. These nations can do little either to help or to hinder the United States; yet for several decades the United States has been involved in frantic efforts to obtain their support and blunt their hostility. The resulting policies have been both unsuccessful and unnecessary, and still no one knows how to devise adequate policies toward these chaotic countries. We recommend abandoning the attempt to devise specific policies for each developing nation; instead the United States should adopt an averaging strategy by which the same policy of friendly benevolence and minimum political involvement is applied to all of them. We begin with consideration of how the international system has been perceived by those who make and debate American foreign policy. This discussion is essential because we believe that the supporters and the opponents of American foreign policy base their positions on images of international instability that are inappropriate for developing countries. Bad policies are the result of bad models. The frantic reflex action of intervention adopted toward nations like Peru is understandable only if one holds an image of a world perched on the brink of disaster unless America acts.

THE INTERNATIONAL SYSTEM

At a low level of analysis the nature of the controversies over American foreign policy seems to be reasonably clear. The "hawks" and the "doves," the unilateral disarmers and the proponents of preventive war, appear to be urging diametrically opposed policies. And so they are, up to a point.

At a middle level of analysis it is possible to discern two opposing models of international conflict. On the one hand, those who espouse the spiral model of nuclear war believe that nations get caught up in a cycle of events in which their responses become involuntary and extreme as they mistakenly believe they have enemies who are out to get them. Each side expects the other to do the worst and, by its very precautions, justifies its initial predictions. The conflict escalates as each party responds to the presumed provocations of the other until the spiral of events gets completely out of hand. The adherents of the rival appeasement model, on the other hand, see a world bully as the ultimate danger. As the great aggressor is appeased, its appetite grows until it becomes so inordinate as to threaten the complete destruction of others. The result is the same as with the spiral model—a final confrontation in a nuclear holocaust. Whether the disputants conceive of armaments and aggressive postures (spiral model) or lack of sufficient armaments and weak postures (appeasement model) as the major cause of world destruction, they agree that if their remedies are not followed cataclysmic events will take place. Although there are more subtle and complex versions of these positions, public debate and official action have been guided essentially by the more blatant models.

At a higher level of abstraction, beliefs about the nature of the international system are powerful determinants of a nation's foreign policy. In a "stable" system, small causes have small effects that generate countervailing influences which return the system to its former equilibrium. In an unstable system, small causes have large effects that throw the system into ever greater disequilibrium as (appropriately) in a nuclear chain reaction. It is evident that since the end of

World War II most American decision makers have considered the international system to be unstable. Hence the United
States has been concerned to halt the advance of communism
everywhere lest a small cause such as a Communist victory
in the Dominican Republic, Guatemala, or the Congo build
up such large effects as to threaten American security. In a
world it believed to be stable, the United States could view
the apparent rise of some Communist regimes as small events
whose consequences would soon be counteracted.

Perceptions about the stability of the international system
are not the only perceptions about the system that influence
foreign policy. In a "tightly coupled" system the component
elements are so closely related that a disturbance of one
link can transmit effects to many and distant links. In a
"loosely coupled" system, however, most effects are localized
in a particular subsystem and do not shake the entire edifice.
If the international system is thought to be loosely coupled,
then the occasional rise of Communist regimes can be seen
as having essentially local impact. The ascendancy of Communists in Ghana or Guinea would be of primary interest
and concern to the immediately surrounding countries (or
at most to the entire subcontinent) but not to the United
States.

Perceptions of the polarization of nations also affect America's foreign policy. Government officials in the United States
feel they are operating in a primarily bipolar (or if China is
included, a tripolar) world. Events, therefore, are interpreted
not only for their intrinsic significance but also for their
impact on the contest between America and the great Communist powers. The world is not only unstable and tightly
coupled, it is also divided into two or three great camps. The
importance of local events is magnified if they are viewed
as part of a larger contest that the United States cannot afford to lose. A retreat here or a failure there is amplified because of its purported significance for whichever camp is
ahead or behind in the cold war. In a multipolar world, however, there may be many contests only distantly related to
one another: The Dominican Republic might be part of a
Caribbean power struggle but it would not automatically
be considered a part of the cold war.

Now the time has come to question the assumptions about the international system—instability, tight coupling, and bipolarity—that have guided the debate about American foreign policy. As a rough operational guide we can say that the international system has gone beyond the bounds of stability if there is a major cost to the United States (like World War II) or a comparable defeat to the Soviet Union. The international system appears in the past two decades to have operated within the limits of stability. Although violence between nations has occurred, it has been contained without spreading very far or involving a direct confrontation of the superpowers. While potential sources of instability exist, they have not yet manifested themselves. Unfortunately, the world may appear stable only to those who lack the wit to sense the disruptive forces building up behind the facade of seemingly insignificant events.

The trouble is that it is either too easy or too hard to confirm the existence of systemic instability. If a moderate level of violence is the major measure of instability, almost any continent where there is some open conflict appears unstable. The absence of revolutionary violence then becomes the only sign of stability. On the other hand, when the analyst must identify the faintly emerging causes of instability its presence is too difficult to verify. (For example, can it be said that the United States is unstable because of its race riots?)

Fortunately, we do not have to confront this dilemma directly. For if the world system is loosely coupled, causes in the developing areas are unlikely to have effects around the globe. Whether or not parts of the world are unstable, Communist victories or other ominous events in Latin America or Africa are unlikely to have continuously amplifying bad effects elsewhere. Instead, evident forces such as nationalism and disorganization are likely to interfere with trends in directions bad for America as well as with efforts in directions good for it.

The question of whether the world is bipolar or multipolar is one of power: Who controls international decisions? Or, differently expressed, it is a question of causal relations: What nations cause events to happen in the international arena? If only two or three nations control international decisions, then the world system may be described as bipolar or tripolar. If many nations exercise power, then the world is multipolar. Stated in this way, however, the test assumes that those who have power have all of it and those who lack it are totally devoid if it. Here it is crucial to specify the areas of policy over which power is being exercised. Actors may be powerful in some areas and lack influence in others. While the Soviet Union and the United States come close to monopolizing control of intercontinental delivery systems for atomic weapons, their ability to control the future of NATO or the international Communist movement is in grave doubt. It seems likely, therefore, that the international system is unipolar or bipolar in some respects, tripolar in others, and multipolar so far as different areas of policy are concerned.

In the unstable, tightly coupled, and polarized international system perceived by many Americans every change is continuously amplified—thereby causing ever greater instability. Forces restoring the system to a more stable position are absent. The United States must provide countervailing power in every instance, therefore, in order to prevent disaster. Those who wish to change American foreign policy must argue, as we do, that a policy of permanent intervention is not necessary, because events in the developing areas are unlikely to blow up the rest of the world.

We believe that developing nations exist in a state of dynamic stability in which there is much action but little overall result. The combination of large populations and high volatility produces internal turbulence but not external force. The image of dynamic stability suggests that the great danger the developing nations pose for the United States lies not in their intrinsic importance but in the temptation to intervene in their affairs. Permanent chaos for them is mistaken for overwhelming danger for us. It would make better sense for the United States to loosen the connections between its national interests and events in developing countries. Instead of rushing to intervene, the United States should be reluctant to get involved. Outside of nonpartisan grants of foreign aid allocated on an objective basis, the American posture should be one of friendly concern but not of direct intervention. We shall attempt to justify these policy recommendations by showing, first, that developing nations cannot affect America's national interests and, second, that America cannot, in any event, devise effective policies toward these nations.

ARE DEVELOPING NATIONS A THREAT TO ANYONE OUTSIDE THEIR AREA OF THE WORLD?

The question of national survival today is dominated by high-yield nuclear weapons, superpowers, and the possibility of central war. Since the concept of central war, in turn, is dominated by intercontinental missiles, submarines, satellites, and aircraft capable of delivering nuclear weapons over long distances, strategic points on the earth's surface are becoming much less significant than they have been. The developing areas lack the capability to engage in or interfere with central war. They are, therefore, increasingly less important in regard to ultimate problems of American survival.

It is not beyond human ingenuity, of course, to perceive overwhelming importance in these developing nations. By insisting that the world is unstable, tightly coupled, and bipolar, the United States can interpret the most minor event as crucial to its well-being. A central war that vastly reduced the strength of the superpowers would obviously enhance the importance of those nations left relatively intact. By then, of course, few Americans would be left to care who was taking their place in the pantheon of nations.

It is still worth considering, however, whether there are less catastrophic but still real dangers emanating from developing nations. Access to their markets, we are told, is essential to the prosperity of the United States. Perhaps America will suffer if these nations ally themselves with hostile superpowers. In the background there is the vision of continents on fire—and the implication that the United States must put out these fires or eventually be consumed in the conflagration. Each of these arguments is worth examination.

Before a nation can be a threat to anyone it must be able to organize itself. Because the developing nations cannot solve the problem of providing adequate government, we believe they threaten no one but themselves.

Adequate government is a supreme human triumph and it

has only rarely been achieved. By adequate government we mean one able to assure internal peace and order, to provide for orderly succession of power, to defend itself against outside forces, and to reasonably satisfy most of its citizens. It seems unlikely that many of the underdeveloped countries will move rapidly toward adequate government. We can learn about the prospects for adequate government from the South American countries; they have not generally achieved it, although their task probably was not as difficult as that which now faces the African countries. We are not, therefore, in a position where with effort, skill, and luck we could bring about a fairly smooth and happy transitional period for the underdeveloped areas. Although we may have the resources to moderate the fate of these countries, many of them are destined for turbulence and misfortune regardless of what we do.

Most of us take government for granted. For us the words "country" or "nation" represent a group of people occupying a fairly well-defined area and having institutions reasonably capable of performing the usual functions of the state. Similarly we assume that power to control the state passes from one group to another in accordance with accepted practices. At least, we feel, control can pass; that is, the country can be taken over, and one can say who is in control. But even this is not always true. There may be no "control" which can make effective use of the resources of a country—which can be taken over, combined, or otherwise figured in the political calculus in the same way as the more familiar integers.

The factors that look so formidable to us as we consider the possibilities for peace, order, and growth in the underdeveloped countries also limit the danger to us from these countries, even if they "go Communist." The developing nations have highly volatile national systems and few national institutions or regularized patterns of action. Their expectations from the past have been disrupted without being replaced by new ones to regularize their social and political behavior. Internal groups exhibit hostility toward one another and do not evidence a strong sense of national identity. Desperate efforts are made to find instruments of nationhood through the army, party, bureaucracy, or some form of secularized religion; communications are poor; talent is woefully scarce. Though terribly small elites can cause large degrees of disruption and coups and countercoups take place with some regularity, nothing much really changes.

Unable to order their national life, developing nations are tempted to look for solutions outside of their territory. But, as they can hardly secure a minimum level of agreement at home, they are quite unable to maintain effective supranational arrangements abroad. Hostile to former colonial rulers, they are no more favorably disposed to neighboring countries in view of traditional enmities or tribal differences. Should a foreign nation (or its ideology) establish a visible presence in or near these developing countries, a counterreaction is likely. "What are these (white, red, yellow) foreigners doing? No doubt they want to enslave us again." It may not be possible to know exactly what the new nations want, but it is obvious that what they do not want is outside interference.

It is difficult for the developing nations to follow any consistent course: They have trouble allying with other nations; their rulers are practically unable to predict the directions in which they are likely to move. It is most unlikely, therefore, that any force will move whole regions and continents in a single direction. These nations are too upset, too conflicted, too inconsistent, too suspicious, and too weak to be a large cause of anything much beyond their borders.

CONDITIONS OF INSTABILITY APPLIED TO DEVELOPING NATIONS

Our argument has been that the chronic weakness of developing nations means that they are unlikely to threaten American interests. Other observers have argued that it is precisely the pervasive disorder of these nations that compels the United States to take defensive measures before the chaos spreads to its shores. This brings us back to the tricky concept of international instability. Perhaps we can move the discussion forward by briefly examining the conditions of instability in the most important case since 1945—Soviet expansion into Europe.

After the end of World War II, Soviet armies had extended

their dominion in Eastern Europe, Czechoslovakia had been toppled by a combination of external threat and internal subversion, and attempts were underway to repeat the process in France and Italy. These attempts were large causes, threatening to have large effects, and the United States responded appropriately in a massive way. The Soviet thrust was contained through active intervention in Greece, threats of force elsewhere, and large injections of economic aid in Western Europe. Had the Communist advance continued, Soviet control of the productive capacity and manpower of Western Europe might have directly threatened the security of the United States. This instability occurred under the following conditions: (1) the presence of a superpower with large ground forces and (2) economic capacity that (3) had already subjugated a series of contiguous nations. (4) These nations were near other threatened nations (5) which possessed trained manpower and great industrial capacity and (6) which had strong local organizations tied to the superpower. Under these conditions, processes with the potential for radically changing the system were clearly at work. These processes were checked by another superpower, which possessed equal or greater resources and was willing to use or threaten limited force, cooperating with local talented economic and political groups opposed to the aggressive superpower.

This set of conditions does not obtain, however, in those areas of the world in which most of the developing nations are located. None of the six potential destabilizing conditions of the European case exist in Africa. There is no superpower in physical possession of territory on the African land mass. No nation has "gone Communist" in the usual sense, though a few countries seem to lean toward one or another superpower. No African nation can be described as a great source of trained manpower with great industrial capacity, like France, Germany, or Italy. Nor are there substantial local Communist parties to invite speculations about whether they are closely allied with Moscow or Peking. Indeed there is doubt whether some of these peoples have the capacity to support "real" Communist parties. Moreover, such immediate success as the Soviets and Chinese appeared to have achieved has been rapidly reversed. Having been kicked in the teeth numerous times the superpowers have temporarily retreated from major participation in the area's internal disputes.

If there is any superpower dominating Latin America it is the United States rather than the Soviet Union. However, an American thrust through Mexico down the isthmus into Central America seems unlikely, to say the least. If the United States does have the equivalent of satellites, it does not seem to be running them very well. The Soviets do not appear to have made anything like a satellite out of Cuba and the Castroites have been remarkably unsuccessful in spreading their brand of revolution. There are Soviet, Chinese, and Castroite groups here and there but these do not seem to be strong. Competition between them, as in Bolivia, limits the chances that any of them will succeed. There is certainly no immediate prospect that numbers of Latin American countries will choose some version of the Communist path. Except for Argentina, Brazil, and Venezuela (in different ways), Latin America possesses only limited economic resources and does not have the trained manpower and organization to exploit fully the resources it does have. From the partial viewpoint of defense of American interests, none of the conditions of international instability in Western Europe in the late 1940s exist in Latin America today.[1]

THE ECONOMIC IMPORTANCE OF THE DEVELOPING AREAS TO THE UNITED STATES

If events in developing nations do not seriously threaten America's political interests, what about the long-standing belief that America's economic welfare depends on cheap supplies of raw materials and privileged trading relationships? We can largely discard the assumption that the United States needs the developing areas as a market (or as an outlet for investments) in order to maintain roughly the standard of living it now has. Only a very small part of the goods and services produced by Western nations are sold in the develop-

[1] We are saving Vietnam and Southeast Asia for later in order to test the relevance of our policy recommendations in the toughest case.

ing areas. Trade with industrial Japan will soon be worth more to America than the rest of Asia combined. Although a good portion of the raw material used by the West is obtained from the underdeveloped areas, technological developments have reduced the importance of this raw material contribution. The increasing substitutability of resources (resulting in part from the ability to synthesize new materials and in part from the generally increased sophistication of modern technology) reduces the monopoly power of any single raw material. Raw materials, moreover, are becoming a less important part of total goods and services. Therefore, the West can afford to pay a substantially higher price for raw materials—or their alternatives—without a major effect on its total economy. For these reasons, hostile control of the underdeveloped areas cannot produce a critical, long-term effect on the American economy.

This analysis is greatly strengthened if it is looked at from the other side. The goods and services which the underdeveloped areas receive from the West are a decisive part of their economies, particularly if they are to raise their standard of living. These countries are far more dependent on selling than America is on buying, as the abortive Arab oil boycott recently demonstrated. We cannot imagine that anyone can organize and control the underdeveloped areas in the next generation to such a degree that they can all be cut off from the West.

CALCULATING GOOD POLICIES

A decision to act should be based not only on a determination that one's interests are involved but also upon a corresponding judgment that one is capable of taking effective action. Having argued that American interests need not be seriously involved in the lives of developing countries, we should like to complete our case with the claim that the United States (like other nations) lacks the knowledge to make wise decisions about individual policies toward developing countries.

In order to exercise political influence in the developing countries we must be able to make the hardest kinds of judgment about their affairs—predictions of the political effects of proposed actions and possible counteractions. Politics in America are stable and familiar compared to the politics of developing countries. Change takes place in small steps so that the political environment possesses a fundamental continuity. Yet it is exceedingly difficult to predict the outcomes of major elections or to discover long-term trends. If picking a winner or judging the extent of racial animosities is a dubious exercise in America, how can we expect to pick winners and judge the extent of racial animosities in West Africa? We can surely fall into evil ways, but we have little reason to believe we can do good except by accident. Merely trying to do good is not enough. We are sophisticated enough to understand that "good can come from evil and evil from good." If we want to play chess with history, we have to be able to think at least one or two moves ahead. Yet we can hardly figure out what went wrong with our past moves, let alone estimate the consequences of future actions.

The formulation of foreign policy is a complicated process. The difficulties for an individual to try to understand the political situation in any one of the developing countries are magnified when all those in our country who participate in determining foreign policy come to grips with the intricate problems of all seventy-five or so developing countries.

Let us suppose that a shift in the situation in Tanzania requires a change in American policy. The first problem would be for those dealing with Tanzania to recognize that the situation is changing, to determine the direction of change, and to predict the impact upon United States goals and policies. (It is not easy to make these judgments: Though there were plenty of reports from Germany during the thirties about the profound changes taking place and the powerful forces at work, no generally accepted understanding of even the basic elements of the situation was arrived at in England or America until very late.) Reports from officials concerned with Tanzania will then have to be considered by the State Department people responsible for making policy in wider areas. It is unlikely that all of the diagnoses will agree.

Since the hypothetical change in the Tanzanian situation requires a shift in American policy, the ideas of Assistant Secretaries of State, policy planners, and numerous other officials will have to be changed. Since there probably was some controversy when the existing policy was adopted, and there is certainly controversy about related situations in other countries, the decision makers will be reluctant to throw out an agreed-upon attitude and will be suspicious of the advice that it is necessary to do so, because of the relation of this advice to other controversies.

The efforts to change the ideas of the policy makers about Tanzania must compete with their concern for seventy-five other underdeveloped countries and the other half of the world. They must also compete for their attention against efforts to carry out the old policy.

If a policy change is to be made and supported, it probably will have to face—sooner or later—opposition in Congress, the press, and small interested publics. Those people who have not learned about the changing facts in Tanzania, or who do not believe them, will oppose the new policy because it is in conflict with their understanding of the facts. In some cases it will not be possible for the State Department to reveal the new facts or the theory which produced the new policy. Thus special interests built up around the old policy will resist change. The change in Tanzanian policy may become involved in irrelevant disputes in Congress or elsewhere.

If two groups in the Administration, the Congress, and the public have different approaches to problems of the underdeveloped areas or foreign policy in general, they are likely to differ on many specific policy questions. These differences will be mediated by our political process, and neither side will win all the time. Therefore, people from all schools of thought must expect that they will consider some of the decisions to be wrong. There is an inherent tendency toward inconsistency in this process of give and take. For the country to "understand" what is happening in the underdeveloped countries necessarily involves a great deal more than the intellectual difficulties confronting any individual.

To some it may appear that the United States is uniquely ill suited to carry out large numbers of discriminating policies for developing nations. The fragmentation of power in the political system militates against fast action and consistent policies. The taking of incremental steps and the use of feedback to judge the next small move—procedures that work reasonably well in a stable, democratic country—may be irrelevant to problems of developing nations. The impatience of the population and the desire for clear-cut outcomes may prevent the careful handling of intractable problems. Yet there is no need to carry analysis further. While the American system has defects, so do the Soviet and Chinese systems, and these nations handle such problems as badly as the United States, if not worse. Indeed, it does not appear that any great power is able to handle these problems. If, as we suggest, the difficulties reside both in the characteristics of the developing nations and the inherent weaknesses of complex organizations like the United States government, the proper course is to devise a policy orientation that takes these sources of difficulty into account.

AVERAGING STRATEGIES

The United States government can adopt three general decision making postures toward the developing nations. The first is to call for the adoption of policies appropriate to the special circumstances of each country under varying conditions. American policy before, during, and after bloody racial warfare in the Sudan would fit in this category. The second posture is to recommend devising individual policies only for a few nations chosen for their special interest or critical position. Whenever a crisis occurred in or near these nations, new policies would be devised; the rest of the developing nations would be covered by general policy guidelines. The preferential treatment once afforded Nigeria, when it was regarded as the hope of the African heartland, belongs in this category. The third posture of decision making specifically rejects creating special policies for each developing country. Nor does it single out a few nations for unusual attention. Instead, this alternative maintains the same policy for all such nations. The rationale for adopting the same policy for an entire class of nations is that the results would, on the average, be better than trying to work out specific policies for all or a few of them.

Averaging strategies originate as a response to conditions that make it prohibitively expensive to calculate new policies for each new situation. As an example, consider the problem that every corporation faces of making sure executives retire before they are too old. We can assume that when people exhibit a certain degree of senility, they should be required to retire; however, people reach this degree of incompetence at different ages. (There is, after all, the "young fogy" problem.) The organization loses out if people are forced to retire either too early or too late. In order to do justice to each employee and to retain the best people, new organizations often begin by considering each case on its merits. Determining "the merits," however, turns out to be much more difficult than it had originally appeared. Not everyone agrees on criteria of excellence in work—on the trade-off, for instance, between experience and vigor. A great deal of time must now be spent working out detailed criteria. The alternative is to act intuitively toward each individual—this one looks good and that one should go—but the absence of formal criteria leads to charges of favoritism. If the man forced into retirement merely feels aggrieved, the cost is only personal unhappiness. But if he happens to be highly placed, or if the decision regarding him is taken as symbolic of a factional conflict, the costs are likely to be much higher. A relatively small matter has now been invested with much larger significance. A campaign for support is initiated; a *cause célèbre* is in the making. Feelings run high almost in inverse proportion, it seems, to the intrinsic importance of the case.

After a number of traumatic episodes, an organization will usually adopt an averaging strategy called an automatic retirement rule. Top executives know that it may be possible to specify the age at which any individual should be retired with more accuracy than the automatic rule provides, but rather than saying to those involuntarily retired, "You are senile," most organizations would rather take the small losses due to early and delayed retirements by making the much less invidious statement, "You are sixty-five." The averaging strategy results in small losses due to people being retired when they might be productive for another few years. On the other hand, considering each retirement on its merits leads to substantial costs of search (investigating each case), decision (time, energy, negotiation), and organizational strain (because fighting over the outcome is regarded as a loss or gain for various factions). An averaging strategy is desirable when the inherent significance of the problem is minor, because the possible gains from correct individual decisions are much smaller than the likely losses from wrong ones. Conversely the high cost of individual bad decisions may be avoided by accepting the low cost of having an automatic policy.

The case for adopting averaging strategies toward developing countries is much stronger than suggested by the problem of executive retirement. No one could doubt the ability of intelligent men to make basically sound decisions about who should retire early and who should be kept on a job. There is no reason to believe, however, that capable men know enough to devise good policies for developing nations. The risk of disaster is always there. And the costs incurred by making these many individual choices must also be measured by opportunities lost to devise better policies in more critical areas.

Suppose that the United States faced a choice of active intervention in one hundred developing nations. Direct action might be justified in fifteen cases. But there is no theory or observation to decide which of the hundred deserve the investment. In order not to overlook most nations deserving of intervention, at least double that number must be tried. Yet some nations requiring direct action must be left out and others in no great need are included. Multiple interventions increase foreign policy difficulties enormously. Instead of seeming active and in control, the United States paradoxically appears insecure and on the defensive, because it is always trying to extricate itself from an unfortunate involvement. It is difficult to know when success has come because it was never clear whether the threatened danger was real or whether it would have been mitigated by local conditions. What is clear is that the stakes of intervention in some cases have dramatically increased because of the importance the United States has ascribed to the case. Yet American ability to control events does not escalate along with its deeper in-

volvement. We need an averaging strategy to bring investments and risks in line with potential gains and losses.

A SPECIAL PROPOSAL

Consider the following major components of the proposed
averaging policy:

1. A policy of abstaining from the internal politics of the
   underdeveloped countries, dealing with each on the
   basis of tolerance and generous correctness. What is
   proposed here is *not* a withdrawal of the United States
   from these areas, but a change in its mode of participation in their affairs.
2. A large-scale economic aid program in which a regular
   part of our national income (or national growth) is committed to helping any of the underdeveloped countries
   that wish such aid.
3. An ability and willingness to fight overt military aggression. The United States should be prepared to nullify the
   effect of Russian or Chinese military power by its readiness to come to the aid of victims of that power. But
   America should be cautious about committing itself to
   providing immediate assistance to nations that do not
   really need the help and use American participation as
   a weapon against their neighbors.

Each case would be decided on its own merits: the ability
of the United States to successfully defend the threatened
nation, its willingness to help defend itself, its importance
to vital American interests, the presence or absence of democratic processes, all these should play a part in the American
decision.

Abstaining from the politics of the underdeveloped countries would mean:

1. Not trying to maintain particular governments in power.
2. Not making alliances, or encouraging countries to commit themselves between the East and the West.
3. Not having particular "friends" or "enemies" among
   the countries of the underdeveloped areas. The United
   States should treat all of these nations with equal respect

and propriety regardless of their policies and personnel. (This does not mean that the government should allow countries to abuse it by provocative acts, e.g., requiring the United States to reduce its diplomatic staff to fourteen people on forty-eight hours' notice.)

4. Finally, abstention would mean not trying directly, except by advice and persuasion, to end any internal political policy such as feudalism or repression. The United States would not, for example, use its aid in order to keep a "good relationship" with anti-Communist governments. The United States would not associate itself in special relationships with particular governments or countries to try to prevent them from "going Communist." The United States would not allocate aid among underdeveloped countries on the basis of which are in the greatest danger of "going Communist."

If the United States approves of some governments and disapproves of others it will be hard for it to avoid having to pass judgment on all governments, and people will read approval or disapproval into everything it says or does. If the United States becomes tied to the success of particular governments by making them, in effect, its protégés, at the same time, if it builds policies that depend on the success of particular governments, it takes on possibilities of defeat in situations which it cannot control, without gaining in return a reasonable likelihood of benefit. This way America loses its freedom of action. It is forced to adjust policies out of loyalty to these governments or for fear of weakening them, regardless of principles or long-run interest. The United States cannot always force reform on governments it depends on, but often, if they do not reform, they fall and the United States suffers. Furthermore, when it becomes associated with a particular government, the United States is tempted to use short-term efforts to save it. When these actions fail, the government never knows whether more intervention will save the day or whether the situation is hopeless.

Of course it would be foolish to treat these prescriptions as absolute rules; rather they should be treated as general rules which the government should be extremely reluctant to violate. In the nature of things there will always be temptations to intervene. There will be a constant series of situations where political action by the United States seems necessary to prevent some terrible thing from happening (or to seize some lovely but fleeting opportunity). But these situations will be misleading. If the value of abstention could be seen in such immediate situations there would be no need for a general rule. The general rule of abstention is proposed precisely because it would be unwise on the whole to do what seems wise in each particular case. The way to stay thin is to abstain from eating too much. Even though each piece of cake tastes good and has no immediately visible bad effect, most pieces of cake must be rejected. The fact that temptation is tempting makes it hard to resist and that is why one must make a resolution to resist.

America's proper attitude towards the underdeveloped countries should be friendly politeness or correctness to all. It should have a large economic aid program whose explicit motivation is benevolence or altruism. The President should decide whether benevolence is a sufficient justification for a large nonmilitary development assistance program (say 0.5 per cent of gross national product per year). If he does, he should present the case for a decision to recognize this obligation of benevolence.

The position should be that the program is justified even if it involves no advantage to the national interest; that the American people can hope in the long run a policy of generosity and benevolence will turn out to be of some value in ways that cannot be predicted. This should be more a matter of faith than of explicit reasoning (like "honesty is the best policy"). Furthermore, there is only a modest chance that more explicit calculations of the national interest would lead to a more effective program, and there are advantages to not trying to make such a calculation.

Selling the program to Congress and the public should stress the argument of benevolence and duty. The case is very simple: They are very poor and we are very rich; therefore we should help them.

It would be consistent with the American character to undertake regular foreign aid as an obligation of generosity. Even today many people think of it in these terms. The altruistic case for foreign aid is a good case. We believe that the American people can be convinced of the merits of a regular foreign aid program on this basis, although a decision of this scope takes a long time to make. There must be widespread public discussion, articles in magazines, resolutions by national organizations and their local chapters. There must be long congressional struggle, hearings, bills, amendments, compromises, debate, delay. But when a decision is evolved out of this kind of struggle and debate, it survives; it is not challenged every year. Social Security and medical care for the aged are good examples of accepted policies. Although it would be the target of regular peripheral sniping, such a major decision on foreign aid probably would become an automatic part of everybody's platform like past reforms enacted amid much controversy.

Once the decision is made that simple humanity requires our giving a small part of our income to the underdeveloped nations each year, there will be no good basis for the annual argument about the need for and value of foreign aid, because every year the situation will be the same: They will be poor and we will be rich. If foreign aid is not considered a way to stop the spread of communism, to induce countries to become our allies, or to assure peace and democracy in the underdeveloped areas, then there cannot be annual debates about whether it is working or not. If there are no short-term objectives there can be no short-term failures. If the aid is to be allocated on the basis of standards which, compared with a crusade against the Reds, seem prosaic, objective, and technical, then Congress will not be so concerned about having a major share in the decision making; the allocation of foreign aid will become a settled policy.

If over a number of years we do not use our aid as a political device, if we give without bias or favor, the nature of our program will come to be understood, and people will learn that our aid is not support for particular governments. All factions in recipient countries will know that if they gain power the aid will continue to come on the same basis as before. To this end, our aid should be allocated and administered on principles designed to minimize as much as possible the relationship of the aid to the particular governments in power in the recipient countries.

A vast bureaucracy is now employed to see that foreign aid is spent for the purposes the United States regards as most desirable. The result is that America courts hostility from the recipient nation in order to achieve an indifferent level of success in securing worthwhile expenditures. The bureaucratic and decision making costs of foreign aid may be virtually eliminated by simply providing grants to whatever government exists on an objective basis.[2] No doubt a fair amount of money might be squandered, but that is the case today. And the United States might avoid the difficulties of trying to maintain control through large foreign-aid establishments abroad. Each recipient nation would have to justify to its own population the use of these funds. Despite evident difficulties, this policy would center responsibility where it belongs—on the nation receiving the funds. If our foreign-aid proposal is regarded as too radical, its essence might be assured by channeling all funds through international organizations, regional associations, and multination consortiums whose major personnel are not American. The amount of aid would still be geared to objective criteria and the amount determined by the United States; how and for what the aid was spent would be determined by others.

The existence of India, with a huge population, and nations like Pakistan, Indonesia, and Brazil, with large populations, raises the question of whether they should be treated as special political cases. Under our proposal they would be treated differently in one crucial respect: since the amount of aid would be determined by such criteria as population size, these countries would naturally get more than others. We could not go beyond this point without endangering the policy of non-

[2] Our objective is to set up a foreign aid system that will (1) commit the United States to substantial yearly expenditure, (2) remove the political costs of supervising aid, and (3) provide incentives to encourage recipient nations to oversee each other. Our immediate purpose is to show how a new foreign-aid program would fit in with our averaging strategy. Considerations of specific criteria—population, birth rates, spending by other growing nations, stability of currency, and measures of effort for development —must wait for a separate paper.

intervention. After a while, the cutoff point for special consideration would be difficult to determine. Population is not the only factor that might serve as a basis for special treatment. Interest in oil or uranium might bring in other countries. The United States would then be in the same situation from which it was trying to extricate itself. The past American enthusiasm for India is a case in point. The Chinese Communists disrupted the Pakistani-American alliance simply by invading India. Immediate American overreaction led to large arms shipments to India. The result was that Pakistan was alienated even though we did not have strong reason to believe that India was really in danger of conquest. The maintenance of special relationships is similarly fraught with danger throughout the world.

CAN THE UNITED STATES MOVE TOWARD AN AVERAGING STRATEGY FOR SOUTHEAST ASIA?

While an averaging strategy might have made sense before the United States became deeply involved in the developing nations, it may appear that its time has passed. Too many commitments have been made. Too many acts of intervention have taken place to permit a policy of self-imposed restraint. Has the original sin become the everlasting flaw? Having once eaten the fatal fruit, must the United States forever choose a steady diet of intervention? The toughest test of our averaging strategy is Southeast Asia.

In the 1950s the United States could have afforded the absorption of South Vietnam by North Vietnam. South Vietnam was not intrinsically important, but the huge American intervention made that nation a symbol of American ability to protect small nations. This action made the possibility of victory for North Vietnam much more costly to the United States than it would have been had we not intervened. One of the benefits that is sought by a policy of very limited intervention is a reduction of the risk of such artificially created costs.

The question before us now, however, is not whether the United States should enter Vietnam but whether it can extricate itself. A policy of helpful and respectful distance will not be applicable to South Vietnam for a long time. But the United States could, over a four- or five-year period, gradually withdraw its troops. This policy requires no coalition government or agreement with the Vietcong or the North Vietnamese. Should the South Vietnamese government collapse, that would end the immediate problem. Should that government survive, the United States would continue to provide military and economic assistance for a decade. The objective of American policy would be to disengage from South Vietnam sufficiently to permit an averaging strategy to be applied in the surrounding area.

There are ample opportunities to move toward an averaging strategy elsewhere in Southeast Asia. If Japan, for example, were in danger of overthrow through internal subversion or external aggression, the United States would have to consider armed intervention. Japan is a potential superpower, and its dependence is of critical importance to the United States. But the Japanese refuse to believe that they are in serious danger. And so long as South Korea remains independent, it will be difficult to convince the Japanese to do more for their own defense. America should not be more interested in the defense of a country than its own people are. Running after a reluctant ally creates a false position, which is bad for American self-respect and Japanese capacity to assess its own interests. Americans may ask whether they really gain anything from a maintenance of military bases in Japan. In order to keep these bases, America now makes disadvantageous economic agreements. (For example, the Japanese sell us their excellent cameras, but we may not sell our superior color film in Japan.) A new policy should be adopted. Having arranged for commercial ship repair facilities and transit rights for airplanes, the United States could move its military bases to Okinawa. Legal sovereignty over Okinawa would be returned to Japan as the United States withdrew its obsolete atomic weapons from the island. Even this limited arrangement should not be made without public acknowledgment by the Japanese government of its own interest in keeping the American bases.

Indonesia is the kind of troubled developing nation with whom the United States should avoid special relationships:

The "low posture" policy currently being followed by the American embassy is excellent, except that it is threatened by the large number of administrators required to do the paper work on foreign aid. Malaysia, which has never received American aid because it manages its affairs too well, should at least get some economic assistance. Nascent nationalism and economic piracy in the Philippines should be met by a marked reduction in America's military and civilian personnel. The historic relationship between the United States and the Philippines might justify continued subsidies in the form of a special sugar quota, but history does not justify vast military bases and a swollen civilian bureaucracy. As rising nationalism leads the Philippines to look for scapegoats for its poverty and injustices, the United States should be making itself scarce. American troops should remain in Korea, however, where a strong and vigorous government is determined to defend its people against the real threat of armed attack. Should the unexpected occur—a full-scale North Korean invasion of South Korea backed by Communist China—the United States might again find itself at war, but one far better adapted to its moral and military strength than Vietnam. The provocation would be obvious, as would the capacity of the Koreans to assist in their own defense. There would then be no need to urge the Japanese to rearm; they would figure out where their safety lay without our help. Over a period of time, therefore, the United States (while still capable of direct action under special conditions) could move toward limited engagement in Southeast Asia.

CONCLUSION

The United States is a great world power and, as such, cannot escape being a prime actor in world affairs. Thus it must inevitably appear to some to be "throwing its weight around." Though history has decreed against escapism, playing a major, often unpopular role in world affairs need not mean total involvement everywhere all the time. A sense of proportion should be introduced into American foreign policy: Distinctions need to be made between major events and minor annoyances. The present overload on foreign policy making machinery, introduced by constant concern about developments in dozens of developing nations, should be reduced. A sense of calm and restraint should replace the frenetic atmosphere that induces intervention as a reflex action. We hope that it will prove helpful to replace the old view of the international system as highly unstable, tightly coupled, and bipolar with a fresh view of it as stable, loosely coupled, and multipolar particularly as regards the developing nations.

We believe that an averaging policy toward developing nations, based on genuine friendship, aid, and respectful distance, will enhance the quality of American foreign policy. Such a stance will facilitate greater attention to more important matters. Armed intervention, if and when it occurs, will take place under more clear-cut circumstances—more likely to enhance support from the threatened nation and from the American people. The self-image of Americans as decent, responsible, and effective citizens will be improved, and fateful days of decision will not be clouded by endless petty squabbles about trivial issues in unimportant places. No doubt developments that might have been headed off by direct action when they were small will grow larger. But such action is as likely to fail as to succeed and to it must be added numerous difficulties resulting from unwanted or unskillful intervention. There will still be failures. But on the average the United States should do better and feel better about what it is doing.

VI Vietnam, Western Europe, Latin America: Where Do Our Vital Interests Lie?

LESLIE M. LIPSON

American foreign policy today is verging on bankruptcy. The time has come to rethink it and restore its solvency. Any policy, domestic or external, becomes insolvent when its declared aims and formal commitments considerably outweigh the means available. Although not the sole instance, Vietnam provides the crowning proof that many of the leading ideas pursued for sixteen years by Secretaries Dulles and Rusk have resulted in a tragedy of errors. In that land of unlimited impossibilities, the Johnson policy failed—not through the poor execution of good ideas, but because the ideas themselves were at fault. No methods, techniques, or gadgetry could accomplish goals which had been wrongly conceived. Too many of the recent programs in Southeast Asia were constructed in a world of self-deluding myth, which hard facts have repeatedly exposed as false. That is why we have had a phenomenon politely called "the credibility gap."

To prevent the repetition of such blunders—a conviction popularly summarized in the phrase "no more Vietnams"—Americans must now re-examine our international position in the light of our vital interests, resources and capabilities. The principal errors in our external policy have been these: (1) We reversed the order of priority in our foreign relations; (2) we affirmed a broad commitment to objectives which, as a people, we could not fulfill; and (3) we exceeded the limits of our power. The foreign policy of the United States will

The only changes that have been made in this article are to accommodate the passage of time since its original publication. ED.

become solvent and, for that reason, realistic only when we have correctly reassessed our various external relationships in terms of the degrees of their importance to us, when we undertake only those responsibilities which lie within our means, and when we recognize that beyond certain limits even the vast power of this great country ceases to be effective. This national effort at reappraisal need not be agonizing. It would, however, be agonizing, as well as intolerable, to continue along the course of recent mistakes and persist in attempts to justify them as a Grand Design.

To begin, we require a candid inventory of our strengths and limitations. It is a fact that the United States, measured by any international scale, ranks as a superpower—a category only one other state occupies at present. As such, we have worldwide interests and a continuing concern that the balance of world power should either be tilted in our favor or at least not be tilted against us. The latter alternative implies another fundamental fact: Our strength, although very great, is not infinite. We are potent, but not omnipotent. There are certain things which even we cannot do; some goals which we might wish to attain, but cannot. An insolvent policy fails to recognize what these are. Realism, on the other hand, requires the wisdom of self-restraint; distinguishing not only between the desirable and the undesirable, but also between the practical and the impractical. Realism also calls for scaling our external relations in order of priority—an order which we must determine according to our conception of where our greater interests lie.

The first priority, of course, is always to maintain those interests which are vital to the United States. Vital means whatever is essential for safeguarding American security by political or military power. Since there are limits to our power, a vital need is always to cooperate closely with governments that most nearly share our basic values and ideals—on the reasonable assumption that it is these whom we can most safely trust and these who would harm us least. Although our interests extend globally (and even nowadays extraterrestrially), they are not all of equal importance. In the protection of vital interests, we should be ready to commit American military forces when necessary. But to uphold interests which, however important, are not vital, our assistance to other governments should always be restricted to the supply of dollars and equipment. Hence we should assess what our priorities are, with the corollary that we should never sacrifice a vital interest to a lesser. All this leads to the concluding query: where should we, as a people, draw the line?

We are living in a world where no one state is so mighty that its government can persist with impunity in flouting the opinions of others, and none so self-sufficient that it can withdraw into a fortress of its own isolation. Therefore one needs allies, among whom, hopefully, one may even find some friends. The pattern of alliances is influenced partly by physical considerations—e.g., the given facts of geography, the potentialities of resources and technology, military apparatus, and so on—but also in part by subjective and political factors —ideologies, attitudes, and opinions. The latter have relevance to the clustering of governments within the framework of alliances because of their effects on mutual understandings and on the willingness or refusal of peoples and governments to pull together.

Hence we should take note of a basic paradox of the American image abroad. Most of the world sees us, at one and the same time, as revolutionaries and conservatives. In our external contacts, we attack the foundations of the established social order while we support the power of its traditional custodians. We plaster the ceiling even as we undermine the floor. To other peoples, we fly in as social revolutionaries—along with our gadgets, know-how, consumer goods, and the fluid individualism of our quicksilver society. Wittingly or not, we travel around the world as restless innovators—disturbing conventional modes of conduct, uprooting ancient relationships, exposing accepted inadequacies, imparting new techniques. Others feel stimulated to adopt us for their teachers and to study us as a model to imitate. Yet when it comes to political cooperation or maintaining diplomatic ties, the stance that comes naturally to us is conservative. Where we have a choice between rival groups to support in a foreign country, almost without hesitation we side with those on the right less disposed to basic social change which

could threaten their ascendancy. In several recent cases where
we have intervened militarily to join in ousting or propping
up a regime, our efforts generally have been directed against
those initiating change from the left. Thus while we automatically oppose the extreme left (whose hostility to us is a
foregone conclusion), we succeed in repulsing and convert-
ing into our foes the moderate left who crave for much of the
social innovation which we represent. Hence many of our
efforts abroad, many of our aid programs, have a quality of
Sisyphus—tremendous effort expended in futility.

Such contradictions in our external posture bear directly on
the solidarity, and thereby the efficacy, of the alliances we
have entered. For, although an alliance stands as a contrac-
tual agreement between governments, to implement it in a
given instance is a political act; its provisions must be interpreted and then applied (if indeed they are) by regimes which
may fear to act positively when they encounter a sharp division in their public opinion. In this context, let us analyze
the network of alliances to which the United States has become a party since 1945. The historic decision of the years
1944–49 to abandon the traditional policy of isolationism was
itself a realistic recognition of the altered power structure of
the mid-1940s. It was endorsed nationally by clear bipartisan
majorities in the Senate and executed by Presidents of both
parties. At some stage, however, the evolution of our postwar policy went astray. We forsook realism for unreality, fact
for fiction, interest for illusion. Where was it that we went
wrong? Can the mistakes be rectified?

The method of our policy has been to construct a system
of alliances which would enlarge the security of ourselves
and others by collective means. In virtually every instance,
because of the relative power of the countries involved, the
United States has emerged as the producer of security among
allies who are its consumers. Largely, these alliances result
from the work of the last two decades. Some are bilateral,
others multilateral. They extend to certain areas of the world
which are of permanent and proximate interest to the United
States—such as Western Europe and Latin America—or to regions more remote which are weak and unstable and could
use some strengthening from outside. Geographically, these

alliances are mostly located near, or around the rim of, the countries ruled by Communist governments. An evident aim in their strategy has been to resist the appeals of communism and contain the expansion of such regimes.

Because of their varied memberships, our alliances differ vastly in character. There is only one, NATO, that has developed any significant cohesion or produced a working organization. NATO is unique in that it provides for integrated training and planning in peacetime as well as for an integrated command in wartime. The other alliances are loose or even tenuous. They have practically no structure and generate scarcely any reciprocal support.

Now let us take a comprehensive view of the formal commitments into which our government has entered since World War II. Under the Charter of the United Nations we share in the general obligation of all members to help in enforcing peace as authorized by the Security Council, where, if we choose, we can exercise a veto. Also we have entered into regional security arrangements under NATO, OAS, SEATO, and ANZUS, and we are committed to assist our various partners (e.g., Japan, South Korea) by a string of bilateral agreements. Under the regional pacts, an attack on any one member is automatically construed as an attack on all and involves an obligation to assist the victim. But, as I shall explain later, there is nothing automatic in either the nature or the degree of that assistance. When you add up all those agreements, together they amount to this: We are committed to help defend Western Europe, the Americas, parts of Southeast Asia, South Korea, and various island states in the Pacific. Count the countries and governments—their total reaches forty-four![1]

Some critics have concluded that our government has been the victim of "pactomania." What is clear in my judgment is that we overextended ourselves, so that what started with

[1] This includes the other fourteen parties to the North Atlantic Treaty, the other nineteen members of the Organization of American States and the Rio Pact—excluding Cuba—the three Asian members of the Southeast Asia Treaty, plus the three states named in the connected Protocol, Australia and New Zealand, as well as Japan, Taiwan, and South Korea.

some misbegotten pacts has ended in some disastrous acts. One is entitled to inquire whether the net result for the United States is collective security or an insecurity policy. We replaced the excessive isolationism of the years before 1941 with a chain of postwar commitments. But in practice, these commitments have led us, because of unsound doctrines and plain errors of calculation in Washington, into an excess of interventionism. Hence it is imperative for us at last to strike a balance between the earlier harmful excess of isolation and the recent harmful excess of intervention. This need is now both pertinent and urgent because of our military overcommitment in one place—South Vietnam. Our government intervened with large-scale warfare in an area which many Americans do not consider a primary interest, and we have appeared, to many of our own statesmen as well as to numerous leaders in other countries, to be acting the role of world policeman. Is this really what our vital interests require?

In essentials, my argument is this: Outside of North America, the vital interests of the United States are linked to three regions which together constitute our primary, permanent, and fundamental concern. These are the North Atlantic (which includes Western Europe), Latin America, and the Pacific Ocean. Other parts of the world—Africa, Eastern Europe, the Middle East, South Asia, and the mainland portion of Southeast Asia—are all important. But none of these is vital to the United States in the sense defined above. I shall begin this review of our relations with other areas of the world by a critique of Vietnam, which is the classic example of what not to do and where not to do it. Since the implications of that involvement will be with us for a long time, they should be analyzed with care if we are to avoid the future repetition of similar mistakes. Then I shall turn to the positive discussion of what we should be doing instead.

The great aberration of the sixties, enlarging on earlier errors of judgment of the mid-fifties, was the notion that the mainland portion of Southeast Asia constitutes an interest so vital to the United States that it must be embraced within the boundaries of the *pax Americana*. Already we have paid dearly for that mistake, at home as well as abroad. Our involvement in that area was officially expressed in the Southeast Asia Collective Defense Treaty of 1954 and its Protocol. This was one of Mr. Dulles' dreams which became our nightmare. It was he who seized on the conceptions of the pacts for the North Atlantic and the South Pacific (ANZUS) and reproduced them in Southeast Asia. But his assumptions were invalid because Asian conditions are so different. Many of our blunders in this region have resulted from the error of reasoning by false analogy—of applying lessons from another region (e.g., the North Atlantic) or another time (e.g., the 1930s) where they did not fit. The Vietnam story is a striking confrontation of fact and fiction. Not until March 1968 did President Johnson finally realize that he could not attain his objectives, so that belatedly he started the movement in reverse—from escalation to extrication. I shall discuss the problem by raising three questions: What is the true nature of the conflict? What brought us there? What are our real interests in that area?

Let me begin with some basic facts. We have been involved in the affairs of South Vietnam ever since the mid-fifties. It all started with economic and military assistance under President Eisenhower. Next, President Kennedy sent military personnel, called "advisers," numbering some 17,000 at the time of his assassination. Then early in 1965, a few months after being elected, President Johnson launched his policy of escalation, including systematic bombing of targets in North Vietnam. By the spring of 1969, some half-million Americans were stationed in South Vietnam. More than 40,000 young Americans are already dead. For over six years military operations have been conducted on a large scale by land, sea, and air. The cost, in the single year of 1968, has been placed at $30 billion. Our newspapers report that a greater tonnage of bombs was dropped on the adversary than on Germany in World War II. No contrast could be greater than that between the opponents, a traditional Asian society possessing for the most part a primitive technology and little modern industry, and ourselves who form the greatest concentration of power in the world. Nevertheless, despite such an effort, we have been unable thus far to bring these operations to a military conclusion. One naturally asks: why?

The answer, in my judgment, cannot be military. Purely in military terms, we should have won long ago. There has to be another explanation, which leaves only one possibility. It is political. Fundamentally, this is a conflict between several rival segments of Vietnamese. It consists, first, in a struggle for independence and unification and, second, in a civil war within a society which contains deep internal divisions and where the stakes are the form of government and social system to prevail in the future. These are the central aspects of the situation in Vietnam: nationalism and civil war. Into the depths of that swamp, our unwise government plunged gratuitously, dragging with it the American people.

When a government chooses to intervene, militarily and politically, in the affairs of another people who differ in civilization, race, and religion, as much as Asians do from Americans, there is one essential requirement for success. The intervention must be on the side of an indigenous regime whose authority is solidly based on adequate popular support. When that condition is absent, no outsider can attain his objectives. Unless he is prepared to resort to direct colonial rule, he cannot run the show himself. Nor can his fiat create those who will govern for him. What we did in Vietnam was to Americanize the war because of the incompetence of the South Vietnamese and the absence, after Diem's overthrow, of any government worthy of the name. As Westerners, we doomed ourselves to fight in the teeth of an Asian nationalism compounded by civil war. Thereby, we intensified the enmity of those we opposed, without really gaining the good will of those whom we backed. Too often, among their compatriots, the latter are branded as our puppets, which vitiates much of what they try to do.

Hence, due to a basic political miscalculation, all our programs, military and civil, have foundered on the same dilemma. Our avowed political aims—those of a limited war—restricted our military means, particularly because we dared not extend the arena or level of conflict to the point of directly challenging the Soviet Union or China; at the same time our military means have stultified our political ends. A staff officer of an allied army, himself friendly to the United States, said to me not long ago: "You cannot use tactical methods to rectify a strategic error." I agree, and would amplify his remark thus: You cannot use military means to rectify a political blunder. War is always a political act; when the politics are wrongly conceived, military victory is unattainable.

Now the second question: Why are we there? The short answer is that, as a people, we are the prisoners of the faulty ideas of a dead man, Mr. Dulles. He originally built this trap into which successive administrations fell ever deeper. Our intervention in the Vietnamese war has been justified by five principal arguments, which may be called the Five Fictions. Among these, two lines of reasoning stand out: one legal, the other political.

The legal case, or Fiction Number One, was regularly reiterated by Mr. Rusk. As he saw it, the government of State A, North Vietnam, committed aggression against the government of State B, South Vietnam, by sending men and supplies across an international frontier to overthrow its neighbor. "It is," we have all heard him say, "as simple as that." He asserted that we are committed to protect South Vietnam under the Southeast Asia Treaty and its connected Protocol and that this government honors its signature and fulfills its obligations. How simple it would be if that were always true! How deeply one wishes that were the case! Others, however, reading both the Geneva Agreement of 1954 and the Southeast Asia Treaty can draw quite opposite conclusions.

In the first place, the Geneva Agreement refers only to Vietnam. Nowhere does it name, or provide for, two separate states of North and South Vietnam divided by an international frontier. It does speak of two zones on each side of the truce line which marked the end of hostilities against the French, and it provided for free elections to be held in July 1956, in both zones to establish a single government for the whole country. The Agreement was silent about how free elections could be held in the North. But the test of that point never came, because Diem, with our support, took measures to prevent elections in the South. This is no war between two states, but a civil war among a people who are emerging from a long period of colonial control by Chinese, French, and Japanese; who are not yet a nation; who have yet to organize a state; and who have been incapable in the South of establishing a competent government on a broad popular base.

Nor is our legal position stronger under the terms of the Southeast Asia Treaty. The true character of that "alliance" is revealed in its membership. The parties were the United States, the United Kingdom, France, Australia, New Zealand, Pakistan, the Philippines, and Thailand. Of those eight, five were not Asian. Excluding China, of the other major countries of Asia (namely India, Pakistan, Japan, and Indonesia) only Pakistan signed. In fact, the Treaty was plainly conceived to bolster up Western influence in Southeast Asia, and two of the three Asian countries which it did include, namely Pakistan and the Philippines, retain strong Western links. Politically therefore, SEATO was bound to run afoul of Asian nationalism and anti-colonialism. Laos, Cambodia, and Vietnam are not parties to the Treaty, but its protection was extended in a separate Protocol to embrace their area.[2] Thus our Department of State has argued that by intervening in the war we are honoring our commitment.

What actually does the Treaty require? The document describes two situations when the parties are bound to render help to one another or to a protected government. One such situation arises in the event of "aggression by means of armed attack in the treaty area," in which case each member is obliged "to meet the common danger in accordance with its constitutional processes." What happened in South Vietnam was that successive Saigon "governments" were collapsing in 1964 under the blows of the Vietcong, and President Johnson after winning his election proceeded early in 1965 to Americanize the war. Only after he put our military forces into action in the South and began bombing in the North did North Vietnam send its regular army units into the South. And so far from conforming to our "constitutional processes," our government never observed that requirement. We have conducted a large-scale war which the President never requested the Congress to declare. What about the solemn

---

[2] The Protocol, like the Geneva Agreement, does not recognize two separate Vietnamese states. What it mentions by name is "the free territory under the jurisdiction of the State of Vietnam."

commitment of our elected officials to honor the Constitution? That provision was written by the founding fathers so as to prevent just such an eventuality as that of a chief executive taking the country into war by his unilateral decision and then confronting the Congress and the country with the *fait accompli*.[3]

The other situation that can invoke the operation of the Treaty exists whenever the integrity of a member is threatened by other means than armed attack (internal subversion, for example). In that event, the only obligation specified in the text is for the parties "to consult immediately in order to agree on what measures to take." But when the Johnson administration decided to intervene in the war in January 1965, no such consultation occurred. That was a strictly unilateral decision for which subsequent endorsement was sought—a way of behaving that was similar to the Dominican intervention a few months later. The response of the other Treaty members has shown what they thought of our action. Of the European countries, neither Britain nor France took any part whatsoever. Australia and New Zealand have both contributed small forces—understandably, because they are paying the premium on their insurance policy with the United States, which is the ANZUS Treaty. Where this country leads, whether wisely or unwisely, they must follow. Of the three Asian members, only Thailand and the Philippines are participating militarily and, of course, both of their governments are heavily dependent on us. Significantly, the lone major Asian signatory, Pakistan, refuses to involve itself. President

---

[3] Those who take the Gulf of Tonkin resolution of August 7, 1964, as legal authority for President Johnson's military actions after January 1965, should note these words of Senator Fulbright: "Many Senators who accepted the Gulf of Tonkin resolution without question might well not have done so had they foreseen that it would subsequently be interpreted as a sweeping Congressional endorsement for the conduct of a large-scale war in Asia. Literally, it can be so interpreted, but it must be remembered that the resolution was adopted during an election campaign in which the President was telling the American people that it would be a mistake for the United States to become involved in a major war in Asia while criticizing his opponent for proposing just that." *The Arrogance of Power*, Random House, Vintage Book, New York, 1966, p. 52.

Ayub Khan, a professional soldier, has declared that if it is the aim of the United States to prevent South Vietnam from becoming Communist, the struggle could last for forty or fifty years. In short, SEATO is a farce. It is a flimsy device which our government has sought to adapt to our ends —not an organization with substance or an alliance with significance. The architects of an unwise policy cloaked their misconceptions of America's interests in the inappropriate language of honor and contract.

So, let us turn to considerations of interest and power, i.e., the political reasons advanced in favor of land warfare in Southeast Asia. A favorite argument in this category—it is Fiction Number Two on the list—is the "domino theory." The theory's major premise is that Southeast Asia is of vital interest to the United States; its minor premise is that the whole region stands or falls together. Whence the conclusion: We must shore up each piece, or all will come tumbling down and America's security will be imperiled. At their best, these are unproven and unprovable hypotheses. At the worst, they are pure fantasy. They are authoritatively asserted as if they were the truth, so that the onus of disproof is shifted to those who doubt them; whereas properly the burden of proof belongs with those who have proposed a doctrine so speculative and novel.

The belief that this entire region is a vital American interest, sufficient to have justified our large-scale intervention in land warfare, has been emphatically rejected by responsible authorities—political, diplomatic, and military.[4] Vital is no term to be used lightly. It should signify that if the balance of forces within an area is tilted adversely to the United States, our security is in danger. Certainly we have no material stake in Southeast Asia—property, investments, and so on —comparable to those which the British, Dutch, and French attempted in vain to defend. As for the assertion that Americans have to fight in South Vietnam in order not to fight at some future time in Hawaii or California, it is political rhetoric and particularly reprehensible when employed to order

---

[4] To name a few: Senators Fulbright and Aiken, Ambassador Kennan, Mr. Lippmann, Generals Gavin and Shoup.

the needless deaths of young men. I shall argue later that the United States does have a permanent interest in maintaining preponderant power in the Pacific Ocean, which means, of course, that our links with island states are vital. But the logic of this reasoning stops just where the water ends and the land begins. The mainland portion of Southeast Asia is not vital to us in any directly meaningful sense. Indeed, I would state the contrary, that to have allowed ourselves to be sucked into land warfare against Asians in Asia is harmful to our vital interests, since we weaken ourselves by an endless hemorrhage without gaining a commensurate benefit.

Similarly, for the thesis that all the pieces are interconnected and that as goes one so go all, the sensible answer is from *Porgy and Bess:* "It ain't necessarily so." In one instance, that of Indonesia, our officials tried to argue that its change of regime and the consequent swing from left to right were prompted and made possible by our stand in South Vietnam. But that is only one more myth out of the Washington wonderland. It was in fact vigorously repudiated by the Indonesian government and press, which insisted that their liquidation of local Communists was a domestic operation uninfluenced by our military stance.

Fiction Number Three derives from the contention that we must stop world communism and affirms that in Vietnam we have met and are blunting its spearhead. This is partly oversimplification and partly delusion. If true, it would presuppose a global conspiracy directed from one central source—something which had a foundation in fact during Stalin's lifetime and then survived in the dreamworld of Dulles.[5] The reality of the fifteen years from 1953 to 1968 was a widening of the split between the Communist states. If anything, however, has served in some limited degree to unite them, it has been our military intervention in South Vietnam, which in this respect was counterproductive as in so many others.

[5] Dulles phrased his dreams thus: Liberate the oppressed peoples of Eastern Europe, unleash Chiang Kai-shek, massive retaliation, go up to the brink of war, conduct an agonizing reappraisal (of our relations with France). All this was empty rhetoric. In practice, he did nothing of the sort. One reappraisal was conducted, not by us but by De Gaulle—and we were the ones to be agonized.

In any case, to the extent that what we are opposing is communism and to the extent that part of communism is its ideology, we cannot hope to combat it by military means. However, since what we have faced in Vietnam is as much a phenomenon of nationalism as of class conflict, it is doubly unfortunate for us that a Communist, Ho Chi Minh, has also been so effective a nationalist. We chose earlier to put our money on the French, who failed; then on Diem, who failed; and latterly on the Kys and Thieus, who would not be where they are without our tanks and dollars.

Fourth comes the fiction that our objective in South Vietnam is to contain China. The logic of this argument I have never grasped because I do not see how the means we employ will lead to that end. There is no disputing the fact that the present regime in China is abhorrent and repulsive to us. Mao's successors at some future date could menace our security. But even so, how in fact would they attack us? The Chinese can only reach the United States across the sea, by air, or through space. I fail to comprehend how our control of the area of South Vietnam would deny, or even discourage, their use of any of those three routes. Conversely, if we should ever need to defend ourselves by counterattack, it is not from sites in so vulnerable an area as South Vietnam that we would launch our missiles against China's industrial centers. In any future war with China, the one military use we could make of South Vietnam would be as a base for dispatching land forces into southern China. Whoever thinks that the way for us to defeat the Chinese would be by land warfare in Asia has lost touch with reality. It is political folly and strategically unsound to challenge an opponent on a terrain and under conditions where he possesses the maximum human and geographical advantages and where all the techniques and assets in our arsenal are deployed at their greatest disadvantage.

Finally, the Fifth Fiction is in the official mythology, which asserts that our action will prevent World War III, that we are doing in Southeast Asia what should have been done in Europe before 1938. Really, this is a classic example of the abuse of analogy. It consists in pretending to discover a parallel in another situation, whose accompanying conditions differ substantially, and then seeking to draw similar lessons from both. South Vietnam in the 1960s is not the Rhineland or Austria or Czechoslovakia of the thirties. Mao is not Hitler. The appeals and aims of Chinese communism are not those of nazism. The culture and technology of China are not those of Germany. Nor can South Vietnam be sensibly compared to Greece and Turkey in 1947, where again the circumstances differed. Those two countries had been long established and were viable entities. At least they had governments able to govern. Their national feelings drew the majority to our side and they share many of our values. Far from preventing the outbreak of World War III, our deepening involvement actually increased, instead of lessening, that danger.

The last point could be expanded at considerable length. So far from bringing any solid, measurable gain, the policy pursued in Vietnam since 1955, and particularly since 1965, has brought heavy and measurable loss. It is we, both at home and abroad, who are the losers. More than any foreign policy of recent times, that of President Johnson tore this country apart. Conscientious opposition has been voiced to a war which never commended itself to the good sense of a large section of the American people. To say and feel "my country, right or wrong" is not synonymous with "my government, right or wrong"—not in a democracy at any rate. Thus loyal and dedicated citizens have criticized a war in which they were never convinced that the United States had a vital interest. Nor for that matter was the public opinion of our friends on other continents persuaded of the merits of the Johnson-Rusk theses. Increasingly during the last four years, many who wish us well and who have willingly gone along with our leadership in the past, have been dismayed at our unwisdom. The reaction of some was ethical. They saw us as a giant trying to smash a dwarf into a pulp, none too successfully, and sympathy has gone to the dwarf. Others have had a political reaction. In their eyes, we just acted stupidly, since few were ever persuaded by the sophistries of the Five Fictions. The erosion of our prestige has been frighteningly rapid, especially in Europe where we most need respect and good will. In recent years I have heard repeatedly from re-

sponsible European leaders—persons who want and work for
close ties with the United States—such remarks as: "Why
don't you Americans learn from our mistakes in colonial
policy? Why do you repeat them yourselves?"

That brings me to the question: What are our real interests
in the area of Southeast Asia? I shall start from two axioms.
First, we must never again allow ourselves to become over-
committed and pinned down in an area where our vital
interests do not lie. Since 1965, because of the deep involvement in Vietnam, we have lacked adequate forces in immediate readiness to cope with emergencies elsewhere. What
could we have done effectively during that time in Europe?
Or the Middle East? Or in Latin America? Second, it makes
absolutely no sense for Americans to collect and seek to sal-
vage the wrecks of fallen empires—be they British, Dutch,
French, or Japanese. When the political trends of this century were working against them—as Washington used continuously to preach in the nineteen-forties and fifties to the sin-
ful imperialists of Western Europe—why should our officials
now suppose that they would work for us? My point is that
we, being what we are, cannot enter on a large scale such
countries as those of Southeast Asia, being what they are,
without recreating the essential relationship of an imperial
power to a colony. Mask the reality by what disguises you
will; the fact remains.

For a case history, look at the current situation in South
Korea, where in 1968 violence continued to erupt along the
frontier with the North. Korea is sometimes compared with
Vietnam, and those who approved our decision to defend
South Korea in the early fifties are asked to see South Vietnam in the same light. But again, the circumstances are different. In Korea there was a clear and unmistakable attack
launched by regular forces from the North. This happened
at a time when we were already stationed in the South because our forces had occupied that area when the Japanese
surrendered. Hence we had no choice but to respond, and
that response received the sanction and authority of the
United Nations. Even so, take a glance at the present Korean
situation, a decade and a half since hostilities ended. Ac-

cording to published figures, the South Koreans now have an army of 500,000 while we keep as many as 50,000 Americans alongside them. The North Korean army reportedly numbers 350,000 without any stiffening by Chinese or Russian troops. Why should the South Koreans, with such a numerical ratio in their favor, not yet be able to defend themselves without the presence of American personnel? How long do client relationships of this kind have to continue?[6] Do we have any real need to expose our personnel to incidents such as the capture of the *Pueblo?*

And *a fortiori,* what does anyone think will be the position in South Vietnam some five or fifteen years from now? In Paris since January 1969, a delegation from the United States, the world's most powerful country, has been seated at a conference table with no less than three squabbling, mutually discordant groups of Vietnamese—and it was our government which unnecessarily involved the American people in their chaotic politics. What sort of sense does this make? That is not America's interest. For how long do we doom ourselves to pay for and prop up a regime in Saigon? Are we not retreading the old familiar tracks of bygone empires?

There is a logic in such questions which implies its own answer. The policy we pursued for the last fifteen years is now bankrupt. We should devise one which will work more to our interest by drawing a line where the political and strategic factors operate to our advantage. The question is: where?

It should be self-evident that our government was mistaken in trying to control positions on the Asian mainland. We have no business being there. On the mainland we have no stake, no vital interest to ensure. But there is somebody else who does. It is the Soviet Union which has real stakes on the Asian continent and faces direct danger from Chinese territorial expansion. The Soviet Union has the need, which the United States does not, to establish a continental balance of

[6] Equally unwise is our involvement in Thailand, where according to press reports another 50,000 Americans are now stationed. The Thai government is much resented in northern areas where another Vietnam may be brewing. Let the Thais defend themselves, with United States equipment.

power. One of the cruelest features of the blundering policy
in Vietnam is that our government sent young Americans to
fight and die for what are essentially Russian interests. That
is a privilege we should have left to the Russians.

Now, what are America's interests? Our security is vitally
concerned with the Pacific. We do need to retain a preponderant position throughout the ocean up to the edges of the
Asian coastline, and technically this is more manageable for
us than to control a slice of the continent. Even in this age
of air and space power, sea power continues to make a difference, and its advantages are decidedly ours. If possible, we
should retain alliances—and, hopefully, active friendships—with
all the island states. However, this does not mean that every
single island state must always remain in alliance with us and
may never withdraw. It would be politically counterproductive
for us to restage in the Pacific Ocean an American version of
Russia's occupation of Czechoslovakia. It is preponderance
we need, not monopoly.

Having drawn such a line, we should seek to exploit the
division between the two great states with Communist governments. As a clue to the making of an intelligent policy,
let me quote from that master of *realpolitik,* Bismarck. When
the French in the 1880s were embarking on colonial expansion in North Africa, Bismarck, rather than opposing, encouraged them. A friend, reminding the Chancellor that the
French were burning for revenge against Germany, inquired
why he did so. The reply was a piece of classic statecraft:
"I have sent the fiery steed of French ambition galloping
into the sands of North Africa. They will find it heavy going."
His prediction, seventy years later, proved to be correct. If
we had more sagacity at the top of our State Department,
this is what we would have tried to encourage, since it is
always in one's diplomatic interest to help a competitor into
situations which will only cause him trouble. The unwise are
those who gratuitously grab the trouble for themselves, which
has been our government's policy. Our aim should be to entice the Russians into the region where we have adventured.
The jungles, swamps, and mountains of Vietnam belong to
the Bear, not to the Eagle. After all, there is a genuine Rus-

sian interest in securing positions in the rear of the Chinese so as to challenge them from both sides.

I would therefore hope that, as the negotiations in Paris lead to a planned withdrawal of American forces from Vietnam, we would welcome the introduction of a multinational peacekeeping force. This should include not only Asian units from countries which have not been engaged in the war, but also contingents from the Soviet Union and Eastern Europe. It is America's interest to help the Russian Bear encircle the Chinese Dragon. Meanwhile on the mainland, our policy should be to assist selected governments with dollars and equipment only. The principal recipient of such help, of course, has to be India. For the rest, among the island states we must recognize the reality of the resurgence of Japan. At present, like West Germany, Japan has strength without power. But its power will come, and it will be felt in the seventies when the Japanese economy will have developed into the third strongest in the world. At that point, a new era will open in Japan's relations with the United States. It is the mutual interest of both that these be cooperative and friendly.

American concern with the Pacific and Soviet concern with the Asian mainland suggest, for that hemisphere, a possible division of spheres of interest appropriate to the vital needs of the two superpowers. But any arrangement for coexistence on that side of the world requires a parallel understanding in Europe where both are also involved. So let us now consider what American policy has been, and should be, in the Atlantic region.

There is no question in my mind that of the three areas with which the vital interests of the United States are linked externally—the North Atlantic, Latin America, and the Pacific —the first of these is first in priority. Now and in the future, the prime objective of our statecraft should be to develop the closest practicable relationship with the peoples and governments of Canada and Western Europe. Indeed, I would assert this axiom for the foreign policy of the United States: Any American policy which reinforces our links with Western Europe is justified in terms of American interests. Conversely, no American policy elsewhere in the world can be justified if it tends to weaken those links. The reasons for this can be simply stated. Foremost of all is the fact that the peoples of Western Europe and Canada belong to the same civilization as ourselves. When we associate with them, and they with us, it is in order to preserve jointly the values that make us what we are. Hence it must always be our top external priority to cooperate with them as intimately as possible. In the future, the destinies of Western Europe and North America will continue to be linked in a special relationship just as they have been in the past. This is not only the consequence of history, culture, and geography; even if we wished, we could not ignore the current realities of world politics and economics. We and the Canadians need an association with Western Europe because that area constitutes in its own right a tremendous center of actual and future power—industrial, scientific, technological, and political. Together, Western Europe and North America can reinforce one another in a world where long-term population trends are decidedly disadvantageous to us.

The truth that the security of the United States is connected, mutually, with that of Western Europe has received formal recognition in the North Atlantic Treaty. Since the United States had twice within a quarter of a century become a participant in world wars originating in whole or in part in Europe, it was understandable that United States public opinion and political parties after 1945 should accept the notion of organizing collectively to prevent a future recurrence of the same. Had Great Britain and the United States given clear, public warning before 1914 that they would oppose any act of military aggression in Western Europe, it is virtually certain that the German government would not have gambled on invading Belgium and Northern France. Had the United States made it unequivocally clear to Hitler prior to 1938 that if he sent his panzer divisions across European frontiers the United States would definitely intervene to oppose him, World War II in Europe would most probably have been averted. This reasoning underlay the provisions of the North Atlantic Treaty signed in April 1949, when Western Europe once again confronted a clear and present danger. That danger was present after the coup by the Communist Party in Czechoslovakia in 1948, an event whose stage managing was quite reminiscent of Hitler, and to anybody who had eyes to see, the danger was clear again in June 1950, after North Korea attacked South Korea. All that it then required was one signal from Stalin to launch a similar movement from East Germany westward. Hence the North Atlantic Treaty rapidly evolved into an Organization—the "O" in NATO, which the French like to emphasize—and the NATO shield was constructed.

Now, twenty years after, we are in a position to appraise its results and thence to make some guesses about the future. Assuredly in terms of its initial objective—to deter an armed attack on Western Europe and North America—NATO has been a success. At any rate, no such attack was attempted, and it is reasonable to hold that this has been due in no small part to the existence of both the Treaty and its Organization. Indeed, so strongly has the sense of security grown latterly in Western Europe that various groups[7] within some of NATO's member states have been increasing their opposition to the Treaty. Moreover, in the case of France, a government withdrew from military participation in the Organization and peremptorily ordered NATO's military headquarters off French soil.[8] A few years ago, it was not uncommon in Western Europe to hear NATO dismissed as "an alliance in search of an enemy."

But the events of 1967–68 have done much to modify this attitude. The two new realities are the continued presence of a significant Soviet fleet in the Mediterranean and the occupation of Czechoslovakia in August 1968 by Warsaw Pact

[7] The reference here is to non-Communist groups. The opposition of Communist groups is, of course, taken for granted.

[8] General de Gaulle did not withdraw, however, from the Treaty, which legally he could not do before April 1970 at the earliest. Contrary to what one often hears or reads, the North Atlantic Treaty could not expire in 1969. All that could happen in that year was that Article 13 be enforced, permitting any member to give notice of its intention to leave the alliance. The departure would then come into effect twelve months after such notice had been given. For those not taking this step, however, the Treaty continues in force indefinitely.

forces, including—blunder of blunders!—troops from East Germany. The Soviet fleet, sailing the waters of the Romans' *mare nostrum,* has reawakened concern in Italy and Greece for NATO ties, while the military suppression of a liberalizing Czech regime has sent a shock wave pulsating throughout the West. For the immediately foreseeable future the argument is irrefutable that the military defenses of the North Atlantic region will have to be maintained until a general plan for disarmament can be negotiated and mutually enforced. Since national defenses are no defense, a single integrated supranational system is required; and this, to be effective, should be organized for purposes of insurance in advance against the events which it is designed to prevent. The Gaullist contention that one can safely defend oneself by an independent national force fails for this reason: Such a force cannot be a credible deterrent to a would-be aggressor because to build it nowadays to a level of credibility would overstrain the means of any state except a superpower. What happened in France in May–June and November of 1968 supplies some evidence on this point. Had the French government devoted less of its resources to nuclear nationalism and the pursuit of prestige, it might have alleviated much of the pent-up discontent whose explosion so weakened France internationally and then compelled cuts in the atomic program itself. And *a fortiori,* what is true of a medium-rank power is truer still of one yet smaller. Even if the Czechs in 1968 had had some rockets and nuclear bombs of their own, surely no one supposes in view of their geography that their allies would have been deterred from invading them.

But saying that national systems of defense in Europe can scarcely be credible does not solve the genuine difficulty to which these are addressed. Granted that the contemporary technology of military security requires ever broader integration of peoples, areas, and resources, one comes back to the stubborn facts inherent in the North Atlantic alliance: namely, that it is constituted as an alliance of the governments of separate nation-states, some of which are understandably reluctant to surrender to another the decisions on which their survival may depend. Such considerations are a blend of the political and psychological. NATO remains the cornerstone on which the external military and political relationships of the United States are built, and within it we are the leader. But, thus far, we have not succeeded in solving the political problems generated by the dynamics of this essential alliance.

The crux of the matter is the inequality of the allies. This grouping of fifteen is strangely composed in that the military strength of one exceeds the combined strength of fourteen, and owing to this disproportion the Organization functions under evident strain. Thus diplomatic formulae which proclaim equality of status, or which announce the right of all to participate jointly in decisions, do not square with basic realities. The United States, of course, can lead unilaterally, in which case the only certainty is that criticisms will be forthcoming. For their part, our allies can debate—which they do. But they can decide nothing unless at least Great Britain, France, and Germany agree, and even if they should agree, they lack at present the wherewithal to lead or act effectively without us. The result, almost inevitably, has been a tendency for several members of the alliance to go their own ways in pursuit of what they conceive (or misconceive) to be their vital interests—as did Britain and France at Suez, France in Algeria, Belgium in the Congo, the United States in Cuba and the Dominican Republic and Vietnam—and then to be pained when allies have expressed displeasure.

When seeking escape from these dilemmas, many take refuge in the idea of consultation as the magic formula whereby the needs of all can be incorporated into the process of decision. But since a right to be consulted is not the same as a capacity to act, the faith in that formula, though it will work in some instances, is bound to give disappointment in others. For at the core of the issue is the very character of NATO—a defensive regional alliance organized with much more structure than any previous grouping in modern peacetime history.[9] Politically it represents a stage in the journey

[9] An ancient parallel is the Confederacy of Delos, organized and led by the Athenians in 477 B.C. after the repulse of the Persian invasion. But that came to a sticky end.

from separate nation-states to a possible supranational entity, along which road no halfway house is ever an endurable resting place.

From this point, the path to the future could fork off in any of four directions. One of these is the road back whence we came. It takes us to the revival of nationalism, the reassertion of "sovereign" independence, the refusal to organize collectively for preventing disaster before it arrives. This is the Gaullist road. In the first half of this century, it led two generations into two World Wars. Why then retrace it?

A second route is to follow the leader, to accept the power of the strongest, to go wherever Washington beckons. Substantially that was what happened in the fifties when Western Europe and Canada acquiesced in American initiatives and leadership, albeit with muttering and grumbling at times. But we are now in the seventies. This emergent Europe—thanks to the efforts both of Europeans and of North Americans— is no longer that Europe. And in any case, after witnessing our policy in Vietnam, Western Europeans will certainly sign no blank checks to join us in global adventurism. They have grown too skeptical of the wisdom of Washington.

A third route avoids detours and brings us directly by a quick short cut to a supranational authority, the region-state of the Atlantic peoples. This would eventually mean transferring the power to provide for the common defense to an agency common to North America and Western Europe. For the institutions to bring this about, we have no lack of models at hand. They already exist in the principles of federal union whose practice this country invented. Is the majority of the American people yet ready for such a step? Specifically, would the Congress agree to relinquish unilateral control over America's nuclear arsenal? We cannot expect others to take this step if we are not prepared to take it ourselves.

The fourth route is that of partnership. Its goal is a United States of Western Europe linked to North America with enough of a structure to execute policies formulated in common. The principal argument in its favor for Europeans is that this alone ensures equality with the United States. Since states of medium size—such as Great Britain, France, Italy, and West Germany—cannot separately attain equality with a superpower, they could do so if they were united with one another and with their smaller neighbors. The obstacle to this does not come from the United States, which ever since the inception of the Marshall Plan has steadily encouraged all programs leading to the integration of Western Europe. It came, of course, from President de Gaulle who employed the language of Europe as a symbol to cloak what he intended as a French hegemony. Although he urged independence of American power, he resisted that consolidation of Western Europe through which alone the power of the United States could be equalled.

Of the four routes, I rule out the first as potentially destructive for all, and the second as unrealistic because it is no longer acceptable to our allies. That leaves open either the third route or the fourth. The former will require that we too abandon some nationalism of our own in the interests of a wider interdependence. The fourth must await a further turn of events on the French political scene.

The choice between the two latter routes makes overt an ambiguity which has been latent in American policy toward Europe ever since 1947. For two decades we have given our blessing both to Western European integration and to Atlantic union. Evidently we assumed that the twain are compatible. One could be in favor of uniting Western Europe and also for uniting it with North America, without either foreclosing the other. Gaullism has at least accomplished this much: it shattered the facile belief that these aims were necessarily harmonious. Had the General been less of a French nationalist, he could conceivably have been the leader of a European movement functioning separately from, and in opposition to, North America. Nor is it impossible that some other statesman of Western Europe might seek this role.

For the United States, as well as Canada, the weightiest issues revolve around the answer to the question posed in recent years on the other side of the ocean: Can you be both European and Atlantic, or must you choose to be one or the other? The difference goes deep to the roots of Western culture. "Either . . . or" expresses the Cartesian logic of the French; "both . . . and" is the pragmatic empiricism of the English speaking. American diplomacy, as should be evident, has to argue "both . . . and." We must contend for the Atlantic association because our security and prosperity are so vitally connected with those of Western Europe—and theirs, as we believe, with ours. At the same time, precisely because we admire the traditions and cultures of the peoples of Europe and because we respect their sense of pride and dignity, we should prefer a partnership with equals to a hegemony over dependents. It is thus that we can understand the message which Servan-Schreiber conveys in his book, *The American Challenge*. His advice to fellow Europeans is to reorganize their economies, as well as their social and political structures, so as to utilize the potentialities of the new technology. For the fact that American corporations have exploited some of these possibilities in Western Europe more speedily than Europeans have done, he blames not the Americans but the Europeans. His argument, in essentials, is not hostile to the United States, but rather a tribute to this country's effective pioneering. To Europeans he is saying: "Learn enough from America to be equal and to do the same."

The concept, however, of a Western Europe united within an Atlantic union contains another implication for American policy of which we should be explicitly aware. De Gaulle has dreamed of a Europe extending from the Atlantic to the Urals. This appealed to many Europeans who resented that manifestation of the cold war—a political line bisecting the continent from north to south. To reknit the severed limbs of Europe, thus permitting easy circulation east and west, was indeed a design grand enough to compete with the alternatives of the superblocs. For several years, the General made some mileage with that diplomacy. But, like Napoleon's *Grande Armée*, it died in Moscow.[10] The invasion of Czechoslovakia in August 1968 by the Soviet Union and its allies in the Warsaw Pact, plus the continued military occupation since that date, have shattered the Gaullist offensive. From 1964 to 1968 there was considerable progress toward an east-west détente, and these moves were initiated independently by the French, Germans, and Italians at a time when the

[10] Did he ever seriously expect the Russians to relinquish what they hold east of the Urals?

United States, hopelessly bogged down in Vietnam, was incapacitated, morally and diplomatically, from effective action in the area where our most vital interests lie.

The Russian action in Czechoslovakia was thus a significant turning point. What it has done is both to alter the perspective and redefine the context of future East-West relations. The Russian position in the center and east of Europe is stronger in the short run, although it may have been weakened over the long. The present Kremlin leaders have put everybody on notice that they will not tolerate a significant degree of internal liberalization—political, economic, or cultural—in any country within their sphere of influence. There will be no more Yugoslavias if they can prevent it. Thereby they indicate their determination to sit on the lid, even at the expense of holding down some resentful fellow Slavs and national Communists. Ultimately, this decision is more a sign of weakness than of strength because it reveals an awareness among Soviet ruling circles of how brittle is the structure of their own domestic power. But for the time being, irrespective of the folly or wisdom of their policy, they possess the definite means to make it stick.

In the light of these events and their political aftermath, the questions for American policy makers are these: What deductions should we draw from their action and how can we turn it to our benefit? The truly significant point for us to grasp is the meticulous emphasis of the Russians that Eastern Europe was their sphere of influence, that they were confining their intervention to their side of the line, and that we should stick to our side. In other words, the Russians were behaving aggressively within their own alliance, but defensively from the standpoint of ours. Let us take it from there, because in this situation is a possible advantage for us which we should be astute enough to seize. It is our interest, as I have argued earlier, to encourage the Soviet Union to cope effectively with Chinese expansionism on the Asian mainland, as it is equally our interest to see the two major exponents of Communist power devoting their energies to one another. But the Soviet Union, spreading from Eastern Europe all across Asia, must always think of its two fronts. It cannot deploy sufficient force, political or military, against China if it feels insecure in the rear. And this is where we come in. It is in our interest to offer the Soviet Union assurances that if they focus their activity on their Asian problem we shall see to it that their defenses in Europe will be undisturbed. We shall stick to our side of the line in central Europe while they deal with the Chinese, whether in the northeast of the Asian mainland or the southeast.

That brings the argument straight back to the future relevance of NATO and our role therein. Again, this is where we differ radically, and must differ, from de Gaulle. He propounded the idea of a series of bilateral arrangements between individual countries, West and East, including the Soviet Union itself. The disadvantage here is that it opens the way to all manner of separate relationships where every single country, whether small or medium, is going to be played off against every other—a return, in point of fact, to the inadequate system of the eighteenth and nineteenth centuries. The one reliable way to arrange an agreement between East and West is to organize it collectively. We need a revitalized NATO as the appropriate instrument for negotiating and enforcing a system of mutual security and détente with the countries of the Warsaw Pact. Then we can say to Moscow: "Go east, and good luck!"

Whether NATO, besides its military and diplomatic roles, can be developed in the future to meet our other vital needs in the Atlantic region is an open question. Because its immediate task was to defend the West in the period of intense cold war, NATO early received an imprint which was heavily military. It has ringed the North Atlantic region with a protective shield, but has not set out to organize an (or, is it "the"?) Atlantic Community. The social and cultural ideals expressed in the Treaty's preamble and in Article 2 have not been vigorously pursued. Neither in spirit nor letter do the present governments of Greece and Portugal conform to the professed values of the alliance; and Turkey, although Westernized, belongs to the Islamic civilization. The economic goals of the Treaty were left to OEEC, the organization for the Marshall Plan. Since then, the notion of transatlantic economic cooperation has been the responsibility of OECD whose membership has been broadened to include the neutrals of Western Europe and also Japan, while economic union within Europe belongs to EEC and EFTA.

Undoubtedly, America's vital interests require a close continuing association, both economic and cultural, with our partners in Western Europe, an association which cannot be truly effective unless it be institutionalized. This is why for the United States the country with the key role to play in the Atlantic region is Great Britain. The British are both European and Atlantic. They form the natural bridge between the two continents. This is exactly why de Gaulle banned them from the Common Market, whose future significance the British government of the mid-fifties was too myopic to foresee. Hence the United States and Great Britain are in fact linked in a special relationship where their vital interests mutually coincide.

As for the eastern perimeter of Western Europe, the German situation has to be faced—and faced realistically. During the fifties and the early sixties, the attitude of Germany's major allies—our own government included—was one of double talk. Officially they were on record in favor of reunification. In practice, they did nothing to bring it about, and could do nothing in the teeth of Soviet opposition. The plain truth was that public opinion outside Germany did not wish to see the two parts rejoined, and the official postures of Western governments were often at variance with what they privately felt. In Eastern Europe, for obvious reasons, these feelings were as strong as in the West, if not stronger. Indeed, one can argue that the United States and the Soviet Union acted in this matter on parallel lines from a sense of common need to maintain the division. Were the two segments of Germany to be reunited, the power thus formed would be too great to be neutralized or bound permanently by treaties of limitation which some future German government could, if it chose, repudiate. A reunited Germany would once again determine the balance of the European continent. If it swung to our side, Russian security would be gravely threatened. If it swung East, our vital interests would suffer. This was a risk which neither Washington nor Moscow could contemplate. Hence for identical reasons, we have sought to link West Germany to ourselves, as Russia has done with the East. By now, even in West Germany, opinion is divided over the merits of being reunited. There are many, particularly among the post-Nazi generation, who shrink from the prospect of reabsorbing East Germany as it has developed under the odious Ulbricht regime, although understandably they desire the freer movement of persons east and west. It is America's interest, therefore, to foster the closest connection with West Germany inside a system flexible enough to be both Atlantic and European.

In addition to the North Atlantic and the Pacific Ocean, the third region of vital concern to the United States is Latin America. This is the unavoidable result of the fact of geographical proximity. Viewed in geopolitical terms, Latin America is "the soft underbelly"[11] of the United States. Latin and English-speaking Americans are neighbors in the same hemisphere. Because the former lag behind in social, economic, and political development, the United States is, or ought to be, concerned with this area for reasons both of altruism and self-interest. The great majority of the countries in Central and South America have never yet passed through the kind of revolution which makes the difference between a modern people and a traditional one. Evidence of modernization, of course, abounds throughout Latin America. But generally these are isolated oases—or, to change the metaphor, a thinly spread veneer—in whose benefits the mass of the population share too little. The social structure and, with it, the economic system and prevailing political order are pyramids rising to a sharply tapered apex. Naturally, therefore, Latin America is explosive. The entire area seethes with the forces of change, while in one country after another repressive authoritarian regimes (many of them military) attempt to maintain control.

The United States is linked to Latin America by commerce and a considerable body of investment. A cultural connection

[11] The phrase is Churchill's. He referred to Italy in World War II as "the soft underbelly of the Axis."

also exists, but this is not as close as with Europe for the simple reason that most of the North American culture does not derive from the Iberian peninsula. Contractually, our bonds with our neighbors to the south are written into the Rio Treaty of Reciprocal Assistance (1947) and the Charter of the Organization of American States (1948). The inter-American system has developed a political arm, which has a skeleton but little muscle. The military arrangements do not even begin to compare with NATO. In this case, the contrast between the overwhelming superiority of one country and the inferiority of the rest is too glaring to make alliance or reciprocity meaningful. The political interest of the United States in what takes place in the Caribbean and south of the Rio Grande can be expressed in minimal terms, thus: We would never want to see the overall balance of forces in Latin America tilted adversely to ourselves.

Granted that the Americas are permanently joined in an inescapable nexus, it is indeed surprising that Latin America has not held a higher position in the external priorities of the United States. Instead of placing this connection where it should be—second only to Western Europe—we have generally neglected it, and in my judgment we neglect it at our peril. Indeed we only begin paying it attention when something unusual happens which we do not understand and, instinctively, do not like—the revolution in Cuba, for example. Moreover, of the aid which has been given to this region too much continues to be military and too much has been given to governments which persistently disregard the legitimate needs of their poor and underprivileged. More than one military *coup d' état* has been conducted there with equipment which we supplied. The Batistas we are able to swallow, and habitually we do business with them. A Castro, however, we cannot stomach, and similarly we draw the line at a "Papa Doc."

In our relations with Latin America during the last decade we have been obsessed with the fear that Castro's style of revolution might spread. Consequently, our government has opposed any drift to the left in which it thought it detected the possibility of another Cuba. This, I suppose, explains, although I would deny that the circumstances justified, the military intervention by President Johnson in the internal affairs of the Dominican Republic in April 1965. Where much still remains obscure[12] about that operation, one aspect is abundantly clear. That intervention was in direct violation of the treaties we had signed. Our government did not honor its commitments in the Dominican case. It broke them.

The announced pretext for intervening was the need to protect American lives and property during a tense internal struggle for power. The real reason appears to have been—as resulted in point of fact—to prevent Juan Bosch from regaining power and to ensure the installation of a group oriented more toward the right.[13] But irrespective of motive, our government's action was in any case prohibited by Articles 15 and 17 of the Charter of the Organization of American States. Nor can it be upheld under the Rio Treaty. Article 6 of the latter agreement allows for collective assistance to any state whose political independence is threatened by other means than those of armed aggression. In these cases, however, the parties are required to consult immediately with one another in order to agree on what measures to take. No such prior consultation was initiated or requested by the United States. Instead, President Johnson ordered this military intervention unilaterally. Only afterward was the OAS consulted—so as to approve the *fait accompli*. Some units were then dispatched to the Dominican Republic from other American republics at the expense of the United States, and

[12] For instance, no convincing evidence has yet been made public to support the belief that the government was likely to fall into Communist hands.

[13] On this topic, Senator Fulbright has written: "Four months later, after an exhaustive review of the Dominican crisis by the Senate Foreign Relations Committee meeting in closed sessions, it was clear beyond reasonable doubt that although saving American lives may have been a factor in the decision to intervene on April 28, the major reason was a determination on the part of the United States government to defeat the rebel, or constitutionalist, forces whose victory at that time was imminent. Had I known in April what I knew in August, I most certainly would have objected to the American intervention in the Dominican Republic." *The Arrogance of Power,* Random House, Vintage Book, New York, 1966, pp. 49–50.

a Brazilian[14] was eventually designated as commander to lend the whole operation a pan-American camouflage.

This episode is of interest for many reasons. It was conducted by an Administration which, seeking simultaneously to justify its military operations in Vietnam, proclaimed repeatedly that the United States was honoring its commitments to Saigon. Even if the latter point were true, a contention I have sought to refute, the Dominican intervention flagrantly belies the argument. Moreover, in August 1968 our government condemned the invasion of Czechoslovakia, which plainly violated both the Preamble and Article 8 of the Warsaw Pact. Washington did in fact apply a double standard during the years from 1965 to 1968. It broke its commitments to Latin America while it professed to be honoring its commitments in Southeast Asia. It condemned the Soviet Union for occupying Czechoslovakia and molding the politics of that government, but asserted its own right to occupy the Dominican Republic and mold their government to our liking. One cannot have it both ways. If one approves what Mr. Johnson did in the latter case, one should condone what Messrs. Brezhnev and Kosygin did in the former. But if one condemns the Soviet action, one should be consistent and condemn the action of the United States. For in essentials, the two were alike. The latter judgment, incidentally, is widely held in Latin America, where in the long run our return to the interventionism so freely practiced before 1933 will probably prove counterproductive to our interests.[15]

In the framework which has been sketched out here, I have concentrated on what appears essential. Various topics were therefore omitted because, although important, they are not vital. The essentials are to draw the line of our security within the limits of our needs and power, and then arrange our priorities according to our interests. Neither the Middle East nor Africa has figured in the discussion because, important though they are, neither is vital to American security. In the

[14] Brazil was governed at that time by a military junta to which we were supplying financial and other assistance.

[15] Instances in the nineteen-fifties and sixties have been Guatemala, Cuba, and the Dominican Republic.

former region, we certainly have a moral obligation to see that Israel survives; in helping the Israelis defend themselves, we have the cogent political reason that the Arabs side actively with the Russians. Now that Soviet fleets are sailing the Indian Ocean and the Mediterranean, we should be in no hurry to see the Suez Canal reopened. Israel manifestly needs no manpower from the United States. Our assistance there should be confined to equipment. With this in their hands, the Israelis are quite capable of looking after themselves.

In Africa, the case is different. There, the crying need is for economic and social development—in which so much has to be done that whatever aid one supplies can never suffice. Of recent years, our international aid programs, in the form of economic and technical assistance, have declined except in Southeast Asia. The decline has been both absolute, as represented in the amounts appropriated annually, and relative, expressed as a percentage of our gross national product. Among the international comparisons, we continue to be the world's largest donor to less developed countries. But in relative terms, the French ranked first in 1968 and we were tenth. At present, our aid has fallen below the 1 per cent of gross national product which UNCTAD has suggested as a target. For the future, our total contribution should be increased and should be distributed as far as possible through UN or regional agencies and less through bilateral programs.

Public opinion in the United States has reacted unfavorably in recent years to the aid program in general, and congressional cuts have reflected this reaction. The reasons are not unfounded. Too much of this aid has been abused by the corrupt or wasted by the incompetent. Moreover, in some situations, aid has initiated a tangle of involvements eventually ending up with a Vietnam. This national mood to lessen the volume of external aid is linked with the realization by the American people that much is wrong with our society at home and that our urgent priority is to set our own house in order. Such feelings were deepened by de Gaulle's actions and utter frustration at the futility of the Vietnamese morass. The danger is that these understandable reactions could run to excess and result in a neo-isolationism. If this should be the immediate first consequence of reversing the recent spate of interventionism, one would not be altogether surprised. But it can never be too strongly emphasized that a neo-isolationism is no solution to our present problems. It is neither viable nor desirable. For a superpower no such escape route is open. The whole theme of this essay is a plea for a balanced view of our interests, for active involvement and creative leadership where they are vital, but for restraining ourselves elsewhere.

At a ceremony in Rome more than twenty-one centuries ago, when Cato was ending his term as censor, the public clerk read aloud the traditional prayer, beseeching the gods to grant that the Roman republic would continue to grow. Cato stopped him, and prayed instead that Rome be allowed to stay within the limits it had reached. May we in the American Republic likewise understand our interests, priorities, and limits. Thus may our foreign policy become successful and solvent.

VII Future Directions for United States Policy Toward the Soviet Union and Eastern Europe

MARSHALL D. SHULMAN

More than anything else in our relations with the Soviet Union and Eastern Europe, we must seek a fresh outlook on what is valid and what needs to be re-examined among the prevailing assumptions that have grown up about these relationships over the past quarter of a century. But if we approach the problem not as historians, retracing the events of the past, but as political scientists trying to identify the main elements of the relationship as it stands today and is likely to move during this decade, a useful way to proceed is to work our way from the broad context of the problem toward the concrete policy problems it presents. Five questions can be asked that will hopefully put into focus some aspects of the future, each directed to a critical plane of analysis, progressing from the background of the problem to the policy choices it presents.

The first question, which begins with the background setting, is: *How will the relationship between the United States and the Soviet Union be affected by changes in international politics during this decade?*

The purpose of beginning in this way is to sharpen our awareness that the problem is not a self-enclosed one. It is not simply a matter of the vagaries of the Kremlin or the clash of ideologies. The rivalry of the two nations which have become the preeminent superpowers of the world in the middle of the twentieth century is deeply affected by the radical transformations now taking place in the environment of international politics. These processes are moving so rapidly beneath our feet that it is difficult for us to appreciate what a revolutionary impact they are having upon our societies and the conditions under which they interact with each other, upon the international system and upon the instruments of power in the world.

Any enumeration of the transforming factors in international politics must clearly begin with the accelerating pace of technological innovation. This has two aspects of immediate concern to us: rapid changes in weapons systems and the evolution of new industrial technologies.

Over the last two decades the pace of both qualitative and quantitative change in strategic weapons systems has surpassed that of military doctrines, concepts of power, and traditional ideas about the relationship between war and politics. Within this period, there are shorter cycles of change to be observed. Until recently, we have had a period of relative stability in the strategic relationship between the Soviet Union and the United States, despite substantial disparities in their arsenals, because each had developed a relatively invulnerable retaliatory force. But lately this stability has been undermined by the introduction of new technological advances which may, if the trend is not deflected by tacit or explicit agreement between the superpowers, result in a period of increased uncertainties, instability and tension, as well as much higher costs. It may also have the effect of increasing the influence of professional military interests and defense scientists on the decision making process in both countries.

So swiftly have new industrial technologies been introduced since the Second World War that we are beginning to appreciate that the world has entered upon a revolutionary stage of advanced industrialization, with a number of unanticipated effects. Among these effects are the profound political and social upheavals taking place within the industrialized countries—a point to which we will return shortly. Also, these advances in technology are beginning to change the power relationships among nations, strengthening the position of West Germany and Japan relative to the other advanced industrial countries, and widening even further the gap between the industrialized and the developing countries.

But not only is the relative order of nations affected; if we take into account both military and industrial technology, it is becoming apparent that even the structure of the world power system is in the process of change. Awesome as the destructiveness of nuclear-missile weapons is, they are of limited usefulness for a variety of political purposes. Therefore, the stark bipolarity of power between the United States and the Soviet Union has not prevented the growth of other forms of power, and much more differentiated degrees of allegiance and independence and influence among nations. What appears to be emerging is a multiple balance of power in the various regions of the world, reflecting the rising potential of Japan, China, and West Germany—or, if the momentum toward integration is resumed, of Western Europe as a whole.

Another background factor in international politics besides technology is the continuing rise of the North-South problem as a source of international tension. The continuing growth of the industrial countries of the northern hemisphere contrasts with the many difficulties that the developing countries of the southern hemisphere have had in the nation-building process and population growth patterns despite improvements in agricultural techniques, and taking into account the many potential sources of conflict in the developing areas—racial, religious, tribal, and political. Thus it seems likely that continuing turbulence in these areas will be a feature of international politics during the coming decade, and that the industrialized countries will inevitably be drawn into these conflicts. The effect of this upon the Soviet-American rivalry may however be twofold. In some areas—as for example in the Middle East today—the local conflict may intensify the Great Power competition, while in other areas they are likely to find themselves back-to-back, with common interests in damping down or limiting the spread of local conflicts.

This list of elements of change in international politics is far from exhaustive, but it would be particularly incomplete if it did not at least mention the effect of intensification of social and political changes within the industrialized countries. For reasons partly stemming from advancing technology and for reasons still partly obscure, the upheaval of domestic forces is having an increasing impact upon the relations among nations. One obvious manifestation of this upheaval is the rejection of traditional values by a young generation in search of new political formulations, but this is symptomatic of a groping process which is by no means limited to the young. The shifting coalitions in many of the West European countries, the almost universal preoccupation with domestic problems, the increase in social tensions expressed in violence —these are widespread manifestations of the pressure to adapt political institutions to the new conditions of life. One aspect of this process that is particularly relevant to our concerns is that in both the Soviet Union and the United States today, we witness the paradoxical rise both in a need for change and in a stronger conservative resistance to change, with the result that political developments in these countries tend to follow a jagged course, rather than a smooth continuum of ameliorative reform.

This leads directly to our second question: *How will developments in the internal life of the Soviet Union and the United States affect their relations with each other?* The assumption that lies behind this question is that one of the most productive, although most neglected, ways of looking at this relationship is as the interaction between two complex political systems, each of which is changing in ways that also affect the other.

The polarization of political life in the United States and the rise of domestic tensions are manifested in many ways: student activism and the Vietnam war, greater militancy in the Negro civil rights movement and in protests regarding poverty, urban environmental problems, and in general a mood of irascibility and anger, with more than occasional violent expression. As was suggested earlier, these impatient pressures for change have begotten a backlash movement of ascending strength, which expresses itself in a pendular swing toward conservatism in the political life of the country.

Developments on the economic side intensify this chain of events, for it is marked by contrasts between the extraordinary vitality reflected in the introduction of new technological processes and the expansion of economic operations abroad, and on the other hand the struggle to check a persistent inflationary trend by monetary controls during a period of decline in the growth of the gross national product. At stake in this struggle is the profound effect upon the political life of the country that is likely to result if the impending recession and serious increase in unemployment are not checked.

Although this is most definitely a period of domestic preoccupation and foreign policy questions are not in the forefront of the nation's attention, there are some exceptions to this general rule. It is difficult for example to assess all of the scarring domestic effects of the Vietnam war, which have stimulated both general disaffection and also specific pressures against foreign commitments and the military establishment. Until recently, military procurement decisions were the concern of a limited group: professional military men and their suppliers in the business community, together with a small circle of those in Congress who had special interests in military affairs. Currently, as a result of Vietnam, tax pressures, and the educative effect of public debates over the antiballistic missile systems, a countervailing force has been developing which cuts across the political spectrum, drawing upon a growing antimilitarism from the liberal side and opposition to the expansion of the federal budget from the conservative. The relative strength of these various pressures depends upon the international situation; such shocks as Czechoslovakia or hostilities in the Middle East affect this balance, at least for a time, in favor of a higher military capability. In the absence of such shocks, however, the nation appears to be moving slowly toward acceptance of a gross parity in strategic weapons with the Soviet Union. This has involved a profound change in concepts of security from the frontier tradition that there is no safety except in having the modern equivalent of a six-shooter at the hip—that is, a substantial margin of strategic superiority.

Gradually, this tradition is being replaced by a growing appreciation that the nation's security is best advanced by a strategic balance with the Soviet Union at moderate levels. Unlike the situation of a decade or two ago, the manipulation of the idea of an imminent military attack from the Soviet Union is more skeptically received than it was, although the competitive urge is still a strong residual force among military proponents on both sides, and this still provides a dynamism to the arms race. This point illustrates the interdependent effect of the balance of political forces within each country upon that in the other.

Turning to the internal developments in the Soviet Union, we find that the most divisive problems are to be found in the political implications of economic issues. Although the economy as a whole continues to grow at a rate comparing favorably with that of the United States and most other industrial countries, this rate of growth has declined in recent years, and there have been notable shortcomings in capital construction, labor productivity, agriculture, and consumer goods. This has led to differences regarding ways of overcoming overcentralization in planning and decision making within the economy, and there has been slow progress in implementing economic reforms proposed as far back as 1965.

Of more fundamental importance than this, however, have been the increasing difficulties of the Soviet system in keeping up with the innovations in technology and management discussed above. Except in some aspects of military and space activities and in certain sectors of metallurgy, the Soviet Union has not been keeping pace with the technological revolution in Western Europe, Japan, and the United States. This has created divisive political issues, for it raises questions about the ability of the Soviet system as it is now constituted to cope with the complexities of advanced industrialization. A tendency has arisen in the Soviet Union to press for an adaptation of the system, to eliminate some of the archaic impedances, the cumbersome bureaucracies, the overcentralization, and to introduce more modern management and organization. This has given rise to an opposing movement in the Party bureaucracy, a kind of conservative backlash if you will, of people who are accustomed to the old ways of doing things by coercion and exhortation, and who fear that the proposed innovations will have the effect of weakening the central role of the Party and its bureaucracy.

This conservative backlash now appears to be the ascendant force in Soviet political life, and it is not confined to the economic sector. It has forced the ultraconservatives in the Communist Party to form liaisons with the more dogmatic tendencies, the police and the military. It has created an air of orthodoxy which has narrowed the latitudes imposed on artists, writers, young people, and nationality groups. It may also be responsible for the way in which the Soviet Union has been responding to problems in Eastern Europe, for the orthodox wing of the Party bureaucracy does not have the resilience to allow the range of economic experimentation tried in Czechoslovakia and elsewhere in Eastern Europe. This is not to say that the Soviet Union does not have its share of talented economists and scientists, but if the Soviet system is to adapt itself effectively to the new technology, it will require a political leadership of greater vitality and flexibility than it now seems to have.

It is important to bear in mind these internal developments when thinking about relations between the two countries. The political tides within each of the countries produce quite different patterns of behavior than might be expected if other political forces were ascendant, and to evaluate either country even slightly on the basis of a monochrome stereotype is an easy trap to fall into. The presently ascendant Soviet orthodoxy sets limits on what can be expected in the current period in the widening of overt contacts between the two countries; it is less likely to resist the military pressures against a damping down of the strategic arms race with the United States; it permits a harsh and dogmatic tone in the Soviet press' treatment of life in America; and it is less likely to consider it beneficial for the Soviet Union to lower its levels of tension in her relationship with the United States. Still, it is worth remembering that there are other forces in Soviet political life that may in time reflect a different view of Soviet self-interest; the path toward this development may be uneven and full of setbacks rather than a smooth evolutionary continuum as some have expected, but in the meantime we must be aware that the role played by the United States affects this development to some degree.

This brings us to the third question, which seeks to make more explicit some elements of the military competition already introduced into our discussion: *How will the recent developments in military technology affect each country's approach to its security, and what will be the prospects for strategic weapons limitation agreements?* On the face of it, the strategic arms competition between the United States and the Soviet Union is illogical and is contrary to the interests of both countries—and yet the results of efforts to reach arms control agreements have so far been meager. It seems likely that the strategic arms limitation talks may not begin to show substantial results for some years at best, and in the meantime the probabilities appear to be that the upward spiral of the strategic arms race will continue until a new equilibrium is reached at a higher level.

One of the reasons why it has proved so difficult to abate this senseless competition is the increasing complexity of modern weapons systems. Even the simplest proposal for a standstill agreement quickly runs into intricate discussions of the equivalencies of weapons systems that have widely different performance characteristics—although in fact it would now appear that in calculating the effectiveness of deterrents the margins of safety are not narrow. The technological innovations described earlier tend to be an exacerbating factor, partly because pressures develop to realize any new technical possibility, and we find ourselves being led by the nose upward through new weapons developments and refinements. The fact that many of the newer innovations are of such a character as to weaken the relative invulnerability of both sides' retaliatory forces—for example, by improving greatly the accuracy of missile guidance systems—also tends to make a stabilization of the arms competition more difficult, because it raises fears on each side that the other might be preparing for an attack on its adversary's retaliatory weapons. Although such an attack seems a remote possibility—it is not likely to be successful—these fears are difficult to dispel and they provide ammunition for each side's continuing arming.

Such fears as these continue to have force because the level of mistrust by each side of the intentions of the other remains high. In the United States, many people feel reluctant to accept strategic parity with the Soviet Union for fear that the Russians would behave more adventurously in such crisis situations as we have had around Berlin or Cuba, or may yet have in the Middle East. On the Soviet side, the prevailing ideologically shaped stereotype of "American imperialism" that is still popular among ideologues in the Soviet press operates together with pressures from the military establishment to feed apprehensions about the intentions of the United States. Since each side has to plan at least five years or more ahead, and since each is led by its apprehensions to base its planning on the worst possible expectations of the other, the dynamism for an arms competition tends to be built into the interacting cycle. The fact that each country also has apprehensions about potential Chinese nuclear capabilities makes it even more difficult to find ways of damping down the effects of internal pressures and mutual fears.

There are, however, some factors that may in time work toward restraint in the arms race. There seems little doubt but that the political leadership of both countries fully appreciates the destructiveness of nuclear war and wishes to avoid it. The fact that SALT actually began is itself a source of some encouragement, for even if substantial formal agreements are difficult and take a long time, the process of discussion will hopefully have an educative effect in the long run, and may even result in some tacit restraints. Since the new weapons systems are enormously costly, the budgetary pressures on both sides may in time exercise restraint and, particularly in the Soviet case, the effort to improve industrial technology may stimulate the desire to reduce the drain of military technology upon research facilities, scientists, and materials. Another favorable factor is the acceptance by both sides of satellite reconnaissance photography, which has the effect of reducing uncertainties of what the other side is up to, and also reduces somewhat the need for intrusive inspection, heretofore an obstacle to arms limitation agreements. Even the developments in accuracy and yield and in multiple-warhead missiles may have some useful effects, if they lead to a more stable deterrent balance based primarily upon submarine-based missiles—at least until the time when anti-submarine techniques are more highly advanced than they now are.

To slow down the strategic arms race takes time because it involves a process of learning, for the two superpowers as well as the rest of the world. Each side needs to overcome old habits of thinking and to redefine concepts of security in the light of modern weapons systems. In the Soviet Union there is no circulation of defense scientists in and out of government, which has provided in the United States an arms control lobby of independent and knowledgeable critics; nor is there as large a number of civilian military theorists as there is in the United States. The process of learning may therefore take some time. Also, it is natural that professional military men on both sides should press for maximum programs to support their respective services; the decisive factor, however, will be the relative strength of civilian political leaders who can weigh these claims against the overall interests of the country, in the light of a broader concept of security that emphasizes stability and moderation as important considerations.

We now turn to the political rivalry between the superpowers, and to our fourth question: *What are the prospects for codifying and moderating the political competition between the two countries in various regions of the world?* There is a popular impression in some parts of the world—a hope in some countries and a fear in others—that the strategic arms talks between the Soviet Union and the United States reflects the existence of a "Big-Two Condominium," and that it may lead to a spheres-of-influence agreement about their political competition. In fact, this does not seem to be a likely possibility since the nuclear-missile systems have very limited political applications and the level of political rivalry may not be greatly affected even if there were to be some restraint exercised in the strategic competition. Objectively, the two countries do have a mutual interest in reducing the strategic arms race, even when political tension between them is high.

Over the past decade and a half the Soviet Union has been increasingly conscious of its new world role as one of the two Great Powers, and it has been seeking to increase its relative influence in various parts of the world. Many of the general trends discussed earlier in response to our first question concerning the background of international politics in this period are manifested with particular sharpness in Europe: the upheavals and shuffling of political forces in Western Europe, the loosening of West German policies toward the East, the Soviet interest in technological contacts with the West, the instabilities in Eastern Europe stimulated by economic shortcomings, and the revived spirit of nationalism. To these factors is added one more which has encouraged Soviet efforts to stimulate neutralist trends in Western Europe—the recent decline in American prestige and influence, and the decline of Western European confidence in the stability of American society and the dependability of the American guarantee of West European security. The main focus of this Soviet effort is West Germany, whose growing economic and industrial power is a source of increasing influence in European developments. In the postwar period, Soviet policy has sometimes sought to isolate the Federal Republic by harshly attacking it for militarism, revanchism, and neo-fascism; but at other times—as in the present period—it has sought by blandishment to attract Bonn toward a more neutralist policy and cooler relations with Washington. This is one of the functions of the Soviet proposal for a European Security Conference, which seeks at the same time to tap the Federal Republic's capital surpluses and technological experience while shoring up the position of the German Democratic Republic and gaining acceptance for the Soviet position in Eastern Europe. Whether or not such a conference, or series of conferences, is held, it seems likely that popular sentiment is moving toward a multiplicity of contacts between East and West Europe, and a *de facto* softening of the dividing line between the two. These functional forms of association may in time intensify Soviet problems in Eastern Europe, but the Soviet hope apparently is that they will have the useful effect, from its point of view, of increasing Soviet influence in Western Europe relative to that of the United States. Because of the enormous concentration of industrial power in Western Europe, this trend, if it were to be realized, would result in a substantial shift in world power relationships.

With regard to the less industrialized parts of the world, the Soviet Union has been moving substantially but cautiously to increase its influence by means of trade, technical assistance, and in some selected areas, military aid. The Middle East is a partial exception to the degree of caution exercised elsewhere in the developing world. Here and in the Eastern Mediterranean generally, the Soviet Union has been accepting a higher level of risk of direct military involvement—or at least has been operating closer to the margin of such a risk—because the possible gains seem particularly attractive. Whereas a decade and a half ago Soviet policy sought merely to achieve a reduction or denial of Western influence in the area, it now seeks a positive influence in the Arab world, and with it access to the resources of the Middle East (which have important potential leverages upon Western Europe) as well as access to all of Africa and through the Suez Canal to the Indian Ocean, where a Soviet naval presence has been established in anticipation of the reduction of British influence in that area.

The Soviet Union has also been energetically expanding its efforts in Asia, with two apparent purposes in mind: to contain the rising influence of China and to take advantage of the diminishing American influence they anticipate in Asia. In addition to an expansion of its bilateral contacts with Japan and other countries around China's periphery, the Soviet Union has lately been talking about the possibility of an Asian Collective Security System, although a clear design for such a system has not yet been made apparent in Soviet diplomacy.

An interesting point in this connection is that Soviet diplomacy in Asia has for the most part proceeded along traditional nation-state lines, seeking to strengthen its contacts with established governments primarily for the purpose of influencing the orientation of their foreign policies. This has been in marked contrast to the recent policy of China, which has chosen rather to support revolutionary elements and to articulate a revolutionary ideology and strategy for a variety of protest movements. One effect of this distinction is that in some areas, as for example on the subcontinent of India and Pakistan, there are some elements of parallelism between Soviet and American diplomatic and economic support for established governments, even though the ultimate interests of the two countries may be widely divergent.

In short, it appears that the political rivalry of the two superpowers has quite a differentiated character in the various parts of the world, and that it mainly centers upon the shifting degrees of political influence which are affected by the particularities of local conditions.

Now we come to the fifth and final question. In its broadest terms, this question would ask how—given the revolutionary changes in international politics and in the domestic politics of nations, and given the military competition and political rivalry between the two superpowers—the international system can be made to accommodate the processes of change now under way peacefully and without allowing any country to establish a political hegemony over any other? But this would be a very large question indeed, the ultimate question in international politics. Within the scope of our present paper, we will limit ourselves to one vital aspect of the problem, and so question number five stands: *How can United States policy reconcile its desire for reduced tension and improved long-term relations with the Soviet Union, with its desire for a greater degree of autonomy in Eastern Europe?* The question has both moral and practical dimensions, for it has sometimes been advocated (and is now being strongly urged by the Soviet Union) that the basis for improved relations with the Soviet Union and a stabilization of European affairs should be a recognition of a Soviet sphere of influence, if not control, in Eastern Europe. But to do so would be contrary to the direction in which we would like to see the international system evolve, and it is not likely, moreover, that this would in fact contribute to stability in European affairs.

We have seen that the Soviet leadership is faced with the prospect of continuing turbulence in Eastern Europe, stemming from persistent nationalist sentiments and the need for economic reforms. As Czechoslavakia has shown, the present Soviet leadership seems disposed to try to respond to these pressures by coercion, by removing the dissident elements, and by political exhortation. These are the tried and true methods of the orthodox wing of the Party bureaucracy, which came to maturity in the days of Stalin. But while repression may still the voices of dissent, it is not likely to win the allegiance of the people, nor to raise economic productivity, and so it is likely that this turbulence will go on—and would go on, even if the United States were to give full formal recognition to a Soviet sphere of control in Eastern Europe. In other words, even if the West were to grant the Soviet Union the hegemony it seeks in Eastern Europe, it does not seem likely that this would contribute to stable and productive conditions in this part of the world.

It would seem that the Soviet Union could maintain a longer-lasting and more beneficial relationship with Eastern Europe by distinguishing between her own security interests in that area and her need and her right to control the political and economic life of each of those countries. It has already been made clear by the invasion of Czechoslovakia, and before that, of Hungary, that the United States is not disposed to try to challenge the Soviet position in Eastern Europe by force of arms, even in times of trouble. Nor does the United States seem committed to ignore the geographical situation of these countries and to try to replace Soviet influence with American influence in this area. What are involved are questions of degree of autonomy and evolution over a period of time. During a period in which many ties are developing between East and West Europe, political, economic, and cultural, the prospect of a greater degree of independence for the individual countries of Eastern Europe to enter into relations with the outside world should not be used by the West nor feared by the Soviet Union as a thrust against Soviet security. Given a reasonable degree of accommodation on both sides, these multiple forms of association would not lead to the establishment of regimes in Eastern Europe hostile to the Soviet Union; on the contrary, it is likely that such ties would be productive for the Soviet Union itself, and offer a more reliable prospect for stability than the present effort to stamp out dissidence with repression.

If events were to move in this direction, it would become possible to envisage a longer-term evolution of the Soviet-American relationship, moving through a series of stages to a point that could be less threatening and more productive, even though many differences are likely to remain. In the immediate period before us, the most urgent necessity is to damp down the strategic competition between the two countries. In some intermediate stage, the main possibilities would be to codify and moderate political rivalries in various critical regions of the world such as the Middle East and Southeast Asia, while at the same time moving toward an expansion of trade and technological and cultural exchanges, and enlarging both Soviet and American use of the United Nations potential for peacekeeping, in economic development and in environmental problems. And this, in turn, would open up the way for a longer term stage, in which genuine cooperation would be possible between the two countries with regard to such problems as the environment and assistance to developing areas.

This need not mean that the two countries would converge; they may both face some of the same imperatives of industrialization, but the differences in their political culture are likely to persist for a long time. This need not be a bar to their learning to keep their political competition within reasonable bounds, because both countries, whether they recognize it or not, have a self-interest in moving toward an international system which can accommodate itself to the rapid processes of change in the twentieth century, peacefully and productively.

VIII   NATO in the International System of the 1970s

MORTON A. KAPLAN

Since we can only surmise what the international system of
the 1970s will be like, we cannot say with confidence what
place NATO will occupy in it. For policy purposes, projections extending through the next several years are less hazardous but also less significant.

The world in the early 1970s is not likely to differ greatly
from the world of the late 1960s. If the policies of the Nixon
administration are shaped by the expectation that the world
will not radically change after 1972, however, it risks adopting military and diplomatic postures that will be grossly inadequate for the problems of the mid-1970s. The long lead
time for the development of weapons systems or for the in-
stitutionalization of structural changes in international instruments invalidates the expectation that postures adopted for
foreseeable problems will be adequate to the surprises almost
sure to confront us. On the other hand, the surprises may be
so diverse in nature that policies adapted to any particular
segment of the possible range could be even more inadequate
than policies based on the expectation that things will continue as they are.

Are we then led into a cul-de-sac from which there is no
exit? Or can we take prudential measures that will optimize
the flexibility of succeeding administrations? Perhaps no
firm answer can be given to such questions. However, we
shall be in a better position to respond if we examine briefly
the reasons for the formation of NATO; the changes in the
international system that have compounded NATO's difficul-

ties; the structural features of the international system that are not likely to change greatly over the next five to ten years, and the range of surprising developments that might either enhance our security prospects or confront us with a threatening crisis.

I

NATO was both a cause and a consequence of developing international bipolarity. The institutional reforms NATO undertook during the Korean war established an American ground presence in Europe that during a period when the Soviet nuclear arsenal was small and ineffective constituted a tripwire for our nuclear force. The members of NATO were bound together by long-term interests in a way that protected them against the organizational and military capabilities of the Soviet bloc. It was NATO and not the United States that assumed the chief responsibility for guarding the world against the outbreak of major war in Europe. NATO protected the individual nations of Western Europe against the divide-and-conquer tactics that Joseph Stalin utilized in his treatment of the satellites and of party and government factions in the Soviet Union.

The reasons for the weakening of NATO are several. The perception of an imminent Soviet military attack against Western Europe diminished as the Cold War receded. Eventually, most Western interpreters of Soviet foreign policy came to believe that such fears had always been nourished by misconceptions about Soviet goals in Europe and elsewhere in the world. The nations of Western Europe recovered economically from the war and, in most cases, went forward to new and unprecedented prosperity. As a consequence, their dependence upon the United States declined, and their irritation over American dominance in NATO correspondingly increased. The peculiar but definite perceptions of the world and of the nation-state held by General de Gaulle further weakened NATO. The incomplete but effective military rupture of France from NATO made the conventional defense of Western Europe more difficult. As NATO became increasingly dependent on the United States nuclear deterrent the unreliability of this safeguard came to the fore.

Although the United States officially insisted upon the reliability of its nuclear protection of Europe, its attempts to delineate the differences between a deterrence posture and a war-fighting posture seemed to many Europeans to call into question American willingness to use nuclear weapons. Moreover, Europeans were aware that a prolonged crisis in Europe would provide the United States with the opportunity to consider in vivid detail the vulnerability of American cities to nuclear weapons. If the equities of the crisis were not absolutely clear—and they were not likely to be if the Soviet Union developed the crisis intelligently—the United States would, in all likelihood, exert pressure on the most threatened European nation to make concessions contrary to its interests.

The alliance-splitting potential of a crisis would operate even more gravely against European members of NATO which were not at the center of the controversy. Such countries, lacking the second-strike nuclear capabilities of the United States, would be subject to greater pressure than the United States and would be more prone to press for concessions, or to leave NATO at the height of a crisis. It is no accident that West Germany, which would probably absorb the initial blow of any Soviet move in Western Europe, has been the Western ally most willing to coordinate its policies with the United States. Although the artificial division of Germany also plays a role in its alliance with the United States, West Germany, unless it makes a deal with the Soviet Union, is the West European nation least able to divorce itself from crisis in the heart of the continent.

The failure of the United States to provide either a joint-NATO nuclear force or a European nuclear force—either of which would minimize the alliance-splitting potential of a Soviet-inspired crisis or nuclear blackmail—is one of the major causes of the crisis in NATO. The search of the United States for détente with the Soviet Union is another. There are few, if any, accommodations with the Soviet Union that the United States is capable of making that would not threaten some existing West European interest. The nuclear Nonproliferation Treaty is a specific case in point.

It may appear paradoxical to some that West Europeans, who were disturbed by the reputed American Cold War psychology and who demanded changes in the American perspective, are now frightened by the change in perspective they appeared to ask for. Apart from inconsistencies in human personalities, motivations, and reasonings, the answer to this seeming paradox is not particularly difficult. As long as the Cold War continued, many Europeans feared that American differences with the Soviet Union might thrust Western Europe into the maelstrom of nuclear conflict. They were fearful that what they regarded as American intransigence would provoke war. As the United States began to accommodate its objectives to those of the Soviet Union, they began to perceive another and a larger danger: the compromise of their interests that might result from détente. They now discount the possibility of war and see as increased the possibility of a settlement at their expense.

Other concerns influenced their reactions to American warfighting strategies. Deterrence in the view of many Europeans avoided war. They did not like to ask what would happen if war actually occurred. War-fighting strategies raised the specter of actual war—a war that would be fought on their territories. Discussion of tactical nuclear war, an enterprise that is quite dubious in my opinion, further enhanced these perceptions.

A similar explanation may be given for their misperception of the problem of ballistic missile defense. Although BMD increases the likelihood that the United States would actually live up to its commitments in Western Europe by reducing the Soviet threat to the continental United States, it brings home to West Europeans the possibility of an actual nuclear war—one in which the United States would have some protection and in which they would not.

II

What are the structural features of the international situation most directly relevant to NATO that are not likely to change surprisingly in the next five to ten years? Only the

United States and the Soviet Union will possess major stable nuclear forces. Only the United States and the Soviet Union will possess second-strike capabilities, although the introduction of MIRV (Multiple Independent Re-entry Vehicles) might raise the possibility that one or the other superpower might gain a credible first-strike capability. BMD installations in the United States and the Soviet Union might deprive those West European nations which possess unstable nuclear forces of posing even the threat of a penetration capability against the Soviet Union or the United States.

It is likely that Great Britain and France will continue to deploy unstable and provocative nuclear forces. By the end of the 1970s West Germany may have an unstable nuclear force. Developments in ASW (anti-submarine warfare) and in orbital weapons may further increase the first-strike potential of the United States or the Soviet Union.

Increasing prosperity in the developed nations may reduce the incentive for external adventure. Improvements in logistics, large increases in world trading combines, and increased economic interdependence among all developed nations, and between the United States and the Soviet bloc, will create a disincentive for external adventure.

The Soviet Union will retain an authoritarian regime. Decision making will be centralized in a small body of men who in turn will be dependent only upon a technocratic class that will be relatively uninterested in acquiring political power and that will be less shocked by Soviet external adventure than were the emerging humanistic and technological groupings of the mid-1950s.

These last two considerations are not contradictory, although they lead to inconsistent consequences. Economic interdependence reflects a characteristic of economy and technology in a world that is becoming smaller. The attitudes of particular elites toward particular kinds of actions reflect the development of a social consciousness within a particular milieu that creates certain kinds of rewards and incentives. Thus the difference between Soviet intellectual reactions to Czechoslovakia in 1968 and to Hungary in 1956 is striking. Part of the difference may result from dissimilarities between generations and the increasing accommodation of the intellectual class to the post-Stalinist regime. Part of it may lie in the fact that Hungary was the first case of such intervention and thus was much more shocking than the second occasion to the susceptibilities of certain kinds of Marxists. Perhaps this last factor should not be placed among the structural features, for, should the Soviet Union fail in Czechoslovakia, there may be another reshaping of attitudes toward such events.

III

We will now briefly consider the wide range of possible surprises this decade might bring and then sketch the possible relevance of these for NATO. We will finally adumbrate a few of the measures that might improve the operations of NATO in the existing world and in the expected world of the 1970s and that might be adaptable to some of the consequences of the surprising, although not entirely unexpected, worlds.

Consider a world in which the Soviet pressure on China is successful, in which tight Soviet control over Rumania is restored, and in which Yugoslavia is occupied or otherwise brought back within the confines of the Soviet bloc. Despite the prosperity prevailing in Western Europe, this world would have a much more frightening aspect for Western Europe than did the situation after the close of the Second World War or even at the height of bipolarity. A conventional defense of Western Europe would not seem feasible. The credibility of the United States nuclear guarantee would be subject to serious doubts. Moreover, it is unlikely that Soviet pressure, under the sponsorship of a younger and more confident leadership, would be used in ways that would confront the United States with a situation clearly justifying the use of its nuclear deterrent. The Russians could be expected to employ the processes of "chemical dissolution" so powerfully applied by Adolf Hitler against the Czechoslovak Republic in 1938. Local Communist parties would be used as fronts to create incidents giving rise to plausible grounds for Soviet intervention. Threats would be employed that would not be fully explicit. Members of NATO, other than the one directly threatened, would be reassured of Soviet good intentions toward them. Only if the members of NATO were bound indissolubly or if the threatened member had a credible deterrent of its own would the prospects for organizational survival and the successful blunting of Soviet demands be reasonably high.

Consider a world in which China and the Soviet Union are reconciled after the death of Mao and Lin Piao. In this world it is likely that the pressures against Japan and India would be increased, thus diverting American attention from Europe. By maintaining a passive policy against Western Europe, the Soviet Union could play upon the fears of West European nations that in the Orient the United States might drag them into adventures contrary to their security interests. Moreover, despite the absence of Soviet threats or overt pressures, the existence of a unified Communist bloc would be likely to stir in Europe fears of a military nature stemming from entanglements with the United States and doubts concerning the long-term viability of democratic systems. The temptation to move in a socialist direction and to multiply entanglements with the Soviet bloc would increase. In this case, the prospects for NATO would be high only if Europe had an independent military capability. Thus a European nuclear force or developments leading to the beginnings of an Atlantic Union would minimize, but far from eliminate, the dangerous consequences of this particular surprise.

Consider a world in which the Russians decide to settle accounts with the Chinese. They bomb the Chinese nuclear installations and allow volunteer groups to invade Mongolia and Sinkiang in support of dissident nationalist forces in those areas. In this circumstance, a number of requirements would confront American policy makers. The United States ought not to be so tightly bound to NATO that any action it takes elsewhere in the world would appear to involve its allies. Unless Washington loosened the integration of NATO, there might be enormous and perhaps successful pressures from our allies to halt American activities in the Asian theater. Given the demonstrated Russian willingness to take extreme measures, the United States might deem it a prudent move to place its fleet between Taiwan and the mainland and thus prevent the Nationalists from intervening counterproductively, inasmuch as they have little or no remaining support on the mainland. Whether the United States would wish to send supplies to the Communist Chinese government or to act in a manner that severely limited Russian objectives would depend upon the circumstances. If we were too eager, our aid might be accepted but at the cost of great suspicion. Yet the opportunities for intervention which could produce a more favorable world environment for the United States would probably be present. If any important faction of the Chinese Communist Party or military decided to cast its lot with the Russians, then a much more threatening situation would arise for the United States; it would increase the incentives for direct intervention, but limit the opportunities.

Consider a world in which there is a left-wing socialist revolution in Japan and in which Southeast Asia goes Communist. Even if the Communist nations remain disunited, the establishment of what would appear to be a "wave of the future" would increase the pressures against Western Europe enormously. The more closely Western Europe was integrated in NATO and aligned with the United States, the more secure American security interests would be.

Consider a world in which one of several events occurs. There is a revolt in East Germany that arouses sympathy in, and possibly intervention by, West Germany. Alternatively, in an effort to build consensus behind a shaky East German government, there is an East German invasion of either Poland or West Germany. A revolt in East Germany that appears to invite West German responses would engender great pressure from France, Britain, and the small members of NATO to prevent Bonn's intervention or, alternatively, to loosen the bonds of NATO. Measures that maintained centralized control of NATO military forces would, in this case, reduce the centrifugal forces of the alliance. In the case of an East German invasion of West Germany, such centralized measures would increase the likelihood of the cohesion of the alliance in resisting the invasion. In the case of an East

German invasion of Poland, German integration in NATO and, more particularly, in a united Europe would diminish the chances that nationalistic pressures could force West Germany to support the East German move and thus threaten the stability of the existing Bonn regime and of its alignment with the West.

Consider a world in which the West Germans regard a solution for the problem of German reunification out of the question as long as they maintain cordial relations with the West. In this world the Germans would feel betrayed by both the French and the Americans. They might feel discriminated against because they lacked nuclear weapons, although in other respects they would have great power status. In an effort to resolve their problems and to demonstrate their independence as a great power, the West Germans make a deal with the Soviet Union at the expense of East Germany. In this world, France is likely to return to NATO. However, the rational grounds for conventional defense, weak though they may previously have been, are now despairingly inadequate. Nuclear defense or deterrence must be relied upon, but this is likely to work only if the plan for its use approaches automaticity. Thus it is likely that the conditions for the use of nuclear weapons must be spelled out and vetoes removed from the hands of political leaders.

Consider a world in which France, alarmed by German resurgence, makes an alliance with the Soviet Union. A ground defense for the remaining NATO nations would hardly be feasible, and a collective nuclear defense might be difficult to implement. The existence of a stable independent nuclear deterrent in German hands might in this case be the only plausible alternative for United States policy.

Consider a world in which there is a major revolutionary upheaval in Latin America. American attention would naturally shift to the south. If NATO had not yet become a more viable instrument, armed with procedures for consultation and integrated militarily, it might easily be allowed in these circumstances to wither away, thus opening up Europe to Soviet pressures. In all likelihood, the existence of a European nuclear force would serve to protect important American security interests. If NATO remained intact, the existence of such a force would enable the Europeans to assume an increasingly important role in it while the United States turned its attention to the Western Hemisphere. Given such a force, NATO might remain viable even in the absence of forceful American leadership.

Consider a world in which a minor nation uses a nuclear weapon against another minor nation. Although this occurrence need not directly involve either the Soviet Union or the United States, it would constitute a precedent threatening to both. Yet unilateral intervention by either might appear dangerous to both. In such a world, there would be major incentives for the United States and the Soviet Union to establish a condominium, at least with respect to the nuclear weapons issue and probably with respect to quarrels that grew so intense that a danger of nuclear escalation arose. If such a condominium were instituted, it would introduce severe strains between the United States and its Western allies—unless NATO were so organized that various consultative measures could reduce the fears of the West European nations that important interests of theirs would be sacrificed to the requirements of the American-Soviet détente. It would probably be important in this circumstance to exclude Europe from the condominium and to support the creation of a European nuclear system.

Consider a world in which China becomes a substantial nuclear power, and Japan and West Germany acquire nuclear weapons. These weapons systems are likely to be unstable. The Soviet Union would probably be deterred from overt military action and its power of blackmail would be greatly reduced, even though the nuclear weapons systems were not enormously effective against the defenses of the Soviet Union. In this world, NATO would not be important, although its absence might lead to political instability. The possibility of provocation in such a world is reasonably high. The Eurasian land mass would constitute a zone of extreme danger. It is most unlikely that the United States would desire to be bound to it by stringent security treaties. One way to avoid this contingency would be to have previously prepared the way for a European nuclear system or for viable national nuclear forces through the transfer of know-how or perhaps through the actual transfer of weapons.

Consider a world in which the Czechoslovak invasion of 1968 was a last gasp by the Soviet hardliners. Increasingly, Soviet domestic policy is moderated and Soviet controls over the bloc are lifted. Although a Europe from the Atlantic to the Urals still seems a figment of the imagination, the prospects for favorable political developments would be eased by a loosening of the bonds between the United States and Europe. The greater the extent to which Europe could transfer its attention from West to East, the greater the likelihood that developments of this type would strengthen American security. If there were, in addition, a democratic revolution or nationality uprisings in the Soviet Union, the quick dissolution of NATO might enhance favorable prospects.

IV

It is obvious that we cannot protect ourselves against all the contingencies considered above by the same measures —at least not equally effectively. In some cases, NATO becomes a liability for American security and interests. Nonetheless, certain minimal requirements common to most of the surprising worlds stand out. It seems that NATO cannot remain viable either in existing circumstances or in our "most surprising worlds" unless its decision making machinery becomes more consultative and less dominated by the United States. Although the United States should not permit NATO to be in a position to circumscribe American actions over the entire globe, it must find some way to insulate the consequences of these extra-European actions from the European sphere. A more or less united Europe facing the United States within NATO as a relative equal would both increase European bargaining power in a desirable fashion and facilitate distinctions of spheres of activity, thus to some extent insulating Europe from the consequences of American actions elsewhere in the world. This means that Europe would not be expected to come to the aid of the United States in such cases, a reasonable price to pay to secure the compensating advantages.

Possession of an independent nuclear capability by a united Europe would permit a degree of disengagement between United States strategic forces and NATO strategic forces. Although the insulation of the two forces from each other would not be automatic and complete, the distinction could legitimately be made. It may well be in the interest of an enemy of the United States to recognize the distinction and to observe it. Thus, the involvement of the United States in Asia would not automatically invoke the involvement of the West Europeans. This would decrease European fears of America's extra-European ventures. Although Europeans would still be likely to pressure the United States to disengage itself from Asia, these pressures would be greatly diminished by Europe's possession of an independent nuclear force and by the strength resulting from unity.

Even in the absence of West European unity, a European nuclear force with appropriate control machinery would have many of the same desirable advantages. If the European nuclear force were programed in advance for use either if the Russians first used nuclear weapons or if they invaded Western Europe and failed to withdraw within a stated period of time, then the demands for a political veto on use of the force would be diminished. This doctrine of nuclear control would be further improved if it were linked to the doctrine of limited strategic retaliation. The establishment of relatively autonomous command and control procedures not subject to veto before crisis would diminish the blackmail capabilities of an enemy state. The European nuclear force, used under these two circumstances, would appear to be adequate to meet most of the various contingencies posed earlier. For the United States, the existence of such a force would reduce the nuclear risks of involvement in the alliance. But it would eliminate neither the risks nor the rationale for American membership.

If a European nuclear force should be infeasible for political reasons, then one possible alternative would be to aid West European nations to acquire national nuclear systems with second-strike capabilities and adequate command and control systems. Although such a solution would satisfy fewer of the contingencies considered, it would be responsive to a number of them. It would reduce the dangers of American involvement in the NATO system that would result from the acquisition by West European nations of unstable and provocative nuclear systems. Stable independent national nuclear systems would probably deter the Soviet Union—even if, later, NATO were to be loosened or dissolved.

If this alternative is politically infeasible, then a last fall-back position might rest on American development of a capacity that would permit the transfer of nuclear weapons to a threatened ally at the inception of a crisis. Polaris-type submarines may prove to be the only satisfactory way to achieve a quick transfer capacity; the effectiveness of such a capacity would depend on the prior training of crews from the relevant nations. None of these measures would be inconsistent with the dissolution of NATO in those cases in which the Communist bloc breaks up and the internal Soviet system "mellows." However, the acquisition of independent national nuclear systems would transfer to Western Europe the capabilities that would be useful in deterring the Kremlin if further "surprises" revived a Soviet threat to Europe.

In the absence of appropriate European nuclear capabilities, it is likely that increased consultative arrangements for the West Europeans, as proposed by some, would serve primarily as a brake upon United States actions elsewhere in the world. Moreover, in the absence of a unified Europe, such increased power for the European allies of the United States would probably inhibit rather than enhance military support for a threatened member of the alliance. Thus, there is some reason to believe that West Germany would be exposed rather than protected by a decrease in American dominance within the alliance; this, in addition to other factors, might tend to move the West Germans toward a deal with the Soviet Union.

In political organizations political power and military weakness only rarely constitute desirable coordinate attributes. NATO is unlikely to be an exception to this rule. Reforms of

NATO that increase consultation and collective control instead of strengthening the organization may bring to a focus
conflicts of interest and different perceptions of the situation.
Such reforms are more likely to enhance the complexity of
organizational charts than the activities of the alliance.

NATO is far gone on the road to extinction. Yet unified
American direction and military policy still preserve some
organizational potential. The defects of American dominance
give rise to the tribulations of the alliance, but it is far from
clear that coordinate control will remedy NATO's ills in the
absence of coordinate military capabilities. If it is true that
under present circumstances—as contrasted with those of the
immediate postwar period—NATO requires political as well
as military goals, it still does not follow that political goals
can be implemented in advance of the solution of the security problem.

A joint-NATO nuclear system would enhance the unity of
the organization at the expense of the ability of the United
States to act in Asia. A European nuclear force attenuates
the relationship between the United States and Europe, but
it enhances the prospects for a viable European response
while increasing the potential of the United States for extra-
European intervention. The dependence of Europe upon
American know-how and transfer capabilities provides a rationale for NATO and leaves open the prospect of large areas
of mutual political interest not directly involving a war in
Europe. Independent national nuclear forces greatly increase
the risk of the fragmentation of NATO. However, they also
decrease the likelihood of military pressure and therefore
diminish the prospect of crises that would accelerate the centrifugal tendencies in the alliance. Thus, this prospect permits, although it does not facilitate, the development of joint
political goals.

A quick transfer capacity is perhaps the least promising but
the politically most feasible of the alternatives. Furthermore,
the knowledge that such a quick transfer capacity exists diminishes the likelihood of a deliberate escalation of a crisis
by an enemy state. In addition to the deterrence provided by
the American SAC, the actual transfer of nuclear weapons to
a West European state will be undesirable from the stand-

point of that enemy state. Thus, there will be an effort to avoid triggering the transfer. This, in turn, is likely to damp political crises and preserve the prospect that NATO members will be able to attain common political goals.

A failure to find even a "jerry-built" solution to NATO's security problems is hardly likely to facilitate the attainment of joint political goals. At the same time, an increase in consultation and joint control in the absence of appropriate military measures is likely to be counterproductive.

IX Toward a Reappraisal of United States
Foreign Policy in Latin America After Vietnam

MARTIN C. NEEDLER

THE CHARACTER OF THE CURRENT PERIOD IN
UNITED STATES-LATIN-AMERICAN RELATIONS

This is a particularly appropriate time to be re-examining
United States policy toward Latin America, not only because
a general re-examination of United States commitments in
the world is currently taking place but also because political
realities in Latin America which United States policy must
take into account are at the moment undergoing crucial
changes in character. Of course, in principle a nation should
be re-examining its foreign commitments continuously. This
is especially the case for the United States, a nation relatively new to world power and influence and still involved in
the expensive process of discovering through trial and error
what its national interests are. For too often what has become accepted as a necessary and integral part of the national interest turns out on inspection to be simply the residue of an accumulation of past accidents and mistakes.

Traditionally, the United States position vis-à-vis Latin
America has in effect been one of hegemony in Central
America and the Caribbean and of a less precise suzerainty,
or ultimate overlordship, in South America. Although this has
been the effective political situation, Americans have not
usually conceptualized it in these terms, for several reasons.
First, the economic power wielded in the region has been
that of private rather than state interests and thus has been
less explicit, more diffuse, and less clearly national in character. Second, United States political domination of the area

has not always been clearly apparent because United States policy toward the area has usually been indecisive, passive, and self-contradictory. Finally, the fact of ultimate North American power in the area has been further screened from public view in the United States by a facade of Pan-American ideology, an ideology positing a community of interests among the independent states of the Western Hemisphere based on a putative common set of ideals of freedom and democracy.

From time to time Pan-American ideology has even won some acceptance among members of the Latin-American political and economic elites, at least at the verbal, or oratorical, level. This occurred partly because the traditional elites have had economic interests identical, or at least compatible, with those of the United States, but also because it was hoped that the ideology of Pan-Americanism could be urged as a restraint on the use of United States power. Nevertheless, on those occasions when allowing events in Latin America to take their normal course seemed as though it would jeopardize United States interests, the United States has directly intervened with military force, and Pan-Americanism has been left to adapt itself to the situation as best it could.

Today in Latin America the various elite groups which have traditionally shared power or contended for it among themselves no longer have exclusive control of national political life. The rapid increase in population, urbanization, and improvements in communications and education have led to the mobilization of large segments of society traditionally passive and at the margins of the political system so that today the masses are an important factor in the politics of almost every Latin-American country. This is not to say that authentic representatives of the masses rule everywhere, although they do in some countries. But almost everywhere the desires and needs of the masses must be taken into account in the calculations of the political class.

The mobilization of the masses has created a difficult situation for political leaders. Now that government is regarded as responsible for the way in which the national product is distributed, questions of economic policy have become particularly acute as newly mobilized groups confront each other and the still-powerful forces that have traditionally dominated the country. The threat of overt conflict that this invites becomes the more acute since the economic production of the society typically rises slowly, and thus it is hardly possible to finance appreciably larger economic shares for the masses exclusively out of the growth of the national product.

In this situation, the way out of acute social conflict seems to be offered only by a nationalist policy which, at the ideological level, stresses national unity and minimizes internal conflict; at the psychological level, directs aggression outward, against foreigners; and, at the economic level, makes more resources available for the satisfaction of demands without domestic political costs through the expropriation of foreign property. Of course, expropriation results in an increase in resources only in the short run, as the productivity of nationalized enterprises drops and as the further entry of foreign capital is discouraged. However, it is in the short run that riots are avoided and elections are won. In this way, nationalism is currently replacing Pan-Americanism as the prevailing ideology of the Western Hemisphere.

The change taking place in the dominant mood in inter-American relations is visible even in that citadel of Pan-Americanism, the Organization of American States. The recently retired Secretary-General of the OAS, José Mora, was an adept practitioner of Pan-Americanism; his approach was to blur conflicts of national interest and confine OAS activities to trivial and non-political areas, except for a purely verbal concern with economic and social questions that became *de rigueur* after the inception of the Alliance for Progress. His successor, Galo Plaza, although scorned by nationalists during his election to the post as "completely sold out to the United States," in the private words of one Latin-American diplomat, has made it clear that he views his role as that of the spokesman for Latin American interests vis-à-vis the United States and not the representative of the United States vis-à-vis Latin America.

What should be the policy toward this new nationalist Latin America of a United States attempting to divest itself of inflated rhetoric, naive misconceptions about the world, and the habit of supplying the absence of a well-thought-out national policy with a vulgar responsiveness to the urgings of private economic interests?

THE GOALS OF POLICY

It seems fairly clear what the fundamental goals of United States policy toward Latin America have been historically. Although under different administrations different orders of priority have been established among them, the goals to be pursued have always been those of national security, economic advantage, and the promotion of freedom and democracy. In an earlier, more simple age the policies of a given President were dominated by one objective or another. Thus one can say that Theodore Roosevelt was primarily concerned with national security, William Howard Taft with economic advantage, and Woodrow Wilson with the promotion of democracy. Recent Presidents have attempted to incorporate all three objectives into national policy, but the character of each President's policy has reflected substantial differences in priorities and emphasis.

To talk about these three objectives as distinct from each other is a helpful analytic device, but it should not obscure their very real interdependence. Thus, for example, a United States strengthened economically is also strengthened militarily. And most important to appreciate—since it is too often overlooked—countries which are constitutional democracies are less likely to act irrationally and arbitrarily and more likely to be bound to the United States by ties of mutual sympathy. For all of the failures of perception and lack of realism for which Woodrow Wilson has justly been criticized, this fundamentally sound insight of his is one that we very much need to recapture.[1]

[1] It is gratifying to see this point explicitly affirmed in Governor Rockefeller's report on his recent mission to Latin America: "Practically, nations with broadly based political systems of a democratic type are more likely to have outlooks and concepts compatible with the style of the United States and its people and more willing to cooperate with us in establishing an effective world order." Nelson

A sophisticated understanding of national security, in other words, one which goes beyond a limited conventional conception in solely military terms, can subsume many elements of traditional economic and ideological objectives. It is worth remembering in this connection that the nation which gave national security an absolute priority over all other considerations but also interpreted it in a narrow and purely military framework, Imperial Germany, was also the nation that brought war and defeat in war most surely upon itself.

I dwell on this point because one of the characteristic failings of United States policy—and not only in Latin America!—is to accord the goal of national security, conceived of in a narrow military sense, an absolute priority over other objectives and an absolute authority to override all considerations about the means to be used in implementing policy. Now of course any individual person is at liberty to establish his own rank-ordering of the values that he wishes national power to pursue, and to speak, act, and vote accordingly. However, in the conventional wisdom of international relations theory—to dispute which would, at this juncture, take us too far afield—the responsible government leader has no choice but to make the interests of the collectivity he represents, and especially its continued existence, his first concern. Yet even if, for the sake of argument, one concedes first priority in the national policy calculus to national security conceived in a military sense, it remains true that this priority ranking should not be absolute. That is, even for the most fanatic apostle of national security, an extremely minor and problematical increment in security should not justify a policy that leads to a substantial loss in the attainment of other objectives. The priority ordering of goals should always be relative; there must always be room for calculation of degree.

A. Rockefeller, *Quality of Life in the Americas: Report of a U.S. Presidential Mission for the Western Hemisphere,* Agency for International Development, November 1969, pp. 45–46. Unfortunately, this comment appears to be only a *pro forma* aside, inasmuch as the main thrust of the report lies in quite the opposite direction, in an acceptance of the thesis of the "progressive military regime," discussed below.

HOW THE NATIONAL SECURITY PROBLEM
HAS BEEN MISUNDERSTOOD

However, even in questions of national security conceived of in a military sense, any attempts at the calculation of degrees of cost and benefit have typically been vitiated by inaccuracies of perception. In the first place, the amount of damage that can be done to United States interests by events elsewhere has usually been exaggerated. In the second place, it has usually been assumed that any change introducing new elements into the situation is likely to be disadvantageous to the United States and is therefore to be opposed. This view fails to appreciate the fact that in a continually changing world a status quo artificially maintained becomes increasingly unviable.

In the third place, it has typically been taken for granted that the overriding threat to United States national security is posed by "international communism." Yet "international communism," as traditionally conceived of by Americans, has in fact ceased to exist. The diversity of views and tactics among the various tendencies within the far left means today that it no longer makes sense to view the strength possessed and the "threat" posed by a Communist group in any one country on the premise that it forms part of a larger international movement. Thus, for example, the traditional Communist Party of Chile is today a fairly moderate party working within the framework of the established constitutional system and condemning tactics of violence and armed uprising urged by groups further to the left. The Communist Party of Venezuela, similarly, has condemned the small guerrilla groups operating in the country and has engaged in harsh polemics with Fidel Castro. Castro, in his turn, has denounced the leadership of the Bolivian Communist Party as being responsible for the capture and execution of Che Guevara. In other words, it is necessary today to evaluate Communist and other leftist groups in each country in terms of their activities, aims, and tactics in that country instead of regarding them as necessarily on the side of the enemy in an international civil war.

And just as it is possible for the United States to cooperate with the Soviet Union from time to time on matters of common concern, so it should be possible for the United States to view with equanimity the participation of traditional Communist parties that are willing to operate within the established constitutional framework in the politics of Latin-American countries. Indeed, there seems no reason today to assume that a government led by a Marxist party need automatically be considered a threat to the United States. For example: It is likely that covert operations of United States and British intelligence services were responsible for the public disturbances that led to the removal of the government of Cheddi Jagan in British Guiana (now Guyana). Yet, in a personal interview with President Kennedy in which he asked for the inclusion of Guyana in the Alliance for Progress program, Jagan had undertaken to respect civil liberties and operate through constitutional procedures—his was the legally elected government—and the economic program his government was pursuing was precisely what United States advisers recommend to governments in his situation. It would be refreshing, although it is probably too much to hope, that if Jagan should again come to power in Guyana the United States government should respond not as a conditioned organism responds automatically to a stimulus but as a rational group of men considering the actual situation that exists in the light of the real interests of the United States.

But of course there is always the example of Cuba. "We cannot have another Cuba" has now become the rationale for mistake after shortsighted mistake that has been committed by United States policy in the hemisphere over the last few years. Avoiding another Cuba was the reason for United States intervention in the Dominican Republic in 1965, which prevented the return to power of a liberal democrat and friend of the United States who had been elected by an overwhelming proportion of the vote in the only free election in thirty years of Dominican history, and instead perpetuated in power the uniformed gangsters who constituted the leadership of the Dominican armed forces.

It does not help the situation that President Johnson's principal adviser at the time of the intervention had said ten months earlier, speaking of the Marine interventions in the Caribbean in the early twentieth century:

> Our interventions were, in the Latin-American point of view, patronizing in the extreme. By making the United States the sole judge of Latin America's political morality, they were degrading to proud peoples who believed that, in their own wars of independence, they had earned the right to manage their own affairs—to be masters in their own houses. They produced schismatic tendencies in the inter-American family and brought our relations with Latin America to an all-time low.

> These historical experiences suggest two things: Unilateral United States interventions in the hemisphere have never succeeded, in themselves, in restoring constitutional government for any appreciable period of time. And they have, in every case, left for our country a legacy of suspicion and resentment which has endured long after our interventions were abandoned as impracticable.[2]

THE "THREAT FROM CUBA"

It is with respect to Cuba itself that the character of the putative threat from international communism in the hemisphere can most accurately be analyzed. In Cuba, with the establishment of a self-designated Communist state "only ninety miles" from the United States coast, we have the posing of this threat in its strongest form. And indeed a military threat to the security of the United States *was* posed from Cuba. It took two forms: The first was the emplacement in Cuba of intermediate-range Soviet missiles; the second was the organization and financing of a campaign of guerrilla warfare designed to overthrow the governments of South America.

With the emplacement of the missiles, the military threat was posed in the sharpest terms possible; a greater military threat to the United States from Latin America can hardly be imagined. And yet the threat was posed and met, and the

[2] Thomas Mann, Commencement Address at the University of Notre Dame, June 7, 1964. (State Department, mimeo.)

danger passed. Given the Cuban experience, the failure of which was one of the factors that later cost Khrushchev his post as First Secretary, it appears extremely unlikely that the Soviet Union will attempt something of the kind again.

After the failure of the missile gambit, but still fearing the hostility of the United States toward him, Castro turned to the other military strategy available to him for a serious attack on the United States and its interests. In the poorest country of South America, a country having land borders with five of the other states of South America, including the two largest and most important, Brazil and Argentina, a guerrilla "focus" was created, led by possibly the most able man produced by the Cuban revolution, its master strategist and guerrilla theoretician, Ernesto Che Guevara. It is difficult to see how the guerrilla threat could have been posed in stronger terms. And yet it soon ended in ignominious failure. Again the most drastic threat that could be expected had been posed, and again it had been met with little difficulty.

If we have surmounted the threats of guerrilla warfare and missile bombardment, in what does the threat of international communism in the hemisphere now consist? If similar threats were again to be posed, they would surely be less dangerous and more easily dealt with.

STABILITY AND CHANGE

In actual fact, although the expressed goals of United States foreign policy have typically been those of national security, economic advantage, and the promotion of democracy, all of them reasonable expressions of national interest, these goals have nevertheless been translated only imperfectly into the actual day-to-day operations of policy. It would be no exaggeration to say that the operative goal of United States policy in Latin America is in fact the maintenance of stability. This seems to the officers in the field and in the State Department a reasonable way of operationalizing the rather general goals stated from time to time by national leaders and enumerated above, in that stability creates a favorable climate for economic activity; it makes for peaceful international relations; and, if the facade of constitutional practice is preserved, it is usually possible to link support for stability with support for democracy. The institutional biases of the Foreign Service toward caution, inaction, and unwillingness to take risks contribute to the predisposition of United States diplomats to regard the maintenance of established regimes as a close enough working approximation to the implementation of the goals of national policy. However, this approach, applied unthinkingly, has frequently led the United States to support unpopular or anti-democratic regimes because they were what existed, regardless of the implications for United States interests.

But the signs of change are everywhere, and it is clear to most intellectually active people concerned with foreign policy that it is no longer possible to maintain traditional regimes that fail to appreciate the need to change in response to national needs and popular demands. Accordingly, there has been more recently a tendency for United States policy to try to arrive at formulas that combine continued stability with the capacity to change.

The Alliance for Progress represented the best attempt in this direction. Under the Alliance, moral pressure and material incentives were to be brought to bear upon existing governments in the hemisphere to introduce social and economic reforms. Control of the funds for the program lodged ultimately in the United States government.

Although intelligently conceived and fundamentally aimed in the right direction, the Alliance for Progress has had indifferent success because of a series of factors of various kinds: Adverse economic conditions have canceled out many of its effects; the program has bogged down in a morass of bureaucratic delays and misdirections of funds and effort; the United States has lost interest and pursued goals counterproductive to those of the Alliance; and many Latin-American governments have lacked enthusiasm for the reformist implications of the Alliance and have seen it simply as a conduit for the transmission of funds from the United States. Nevertheless, despite the relatively weak showing under the Alliance, the basic *political* orientation it represented is surely correct and should continue to be the fundamental political line taken by the United States. Substantial administrative and economic changes are however necessary if the economic objectives of the Alliance are to meet with any success. The initiatives promised in late 1969 by President Nixon would, if implemented, represent a modest first step in the right direction in attempting to lift some of the burdens placed on inter-American trade by the United States government on behalf of private special interests, although the usual gap between promise and performance where Latin America is concerned has grown especially wide in the Nixon administration.

But another approach to the problem of reconciling continued stability and the ability to change has recently gained ground; this is the thesis of the progressive military government. Such a government, it is said, can maintain stability by enforcing a moratorium on normal open political activity; at the same time, because of its authoritarian character, it can brush aside obstacles to structural change such as opposition in the legislature and the judiciary that can prove fatal to reform programs initiated by democratically elected governments operating under constitutional restraints. Several distinguished American scholars—not, it should be added, political scientists—have adopted this thesis and it has its partisans not only in members of the military forces of the Latin-American countries but in some civilian political circles as well. Recent United States policy has often seemed receptive to this view, as for example in the unconcealed enthusiasm with which the Johnson administration greeted the assumption of power of a military government in Brazil in 1964. The report of the Rockefeller mission seemed to take this line, although it also warned parenthetically of the dangers inherent in military assumptions of power.[3]

Now it is certainly hypothetically conceivable that a progressive military government might exist and might succeed in putting through lasting reforms. However, the probabilities against it are so great, and the certain disadvantages of such governments are severe, that United States policy makers should be urged most strongly to abandon the faith they have thus far put in this hypothesis, which is so seductive but at the same time so dangerous.

[3] Rockefeller, *Quality of Life in the Americas*, pp. 17–19.

Although a military government of reforming orientation may take power with the best of intentions, it is almost certainly doomed not only to failure, but to making the situation worse than it would otherwise have been. In the first place, military men in power typically lack any real comprehension of the economic problems with which they are confronted and tend to intervene in the economy blindly, with disastrous results. Alternatively, they may be led around by the nose by conservative economic advisers who obstruct the implementation of any serious reform efforts. In either case, the implementation of a rational reform policy is unlikely.

Liberated from the obstacles to reform represented by an active political opposition, the military government is at the same time liberated from the criticism that exposes inefficiency, incompetence, corruption, and abuse of human rights; and after a period in which the honesty and partriotism of the new military rulers are self-righteously proclaimed *ad nauseam,* the regime becomes in fact a mass of scandals.

The unity of the leadership group also inevitably breaks down as the problems of running the country are faced. In the absence of an open democratic process for making decisions on controverted questions, the differences of opinion that are bound to arise over policy questions become matters of secret intrigue, usually leading to coups and countercoups which make nonsense of the regime's claim to have brought stability. This intrigue and factional infighting are heightened by the clash of rival ambitions, which can no longer be adjudicated in the open arena of popular elections.

The whole picture is complicated by the popular opposition that develops. The requirements for public order of a regime that has abolished the normal free play of political life are necessarily stringent—so much so that it is easy for opposition groups, usually beginning with students, to force the regime to overreact in a repressive and heavy-handed way by staging a modest demonstration in favor of some popular or even noncontroversial cause. As the conflict between demonstrations and repression escalates, the issue becomes one of brutality and repression itself, and moderate and middle-class elements become alienated from an increasingly unpopular regime. This has overwhelmingly been the fate of military regimes in recent years, no matter how reformist and well-intentioned they were on coming to power. Inevitably, the reformist military regime either liquidates itself, voluntarily or involuntarily, in a return to constitutional functioning, or else allows its reformist impulse to atrophy and becomes a government of personal or oligarchic power.

It is high time that the Department of State learned the plain lesson of experience on this point and renounced its flirtation with the Latin-American military on the premise that they can be an effective modernizing force.

THE STYLE OF POLICY

Many of the problems encountered by the United States in its Latin-American policy have stemmed not from substantive weakness but from weakness in what might be called the "style" of policy. The hardheaded rationalist stance traditionally adopted by the United States in its foreign policy has tended consistently to undervalue questions of style, technique, and manner of approach on the assumption that the most important matter is to decide on objectives, and that the question of how to go about attaining those objectives is a secondary technical question that will take care of itself if a suitable bureaucracy is set up and a large enough amount of money committed. But in the world of international relations there can be no clear-cut separation between a realm of ends and a realm of means. Objectives are not attained once and for all; the reality is rather that of a state of circumstances which one must continually attempt to modify. Thus too often the United States has seen undesirable situations, for example, as malignancies calling for surgery whereas in reality what existed was a long-term pathological tendency best worked on by means of diet, exercise, therapy, and measured dosages of vitamins.

Traditional American thinking about cause and effect relations in human behavior, perhaps still dominated by the image of the rational and hedonist man of Adam Smith and Jeremy Bentham, has often approached foreign policy problems as though foreign leaders would respond automatically to proffered rewards and punishments like B. F. Skinner's white rats. Thus Congress has decreed that the United States will cut off aid (which is often in reality only commercial credit) automatically if a Latin-American country buys supersonic planes, or trades with Communist China, or expropriates the property of United States citizens without compensation. Aid will be given to countries that draw up comprehensive economic plans, or stabilize their currencies, or overhaul their tax structures. These may be desirable objectives in themselves, but one does not need to appreciate the traditional Hispanic emphasis on personal dignity to understand the counterproductive character of the contempt of national autonomy and sovereignty implied in this type of mechanical "automated" approach to relations between states.

This mechanical Benthamism or Skinnerism which conceives of an unfailing connection between the stimulus and the appropriate response does not take into account the fact that the will to autonomy of states and statesmen may prevent them from simply following the path of least pain and most pleasure. At the same time it overlooks the fact that interaction between states is not confined to a single set of stimuli and responses, so that even if the threat of punishment or the promise of reward is effective in a single instance, over the long run counterproductive resentments and mistrust may be generated by this way of conducting international relations.

The persistent failure to respect the autonomy of the Latin-American states, often only by implicit or unconscious behavior, is one of the chief causes for the development of a nationalism that defines itself in anti-United States terms. Thus the United States no longer openly treats the inter-American system, centered around the Organization of American States, as though it were the United States Colonial Office; but the tendency still exists for the United States to bully its way to favorable OAS resolutions, even when these have no practical significance. So long as this and similar tendencies persist, we make it difficult for self-respecting and patriotic Latin Americans to be friends of the United States, and instead attract as our "friends" the servile, the corrupt, and the self-serving.

The traditional stress on concrete objectives achieved at specific times by the most direct techniques has led to the overlooking of a variety of useful modes of behavior. One of the most useful resources of foreign policy is being able to count on a sympathetic public opinion in other countries. In recognition of this fact, the United States spends considerable sums of money on the United States Information Agency and other "information" activities. The most effective influences on foreign opinion, however, are not broadcast propaganda but acts of policy themselves.

Moreover, very often the most important acts in determining the attitudes of foreign publics to the United States are not those which have concrete and specific consequences, but are those of symbolic value only. Thus the expenditure of millions of dollars for feeding school lunches to children is not able to wipe out the recollection that Secretary of State John Foster Dulles pinned a medal on the corrupt and brutal dictator of Venezuela, Marcos Pérez Jiménez. The United States needs to be conscious of the symbolic meaning of its actions in terms of the hopes and fears of Latin Americans. To do this, one needs a sophisticated understanding as to where the interests of the United States lie, and one needs an equally sophisticated understanding of Latin-American realities, and of the ways in which Latin Americans perceive and attach symbolic importance to specific people and things.

SUMMATION

Let us now recapitulate the arguments made to this point. I have argued that the hypothetical threats to United States national security in the Western Hemisphere from communism, on which a great deal of policy planning and implementation has been based, are actually extremely unlikely to become real. In fact, among the various tendencies and groupings calling themselves Communist in the hemisphere, there are some whose practical objectives are not in conflict with those of the United States at all. The important thing in adopting a policy position in any specific case is to understand the politics of the country in detail and not to jump to conclusions based on ignorance and preconceived notions.

It was also argued that a broader conception of national security must take account of the gains to be expected from governments in sympathy with the United States because the United States is regarded as holding to the same principles; and in an age of increasing political participation and social change, only those governments can find a stable base which are representative of and genuinely concerned with their subjects' welfare. However, other types of government are also to be expected to come to power today, especially the military regime which has pretensions to being an agent of structural change, but which typically is ineffective in its reforms and counterproductive in its management of the country's political development.

One of the features shared by governments of otherwise different orientations taking power in the next few years is going to be their nationalism. Given the dominant role of the United States in the politics and economics of the hemisphere, this nationalism will typically take the form of attempts to secure at least independence of action from the United States, and will in some cases become a consistent policy of anti-Yankeeism. Under these circumstances, when nationalist sensibilities will be so acute, it is of primary importance for the United States to continue to seek a common ground of accommodation rather than escalate and harden conflicts begun tentatively or inadvertently. And very often what is necessary is to modify not so much the substance of policy as its style.

I am not one of those who totals up the political and economic problems facing the countries of Latin America and concludes that the situation is hopeless. Rather, it seems to me that the forces working for long-term economic and political development are stronger than the obstacles, despite the acute turbulence of the period of transition through which we are now going. However, I am less optimistic about the capacity of the United States to develop a more perceptive, rational, and effective policy toward Latin America. How can one hope for a learning process to produce more enlightened policy when an Assistant Secretary of State for Inter-American Affairs can acknowledge that all our experience has shown that American military interventions in the Caribbean are ineffectual and counterproductive and then go on to advise another such intervention?

Perhaps all that can be said on this point is that the issue is still in doubt. All the more reason, then, for those of us who think we know something about Latin America and about United States foreign policy to try to see that the prevailing views are those that represent reasonableness, factuality, and the humanistic values of the United States at her best.

X United States Policy in South Asia After Vietnam

RICHARD L. PARK

It is my belief that there is little likelihood of any sharp policy line emerging to divide the period of Vietnam from post-Vietnam. Our exodus from Indochina and the framing of a Vietnam settlement will be time consuming, despite public criticism of current policies. Issues in dispute in Asia remain in the 1970s much the same as they were in the 1960s. New world problems will arise coterminus with those with which we presently are concerned. Eras overlap. Foreign affairs do not present themselves in convenient packages.

According to President Nixon's State of the World address, the area of South Asia apparently is not of great importance. There were a few lines in the speech congratulating India and Pakistan on economic development, and the hope was expressed that there might be regional reconciliation in the near future. The South Asian section provided an encouraging pat on the back, but without attention to detail. In formal speeches of this kind the implication follows that a relatively low priority is given to South Asia by the Department of State and the President. If that were all there were to the story, we could close now. It is the rest of the story that I should like to discuss. Special attention will be given to the policy's emphasis on India and the reasons for it. Next we will describe United States political strategy in South Asia and assess that strategy. Finally, we will suggest new policies for South Asia.

United States policy in Asia since the end of World War II has opened up new patterns of behavior. The period has been one of involvement, and subsequently our knowledge of the region has increased vastly. We have taken on economic and military obligations in Asia that would not have occurred to us forty or fifty years ago. Why should this be so? After the war, we replaced, at least in part, the influence previously held by the Western European imperial powers. This is not to offer a "power vacuum" theory; whatever influence the United States has had in the Asian region since the end of the war has contended with another, much more powerful factor, namely nationalism. Nationalism and the urge for independence have been integrated into the political styles of the newly independent countries. Perhaps most important of all, the successful Communist revolution in China involved us in the protective political responses of China's neighbors.

As the Western European powers left, having been weakened by the war and unable to perform imperial missions even if they wished to do so, American influence increased, though not in proportion to the old power of empire; the equation had changed: The balance was now altered in favor of indigenous political leadership. Furthermore, the experiences of World War II produced an increased interest in Asia. Tens of thousands of American soldiers and sailors became acquainted with Asia's cultures, and Asia became part of our political culture to an unprecedented degree. In the universities and in government this was a time for increasing skills in the teaching and learning of languages—Chinese, Japanese, Hindi, and others. Scholarship in Asian studies arose from the necessity of increasing our knowledge during wartime, and interest continued into the postwar world.

Another important factor was Japan's prowess during the war. Japan had been preparing itself to compete for world power at least since 1894. During World War II military Japan was able to move through Southeast Asia quickly and cross the borders of India. This was a remarkable performance in a military sense, but even more so in terms of the logistical support and industrial strength that it implied. What was it that enabled the Japanese army to be so well organized and move so smoothly and devastatingly through such a large

part of Asia? Why was Japan welcomed by some of the leading nationalists in the Asian countries occupied by Japan?
The implications of these questions and search for their answers alerted many policy makers in the United States to the
new forces in Asia, of which Japan was the military avant
garde.

Finally, and most dramatically, the winning of the mainland by Communist China in 1949 resulted in a major shift of
policy. The Cold War era opened on a grand scale, and new
strategies were devised for Asia. A good deal of attention was
given to the concept of counteracting the power of Communist China. When it became obvious that Communist China
controlled the mainland and that it was there to stay, the
question of the fate of those countries on China's periphery
arose. "Periphery thinking" is still powerful in the United
States; in the 1950s it was compulsive.

A study of statements on United States foreign policy
from the early fifties will show the broad strategy employed:
Two major Asian countries would be depended upon for off-
setting China—Japan to the east and India to the west. It
was an easy thesis to defend. Japan was selected because of
its great potential for power and its geopolitical position
vis-à-vis China; India was selected because of its size, its long-
range potential for power, and its likely political influence on
its various neighbors.

The strategy worked out in the case of Japan. Almost everything that was expected took place—perhaps more so: Japan's
economy has grown enormously at home and in international
trade; her police force constitutes a substantial military machine; she has regained the political unity that was so well
established before the war; her international commerce and
banking have become major influences in Asia, as well as
in parts of Africa. Japan has played an expanding leadership
role, despite a defense treaty with the United States, and
despite the feeling of many Japanese that they did not wish
to become engaged in regional political conflicts; they preferred to concentrate on educational, commercial, and monetary advancements. Leaving aside rhetoric, from the American point of view the achievements of Japan have met

expectations, minus that measure of direct Japanese political involvement in Southeast Asian affairs that might have reduced American obligations.

India, on the other hand, has not met expectations, including Indian aspirations. There has been a decline in optimism, both concerning the growth of the economy and the establishment of stable political institutions. In the early 1950s, when one visited the Planning Commission of India the sense of achievement was exhilarating. It was felt then that independence had been attained, that the foreigners had been thrown out, that with the people working together toward one end the millennium would be soon reached. Now a more cynical, but more realistic, perspective has characterized public affairs. Instead of the original twenty-five-year sequence of Five Year Plans (from 1950), one must live with the thought that it is going to take at least fifty years to reach "take-off" into self-sustaining growth. This is not exactly the sort of figure that politicians there can latch onto; nor, incidentally, does it please our State Department. This is so because the regional stabilization that was to function in India by 1970 (or at least by 1975) is unlikely to be effective for some years to come. The internal problems of India are too great. She has not yet played a major external role, nor is she likely to do so in the 1970s by acting as a balancing force against Communist China.

We have had two major Asian wars in recent years; one is still going on. The Korean and Vietnam wars were critical but minor tests of the Cold War. They never were and never could be decisive, as far as the balance of power in Asia is concerned. India's fate *is* decisive; so is Japan's. Looking back at 1950 conceptions of South Asia in Washington, there may have been some shrewdness in the early strategy, but only insofar as it applied to the world of the fifties. What happens ultimately to India and to the surrounding countries in South Asia does make a difference in the long run. India thus deserves continued and special emphasis on the part of the United States in long-range Asian strategy.

Let us look more directly at South Asia. I am about to say a good deal below about India that may annoy people with a

Pakistani, Ceylonese, or Nepalese outlook on life. But from the analytical point of view, the keystone to South Asia is India, and India is thus the key to United States policies in South Asia. Though important, Pakistan is a country of the second rank that will be marginal, from a power point of view, in major countries' views of this part of the world. This point is a source of great frustration to the Pakistani government, for it is forced to live as a second-class power in its own region. On examining the history of Pakistan's search for a foreign policy, it will be found that initially Pakistan believed that a Pan-Islamic movement would link her to the Middle East, hopefully with Pakistan playing a leading role. This concept was rejected bluntly by several Middle-Eastern countries that considered Pakistan to be a johnny-come-lately country and not central to the Islamic world in the first place. In addition, Pakistan looked for favored treatment from Great Britain. Pakistani leaders felt that Great Britain had been helpful in the founding of Pakistan both directly and indirectly; they believed that Great Britain might play a special supporting role to Pakistan, at least for the transitional years after independence. The Pakistanis forgot the lessons of history: It is a rare occurrence for the British to give first priority to a minor power when there is a middle power nearby to support. This is basic to the foundations of British foreign policy.

At this point, Pakistan found herself without a protector and in need of one, India being a much larger and more powerful neighbor; at the same time, she felt that India's interests were inimical to her own interests. Finally, Pakistan did not have sufficient internal strength to be fully "independent." From where was the help to come? There were few alternatives: Alliance with the Soviet Union did not fit in with Pakistan's world view; the United States was at the time (the early 1950s) looking for an ally in South Asia, and subsequently interests were joined. When one looks at Pakistan's membership in the South East Asia Treaty Organization or at the 1954 Defense Agreement between the United States and Pakistan, however, one sees that these were strictly opportunistic on both sides. The cooperative arrangements had very little to do with the mutual national interests of Pakistan and the United States. The United States considered Pakistan the final link in South Asia to close the chain circling the Soviet Union and China. The United States needed air landing rights and the wherewithal to gather intelligence. The United States was prepared to pay, and so she entered into agreements with Pakistan. Pakistan, it seems quite clear, was not particularly concerned with the Communist issue, although it was present as a minor premise. The major Pakistani premise was potential trouble with India; so from Pakistan's point of view the agreement seemed reasonable. However, the Defense Agreement fell into disuse after 1962 because of the military aid given by Britain and the United States to India during the Sino-Indian border dispute. This dual action against the Pakistanis was the last straw, as they saw it. They felt that a bargain had been broken, that the Pakistanis had in effect done what they were supposed to do but that the United States had not kept its promises, and in fact had bolstered the military power of India. Therefore, there was no reason for Pakistan to continue the agreement. Pakistan has since developed military and commercial relations with the U.S.S.R. and China, while at the same time maintaining formal but friendly relations with the West, including the United States.

I propose that the key to United States policies in South Asia is India, for a relatively stable political order in Asia is unlikely without India as a partner in the system. This is not to say that other countries in Asia are directly dependent upon India's future, but they cannot help being affected, in some way, by what is physically and politically a subcontinent, in much the same way that the size and internal affairs of Western Europe have a tremendous effect on the international scene. Many countries look to India, for example, not because they wish to emulate it, but because it is clear to them that the political experiment taking place there is decisive in the future policy of South Asian countries. If it fails, many other countries in Asia will be forced to make (for them) demeaning political adjustments with China and the U.S.S.R. The "Indian democratic experiment," as people put it in Cold War terms, and now in somewhat more sophisticated ways, remains crucial. The consequences that would ensue if India were to become a Communist state would be felt for a long time.

India is a country about one third the size of the United States containing about 550 million people, with 14 million added to the population annually. Population is not all asset, and in India's case a large segment, from the economic point of view, may be a liability. But it is a massive country consisting, in a figurative sense, of several "Israels," possibly a "Biafra," several "African states," and two or three "Near Eastern countries," among other examples of behavior. There is a great variety of economic levels of development, of types of people, of world views, and of competence. Sometimes in international relations we think in nation-state terms, but such a listing of polities can be confusing. Functionally, India does not equate with Pakistan or Kenya or Israel; it is very much bigger and much more significant results follow from its politics.

A country such as India is a rarity in Asia: A party-run, constitutional, parliamentary democracy pursuing the efficient operation of a complex federal system of government is quite atypical for Asia. Twenty years ago there were numerous examples of this kind of government in Asia. But if one were to list all the countries of Asia and for each country to describe the presence of a stable government, any attempts at constitutional government and a party system, and all their failures, the picture would be a dismal one, indeed. Pressures of life—economic and political—and forces of social change have made rational, constitutional, party government in Asia the exception. With great difficulty, India has performed this exceptional feat, and considering its size and history, this is a more than modest achievement. Akin to this is the uniqueness of India's political order: It is under firm civilian control and is headed by an intelligent political leadership. India has all kinds of politicians, as we do; they have all kinds of bureaucrats, as we do. But India, more than most of the countries in Asia, has been served well by its elites.

Finally, one must mention the strong nationalist movement in India—it has been long lasting and deep rooted, a crucial feature of the movement. When contrasted with Pakistan, the sad thing is that after more than twenty years of independence Pakistan has not yet built a political base—one with a popular consensus for a national politics. One of the reasons is that Pakistan had a very short-lived organized nationalist movement in which a narrow leadership group developed, and several of the crucial leaders died shortly after independence; in addition, divided elite loyalties, based on the geography of the country, have given it a weak political consensus. One of India's great assets is a nationalist movement that we can trace in depth at least back to the late 1860s. It developed in a natural way, mobilizing first thousands and then tens of thousands and then hundreds of thousands of persons, particularly in the later years under Gandhi. It is difficult to weigh how important an asset this has been, but this fact made it possible for India to live as a democracy through the difficult years since 1947.

At this point, it would be worthwhile to examine some of the basic strategies that the United States has applied in South Asia since World War II. The first of these was a hope, based almost exclusively on the potential power of the individual country, that India and to a lesser degree Pakistan would assume the major roles of leadership in South Asia. There were no indications from examining the documents of postwar India that this expectation would be transformed into government policy; and less optimism on the part of United States foreign policy analysts would have been wiser, since Nehru and his followers, in fact, chose not to pursue a course of world leadership. On many occasions Nehru pointed out that India had too many domestic problems to intervene in the affairs of other countries or groups of countries. Who are we, he said, who have not got enough to eat, do not have enough jobs or houses—who are we to tell others what to do? Only in the last decade or so has India adjusted her policy to permit closer relations with other Southern Asian countries and Japan. For she has come to see that, as a great "middle power" and an even greater potential power, her responsibilities extend beyond her borders and involve taking some risks on behalf of developing countries in her part of the world. In short, while the United States was shortsighted in its initial assumption that India and Pakistan would, perforce of their size and government, assume leadership in South Asia, world events and a more cosmopolitan leadership in India have actually proven that our trust in this potential Asian power has been worthwhile.

A second aspect of our strategy was a regional approach to South Asia. Many political scientists tried to convince colleagues in the Department of State of the importance of this approach. It made sense to look at the region as a whole rather than at the individual countries. The consequence, however, was to overstress Indian interests, to the detriment of the others. Pakistan, suffering especially from this approach, became antagonized and Nepal and Ceylon felt excluded. All three felt that the more logical way was to approach the region in terms of bilateral relations in nineteenth-century fashion. We may have tried to be too sophisticated, examining regional consequences before enunciating policy. We tried to forecast the results of our policies too soon and attempted to act in such a way as to offend nobody. Needless to say, trying to please everybody at once is rarely successful.

We made three exceptions to the regional approach in the postwar period, and these were crucial to our foreign policy in South Asia. The first was the United Nations action taken in 1948 over Kashmir. We followed the United Nations resolutions—the majority view—which were hostile to Indian interests. And as far as Pakistan was concerned, we indicated general support on the principle of a plebiscite. In practical terms, we concurred with the status quo on the cease-fire line, which boiled down to a nonregional approach to Kashmir. Here was the problem: One had to take a position, and no matter which of two parties was favored, each could claim to have been offended for partisan reasons on different occasions. The second time that regional approaches were broken was during the 1954 defense arrangement with Pakistan. President Eisenhower had made a hopeless attempt not to offend India by proposing a defense agreement that would parallel Pakistan's. Nehru, of course, recognized this arrangement for what it was: an affront to everything that India's foreign policy stood for and an insult to the Indian people. So regional diplomacy did not work in that case either. The third instance was the Sino-Indian border dispute of 1962 when India appealed to the United States and Great Britain for military aid. Their direct response to India's request indicated that the United States was not prepared to follow up its general commitments to Pakistan, which felt entitled to special regional considerations under the 1954 agreement. The Pakistanis also felt that the Indians were making more of the border dispute than necessary in order to milk out of Britain and the United States as much military aid as possible. The Pakistanis saw the possibility that such arms might be used against them at a later time, and the Indo-Pakistani war of 1965 bears out Pakistan's contention.

A third strategy in South Asia during this period was American economic aid and technical assistance. In certain practical ways, economic activity was the major foreign policy strategy which the United States had at its disposal, with the exception of the defense arrangement with Pakistan. India, for example, from 1948 to 1969 gained in loans or grants something in the neighborhood of nine billion dollars. This was in the form of what might be called "integrated aid," that is, aid linked to India's overall development plan. This was similar to the aid given to Pakistan—the total amount was less than what India received, but more on a per capita basis. Both were integrated aid plans. The governments concerned calculated their major economic objectives and the United States, in turn, estimated the amount she could contribute. The two parties would then agree on a program of aid, linking together donor and recipient objectives. It is a dangerous procedure, in a way, because the donor country ties itself to other people's aspirations and sense of priority. It is the favored policy to follow, however, if building economies is the major objective.

The contrasting method of aid to developing countries is that most often used by the Soviet Union and can be described as "monumental aid." This program is conducted very well by the Soviets, but it does not rely on total integration into the economy of the country—rather, it is direct assistance appropriated for a specific purpose. Instead of offering a sum of money to be channeled to fill various gaps in the economy, the Soviets contribute aid in the form of services. When a steel mill has to be built, Soviet workers are sent to build it in the most efficient way possible; when a new kind of communal farming experiment is tried, Soviet advisers are furnished to train native workers for a given period of time only. Monumental aid does not attempt to integrate itself into the local economy; it does not attempt to change, however slowly, the existing way of life; and, as a consequence, the developing country need not become dependent on that aid. American aid has been mutually dependent, and therein rests a good deal of controversy between the United States on the one hand and India and Pakistan on the other. The rationale of decision makers here is that the price paid in the inefficiency of integrated aid and possible disruption of an established way of life is more than compensated for in long-term development programs that are designed to put a country "back on its feet" and benefit from modern technology.

Another part of our strategy in this region was to give the area diplomatic priority, an emphasis granted to very few countries by the United States. To those outside the Department of State, this may seem to be a minor objective, but consider the circumstances. In India there has been a series of hand-picked ambassadors, political and economic officers, and heads of specialized missions. There, and to some degree in Pakistan, extreme care was taken in selecting these people on the grounds that, in addition to pursuing their jobs, they might be able to exert influence on the personal level. And to a great extent this has indeed been the case. Along with this, India was granted priority in educational and cultural affairs, a field which experienced much fluctuation in popularity and effectiveness. The Fulbright program, for instance, was at one time quite sizable in Pakistan, but in recent years this has been suspended. And the Indian Fulbright program ultimately became one of the largest in the world. While there have been other cultural programs conducted here with some effect, it is very difficult to measure and judge them. But the fact remains that educational and cultural programs were extended generously in South Asia.

The final policy applied in India and gradually in Pakistan, Nepal, and Ceylon, has been the acceptance of "nonalignment," the new Asian neutralism. A nonalignment policy embraces the concept of dealing with the world as a series of equal units, treating each new problem on its own merits, and not being committed by military arrangements that subordinate national policies to other people's priorities. It is a view that has enjoyed a warm reception in this part of the world.

What has resulted from employing these various strategies? They have been subject to a lot of superficial criticism, and while some of it is justified, fundamentally the strategy was positive and, on the whole, appreciated by people who followed these matters closely. One result has been substantial economic growth over the past few years, particularly in agriculture, but there are signs of improvement in industry as well. These advances are the result of persistent efforts over many years on the part of government agencies as well as the major private foundations. Our newly acquired skills were taught to the recipient countries: Aid became a vital mutual effort. The disappointing outcome is that our financial capacity (or will) to fulfill the ever-increasing needs has declined; it is disappointing because only now are positive results becoming visible. The recipient countries are in a better position now to use the kind of aid that we were providing in abundance eight years ago, and we have become more sophisticated in administering such programs. There is, without question, a considerable residue of American influence in industry, agriculture, education, and management that stemmed from years of experience in aiding developing countries.

Our reductions in military and economic aid in recent years have led to increased Soviet and Chinese influence in the region. The South Asian countries, seeking the kind of investment and supplies they need, have found them elsewhere when they were not forthcoming from the United States. The Soviet Union has been quite helpful, first to India and now increasingly to Pakistan. China, too, has a special relationship with Pakistan in the military realm, and though it is slow in developing, it is important. The Indian military establishment is dependent upon the Soviet Union for its heavy military hardware and some spare parts.

In the space that remains, I would like to review briefly some new policies that I consider beneficial for South Asia. Some of the suggestions have been proposed before, but they still have some utility. First, all indications point to the need for the continuation of the arms moratorium in the region, in spite of the risks involved. No military establishment is going to do what an outside government wants it to, if the local government feels such action is not in the national interest. If Pakistan does not stand to gain anything from the defense arrangement of 1954 with the United States (which it feels it does not), if it cannot acquire easily in the open market the kind of weaponry that it needs because of inability to pay or inaccessibility, but if it still decides that it is in its national interest to possess weapons, then it is going to obtain them. Now Pakistan receives substantial military aid from China, largely because China has disagreements with both the Soviet Union and India, and she finds that it is in her own interest to do business with Pakistan. At the same time, Pakistan can use this kind of military support and is quite prepared to take it and develop an arrangement with China for as long as it is mutually agreeable. India has more military capability of its own—she develops small arms and spare parts itself—but she still needs planes, tanks, and other sophisticated military items from abroad. These come from the Soviet Union. So when one talks about an arms moratorium from one power in a multilateral world, all that is actually being accomplished is the attempted reduction of munitions being used in warfare *inter se,* in this case between India and Pakistan. This worked in the Indo-Pakistani war of 1965 when both sides ran out of armaments. Britain and the United States had stopped sending military supplies at the war's outbreak, and the Soviet Union cooperated in this as well. When the tanks were inoperative and when planes were grounded and small arms supplies declined, the war necessarily came to an end. But in practice, as in the above example, one party does not break an arms race; it takes several. In South Asia, all three major powers—the Soviet Union, China, and the United States—are suppliers of armaments, and any effective arms moratorium will require multilateral cooperation.

Secondly, I would suggest a "hands off" policy in Kashmir. Many have meddled in the affairs of Kashmir, including the United States, and most of the effort has been useless and even harmful. In order to understand the underlying causes of the confrontation in Kashmir, reference to the first two major addresses given before the United Nations in 1948 is all that is needed. Nothing that has happened since offers a solution reasonably acceptable to all parties. Contrary to what the words "hands off" imply, such a policy is in fact a positive policy decision—in this case one that favors India in the eyes of the Pakistanis. For it assumes that the area presently controlled by India, which is the heart of Kashmir, would remain as such, and naturally India would be quite satisfied to leave it that way. Thus a hands-off Kashmir view is likely to be looked upon by Pakistanis as antagonistic. But nothing can be accomplished by the intervention of a major power, except in the unlikely event of military intervention. And nobody, especially the United States, is willing to risk that in search of a solution. Thus it seems that the best policy in this particular case is to let those parties directly involved work out their struggle.

A third principle to recognize is that of bilateral rather than regional approaches in South Asia. This may seem to be a backward step, but I think it is essential for the smaller countries surrounding India. She will see this policy as being anti-Indian, because it is natural for her to take a "balance" in the region to mean her continuation as the preponderant power. For the well-being and sense of prestige of countries like Pakistan, Nepal, and Ceylon (and even Bhutan), it is essential that the view of independence of each country and the proper development of their own national interests be emphasized.

As for economic aid, the logical course is to increase it, not—as many Americans feel—to decrease it. There is no question that this is an unpopular position; there is no constituency in Congress for economic aid. The "rat hole theory" has penetrated the minds of large numbers of people; stories of corruption have become widespread. There are all these negative factors, plus the fact that many of us feel that there ought to be greater concern for our own domestic issues. This is the best excuse possible for the enemies of economic aid to reduce it, while probably not allocating very much to American domestic solutions either. In any event, the need for increased foreign aid exists and it is a tragedy that once we are in a position to do an excellent job of assisting the South Asian countries, who need it now more than ever, we are without the necessary funds. The trend, if it continues, suggests that we are going to dribble away economic aid until it is no longer even mildly significant. At least India and Pakistan have for a number of years been given high priority in whatever aid has been available, so that their cut has not been as drastic as that in some other areas. The level of economic aid should be built up to at least double what it is now. Chester Bowles has been saying that aid should remain at 1 per cent of Gross National Product for some years to come. According to World Bank calculations, however, our contribution is now less than one third of 1 per cent.

A final specific policy should be an increase in scholarship and in educational and cultural affairs. We are in a new era and with it we must shed old concepts of conducting research and related activities overseas. We have worked independently in the past, with only a distant relationship with Indian or Pakistani or Ceylonese associates. The future will call for a great deal more mutual cooperation that will involve respect for other people's sense of priorities in their own environment, a good deal more working together in teams. And along with this new outlook, we must be ready to apply the most sophisticated methods available, since working interdependently invites complications, particularly for academic people who tend to be highly individualistic.

In a world where crisis follows crisis, it is presumptuous, and can even be dangerous, to predict the nature of our policy ten years from now. But we should bear in mind that crises force shifts in policy and they often have deep roots; it is up to us to anticipate where the trends are leading. Crises become matters of public knowledge very suddenly and one cannot ignore them. One can always choose to avoid involvement, but the implications of noninvolvement must be fully understood. In this case, doing nothing constitutes positive policy. What are the crises that are likely to arise in South Asia over the next ten or fifteen years that might involve us in one way or another?

One of the troubled areas of Asia is Bengal. The Bengals—West Bengal in India and East Bengal in East Pakistan—are both unstable regions in the subcontinent. Political conditions in East Pakistan are critical to it. There is subversive discussion in East Pakistan that asks whether: a) East Pakistan should remain with West Pakistan or go its own way; b) East Pakistan should consider reuniting with its linguistic neighbors in West Bengal; c) some other radical political solution exists. These are matters of public debate in East Pakistan, whose conditions are far less stable than those in West Pakistan, and although West Bengal is currently under President's Rule, conditions in the state are close to anarchy. The replaced government was headed by an old and not terribly effective man, a dissident congressman, desperately holding on to power with his Home Minister, Jyoti Basu, a Communist of Peking persuasion and a very tough man. Being Home Minister meant that he had access to the police system and was in the direct line of administrative authority down to the district administrative system. West Bengal is not yet in complete chaos, but it is close to it. From a classical Communist strategic point of view, West Bengal (which houses a variety of Communists, a good many Left Socialists of anarchistic persuasion, and other dissenters) happens to include an area in the Jalpaiguri district that is contiguous to Tibet and thus to China. This opens interesting possibilities of subversion in the northeastern sector of the subcontinent, if I may employ a Cold War term (which is not totally inapplicable when discussing the New Delhi government's outlook on Bengali affairs). The problems festering in Bengal will be among the major social—and ultimately political and possibly even military—problems in the next twenty years. Who can say now what crises may arise in the future that might tie our fate to that of the peoples of Bengal?

Another major problem of the region as a whole is population growth and its ramifications. The slightest pressure on population can become a catastrophe in this part of the world. The efforts that are being made to stem population growth are massive, but statistically they are more or less ineffective. India alone is growing at the rate of about fourteen million per annum. Imagine the work involved in growing food and building houses and schools and providing the water and sewage disposal just for the new mouths that are added to the population each year, not to speak of assisting others in the country who are building toward higher economic goals. Furthermore, rural-urban migration is flowing far more rapidly than industrial jobs can absorb, in part because of the "Green Revolution" that favors well-off farmers and dispossesses those on the margin. Rapid urban growth, poor housing, and inadequate utilities carry with them the radicalization of urban politics, on the left and right. It is a difficult economic time, and as every year passes the population problem is going to become more difficult to combat.

The Kashmir case remains. As far as Pakistan is concerned, it is still the key regional issue, for until this issue is resolved Pakistanis do not feel that they will be able to do business with India. And until India and Pakistan can cooperate, many constructive actions in the economic and social spheres in both countries are going to be held in abeyance.

Finally, there is increasing political instability in both India and Pakistan. From the end of 1958 General Ayub Khan of Pakistan tried to build a political base by means of martial law; he tried in this way somehow to organize the politics of the country. He failed; he had to go. General Yahya Khan is anxious to make his reign a short one, quite genuinely, it appears. He has taken the leash off the politicians, but, as Pakistanis say, politicians are behaving in the same old way. Factionalism is developing. Some of this is healthy, but mostly it is not. India has been favored, in a sense, by the fact that the Congress Party has controlled the central government since 1947 and still holds it. The Congress has been strengthened and may be able to hold its dominance for a time, but in the long run coalition government at the center and in some of the states is likely to be India's fate. In that event, India will have to live with political instability, making it even more difficult, in turn, for governments to deal with crisis areas like Bengal.

President Nixon's State of the World address underrated many of the underlying major issues that are involved in South Asia. While at the moment they are overshadowed by domestic problems of America that have been ignored for too long, South Asian issues are likely to be paramount in the public eye five years from now and cannot afford to be avoided.

XI   American Foreign Policy in Africa
After Vietnam

IMMANUEL WALLERSTEIN

The depressing but crucial fact that we must begin with is that we are not yet "after Vietnam," and developments in the recent past give little indication that we soon shall be. Continued American support of the South Vietnamese government contributes neither to the health of South Vietnam nor of America—nor, let me add, to that of Africa. And furthermore, it is risky to talk of the African future without knowing the terms on which the war will end, and when.

Let me make no presumptions therefore about Vietnam, but rather extrapolate only on the basis of the existing situation and trends in Africa. In the decade of the 1960s, American foreign policy in Africa seems to have had certain working premises: 1) In relation to white-dominated southern Africa, there was a desire to prevent African revolutionary movements from coming to power; discomfort with the more overt aspects of white racism in the present regimes; a desire to witness the gradual incorporation of moderate African leaders in the governmental machinery—in short, a curious utopianism and a *de facto* support of the status quo. 2) In relation to most of independent Africa, there was a desire to be relatively uninvolved in either economic assistance or direct intervention favoring a particular political leader, on the grounds that France and Britain were still overseeing the situation, and that Africa was not very important anyway; but in addition there was *sub rosa* opposition to regimes that appeared too left wing and especially those which sought to support left opposition movements in other African countries—in short, indifference and a *de facto* support of the status quo. 3) In relation to the Congo and, to a lesser extent, Ethiopia, there was strong commitment to certain regimes and a willingness to introduce considerable political effort on their behalf, on the grounds that these countries were geopolitically crucial and that no other Western power could be entrusted to do the task correctly—in short, intervention and a *de facto* support of the status quo. The best that can be said for this record is that it could have been worse, for it is an unfortunate statement of overall policy in Africa. Furthermore, until there have been some significant political changes internally in the United States, it does not appear that this record will change substantially.

Of course, twenty years from now, the United States may have withdrawn from Southeast Asia, China may have had significant economic growth, and various social revolutions may have taken place in influential Latin-American countries and some Middle Eastern countries. In that case, the politics of Africa will have changed accordingly. Presently, however, the political picture of Africa can be summed up as follows: in southern Africa, relative stalemate of the liberation movements; in independent Africa, relative instability, with only minor changes occurring in the form of changes in regime.

Let us look briefly at the dynamics of each area. Southern Africa can be divided into two segments, Portuguese Africa and the South Africa-Rhodesia complex. Although the regimes in both are allied and have basically similar policies, the decision making apparatuses are quite distinct and it is possible to foresee noncongruent developments in the two segments at certain points in time. Furthermore, this functional distinction, a distinction which is reinforced by historical and cultural ties, is recognized by the liberation movements themselves. There are two sets of working alliances among ideologically consonant liberation movements. In Portuguese Africa, there are the Conferência de Organizacões Nacionalistas das Colónias Portuguesas (CONCP) groups movements in Angola, Mozambique, and Portuguese Guinea. They are, respectively, the Movimento Popular de Libertacão de Angola (MPLA), the Frente de Libertacão de Mocambique (FRELIMO), and the Partido Africano da Independência da Guiné e Cabo Verde (PAIGC). A parallel alliance, which is formal but without a special name, is that between the African National Congress (ANC) of South Africa and the Zimbabwe African Peoples' Union (ZAPU) of Rhodesia.

There are two significant differences between the segments of Southern Africa. One is that in Portuguese Africa the actual white settlers are not in political control of the government, which opens up the possibility of Portuguese withdrawal should this one day be in the interests of the Portuguese government in Lisbon. The shifting interests of the metropolitan government historically played a crucial role in the decolonization of Algeria, the Belgian Congo, and Kenya, three white settler areas. It is precisely this metropolitan government which is absent in both South Africa and Rhodesia. The second difference is in military and economic strength. Portugal is a poor country whose internal resources are unimpressive and whose military potential is distinctly limited. It would be even more limited without the present military assistance she receives through her membership in NATO. South Africa, by contrast, is a country possessing copious natural resources, a potentially large industrial capacity, and a strong military arm—one of the strongest military apparatuses of a country that is not a major world power. And Rhodesia is in effect under the military protection of South Africa, at least insofar as Rhodesia is threatened by liberation movements. Furthermore, the topography of Rhodesia and South Africa is less favorable to guerrilla activity than that of Portuguese Africa. This is one reason why, although there is sporadic guerrilla activity in Rhodesia and South Africa, there is thus far no sustained military activity at the level already achieved in Portuguese Africa.

At the present time, the amount of external military and financial assistance to African liberation movements is not terribly impressive. Some African states give money, though not very much, to these movements via the African Liberation Committee (ALC) of the Organization of African Unity. Some also give assistance in military training and, of course, a few lend their territory as staging bases. Aid from the rest of the world (Russia, China, Sweden) is no doubt comforting and useful to the liberation movements, but it is scarcely at a level which is militarily critical.

However, the sum total of this assistance is enough to sustain these movements and seems to be incremental over a long term. That is, it permits them to maintain a sufficient level of activity so that they can consolidate their movements as military and political organizations, occupy regions of the country *de facto*, and bog down Portuguese troops. If the pace can be maintained, a function more of the political cohesion of the liberation movements than of their military possibilities, this kind of slow war of attrition may well be more psychologically demoralizing to the Portuguese (especially those in the metropole) than to the liberation movements.

In addition, it is clear that metropolitan Portugal is entering into a new political era, one whose outcome is not clear. But it is reasonable to speculate that withdrawal from a debilitating colonial war may seem to be an attractive possibility to two very different political elements. The forces of the left (broadly defined to include not only Marxists of various persuasions, but also left Catholics and nonparty intellectuals) may see the colonial wars as sustaining conservative forces within Portugal and thus blocking internal change. It may also be attractive to quite another group, the segment of the industrial bourgeoisie and professional classes that is linked with outside capitalist enterprises (whether European or North American). Whereas one of the fears of the ruling groups in Portugal today is precisely that in case of decolonization American, French, or German economic interests would replace Portuguese interests in a future neo-colonial relationship; Portuguese groups with links to these non-Portuguese enterprises would obviously have little or nothing to fear. On the contrary, they might gain. Thus it is not inconceivable that there might be perhaps a passing alliance in Portugal between these two politically disparate groups which might force a change in the attitude of the Portuguese government. Were such a change in Portuguese policy imminent, those with the most to lose—white settlers in Portuguese Africa, the South African and Rhodesian governments—might react. One way to react might be for the white settlers in Portuguese

Africa to proclaim "independence" with a government securely dominated by these settlers, as the white Rhodesians did with UDI (Unilateral Declaration of Independence) in 1965. This tactic might be more feasible—for both geographical and political reasons—in Mozambique than in Angola; it would be impossible in Portuguese Guinea.

Any such development in Portuguese Africa, whether or not a UDI were to be proclaimed, would of course be very unsettling for the Rhodesia-South Africa complex—a complex because it is difficult to envisage the possibility that, whatever the case in 1965, the South African government would now permit the Rhodesian government to fall. It seems that the liberation movement cannot muster enough military strength to overthrow a regime in Salisbury backed by Pretoria. The key question then becomes the internal civil war in South Africa. The prospects and the timetable are hard to evaluate: On the one hand, the present government is strong—in its will and in its prowess; on the other, the oppressiveness is great, as is the potential for a revolutionary movement.

In many ways South Africa plays a peculiar role in the world. It is not like other African states in that it is a functioning member of the capitalist industrialized world—a minor partner in the center of this world rather than a dominating part of the periphery. Nevertheless, it is also not like other members of the capitalist industrialized world since it is the only one whose numerically huge and ethnically distinct underclass within it, a class with no political rights and hence no political loyalty to the regime, constitutes a majority of the population. Finally, South Africa is peculiar because of its production of a large part of the world's supply of gold, and gold remains a key element in the world banking system. This world-banking system rests on a shaky political base and tampering with South African stability would have an impact on this system difficult to foresee and horrendous to contemplate—or, no doubt, so it probably appears to central bankers throughout the capitalist world.

Thus, the standard neo-colonial compromise by which nationalist struggles have been resolved in Africa does not seem very plausible for South Africa. In most other instances,

European-American interests had a lot to gain and little to lose from granting independence. Not only are settlers in control in South Africa, but European-American interests may calculate that they have little to gain and much to lose in a transfer of power to the black majority. In short, the stakes being much higher for the world capitalist system, the willingness to take risks is correspondingly and understandably smaller.

What then can we anticipate in South Africa? Over the next few years, the South African government will continue to be dominated by the so-called *verligte* (enlightened) wing of the Afrikaner nationalists, as contrasted with the *verkramptes* (cramped ones). The *verligte* viewpoint is that apartheid is both desirable and viable, provided it is applied with a certain limited flexibility in two areas: the policy vis-à-vis the leaders of neighboring African independent states; the policy vis-à-vis "traditional" chiefs in the rural areas. The *verligtes* feel that they can turn these two groups into allies with no significant damage to the economics and social practice of urban apartheid and with significant gains among elite public opinion in the United States and the United Kingdom.

We see this *verligte* policy being effected today in both these areas. South Africa has sought to exchange diplomatic representatives with a limited number of neighboring black independent states, offering them technical assistance, trade, and special exemptions for their diplomats from apartheid legislation, in return for abstention by these states from opposition to the South African regime and acceptance of South African investment. Malawi has been the focus of special attention in this respect; together with Mozambique it is the reservoir from which more than half of South Africa's mine laborers are recruited. It has become the model state for South Africa, and by now four or five other states have followed with a somewhat similar relationship to South Africa.

Internally, South Africa is pursuing the Bantustan program of creating all-black political units in rural areas of limited autonomy. The first one created was the Transkei authority, and since then the government has created several more, with still more planned. In addition, the present regime seeks to win over the English-speaking white population to a more wholehearted acceptance of the Afrikaner-dominated regime. Though the *verkramptes,* mostly small rural Afrikaner farmers and lower middle-class urban whites, are fearful that these overtures represent a betrayal of the Afrikaner's historic cultural self-assertion against the English, the *verligtes* represent that segment of Afrikaners who are sufficiently secure in their social and economic status to wish to bury the hatchet with the English and concentrate on the economic development of a racially stratified society.

All these policies of the *verligte* regime are aimed at one more benefit: moderating negative views about the South African regime in dominant political and economic circles in the United Kingdom and the United States in the hope of expanding economic collaboration and recreating the kind of political and military links with the West that South Africa enjoyed until 1960. In many ways, these policies have been remarkably successful in the short run. However, the system in its present jerry-built form is faced with internal contradictions which must soon strain its equilibrium.

First of all, the system continues to assume that the black elites nurtured by it will continue to accept the social and political inferiorities to which they are subject. But the South African blacks are refused those privileges enjoyed by what must seem to them the far less educated and sophisticated elite of Malawi within South Africa itself. In particular, it is not hard to see the puppet leaders of the Bantustans turning into Frankenstein monsters from the regime's point of view, whenever openings for such transformations occur. Secondly, the system assumes that it can either maintain a growing urban black proletariat at a minimum wage level at low political cost or make economic concessions to this group without encountering high backfire from the large white privileged working strata. At one point or another, the *verligte* regime risks becoming more *verligte* and overthrown by a more rigid right-wing group (risking its international equilibrium and also a union of Bantustan leaders and black nationalist revolutionaries), or becoming less *verligte* themselves and obtaining the same results.

But this is not the crisis of a day's or year's duration, but that of a decade. During that decade, policy direction may shift back and forth uncertainly; and this uncertainty will no doubt be paralleled by United States policy uncertainty. The extreme *verligte* elements will appeal to United States policy makers on the traditional grounds that "beyond us, there is worse" and "help us against our *verkramptes*." The United States may be tempted to assist the regime in its "liberalizing" aspects: financial assistance to economic projects in a Bantustan area, for example; cooperation in economic assistance to neighboring African states, etc.

A conservative United States regime and a *verligte* South African regime are not very far apart in their foreign policy. They are certainly allied in their desire to maintain—at almost any cost—the status quo in southern Africa. It is not unreasonable to presume that they may move in the direction of formalizing those affinities. South African black nationalists will not appreciate this *de facto* alliance; they do not do so today, and will do so even less as the alliance intensifies. The black nationalists may step up their hostility toward the United States government by adding to verbal condemnations physical attacks on United States officials. Under such circumstances, the United States government may be willing to consider the resumption of arms sales to the South African government. And so it can go on.

There is another element to add to this picture, and crucial in its potential power. The process of the politicization and radicalization of black Americans has been going on for some time now and should continue to accelerate. It need not be that a movement like the Black Panther Party will eventually effectively represent all twenty million or so American blacks. We merely have to assume that the BPP or some similar group will hold the "benevolent neutrality" of the majority (no more) of American blacks—a not implausible assumption. When this does occur, there will be turmoil within the United States even more serious than at present, which will take the form in large part of a black-white struggle. Since it is likely to be the same form it will take in South Africa, there probably will be two consequences. First, black Americans will identify and ally with their brothers in South Africa. Second, whites in America, even those ubiquitous

"liberal" whites, will increasingly identify with the white regime in South Africa, or at least with an "anti-liberation-
movement" cause.

In summary, we can most probably anticipate a contin-
uance of the South African government's policy of no concessions and no significant European-American pressure to
change this policy. The prolonged politico-military struggle
that results will inevitably radicalize the black middle class
of South Africa more and more, and further politicize the
working classes. This will probably mean that the liberation
movement in South Africa will come to be the first one that
is profoundly, and not just superficially, socialist. The comparison that is probably most apt is with Vietnam. But, as
with Vietnam, this will mean that the potential loss for the
capitalist world involved in decolonization, and hence the resistance, will be still higher. This could result in a repetition
of Vietnam, though not in a directly parallel way. South
Africa could become the scene of a twenty-five-year struggle
for liberation, during which time the United States may well
become inexorably involved until it becomes the prime mover
rather than a reluctant ally.

Elsewhere in Africa, all will not be quiet. The present situation is one of corrupt and unstable regimes, which change
their top personnel with some regularity largely via military
coups and which are subordinate to European-American economic control; they are beset by secessions and "tribalism"
and are incapable of curbing the growing unemployment and
hunger. This deplorable state of affairs cannot last, especially
if there is a major civil war in South Africa.

There are too many ifs to do more than speculate, but the
two countries most likely to have serious revolutionary movements, socialist in ideology and nationalist in character, are
Nigeria and the Congo (Kinshasha). These countries have
had the purgative effects of civil war, which have weakened
both the indigenous administrative bourgeoisie and the pervasive influence of foreign whites at the local levels, thus
undermining the two main popular supports of a neo-colonial
regime. Nigeria and the Congo are strong potential candidates
for rapid industrialization: they have a resource base, a large
internal market, and mineral wealth. They also have a grow-

ing landless, unemployed proletariat with potential for political mobilization. Hence it is not inconceivable that in the next ten to twenty years either of these countries may have a serious and successful revolution. And if that happens, the effects on the neighboring countries will be immense. (By contrast, when the Congo/Brazzaville proclaims itself a Marxist state, even if that is to be taken totally at face value, the impact is minimal and the viability of the regime doubtful.)

Let us project one step further. In ten, twenty, or perhaps thirty years China will have consolidated herself politically and achieved significant industrial progress. She will be ready, *for the first time,* to engage in an internationally active foreign policy. It is reasonable to expect that she will throw her support behind the African liberation movement in South Africa, as well as behind revolutionary movements in Nigeria and the Congo.

What would Russia do? Here there are many possibilities. She might seek to emerge as the great world arbiter, the beacon of liberalism and reason. No doubt this would be a difficult role to play in the light of past history and present culture and image, but structurally it makes sense and the U.S.S.R.'s leaders might very easily slip into what now seems an implausible pose. Another possibility is that the U.S.S.R. might find herself faced with a revolt of the various nationalities within her borders; in all likelihood the regime we know would prove itself too inflexible to make the suitable adjustments. In that case, the Soviet government might panic and throw itself into the American camp, reluctantly but inexorably coming to oppose the liberation movement in South Africa and revolutionary movements elsewhere in Africa.

After Vietnam, what in Africa? From a cursory examination of our policies there, the possibility of an even bigger and longer "Vietnam" in South Africa is not farfetched. But South Africa is central to the world economic system, whereas Vietnam is quite marginal. Hence, a prolonged, polarized struggle in South Africa could threaten the very foundations of the world system in a way that nothing has up to now.

I am predicting neither apocalypse nor Armageddon. I am projecting a very serious world crisis which, for the first time, will be played out internally in the United States as well as elsewhere in the world. American foreign policy and American internal policy will then be the two sides of the same coin. Americans will have to evaluate what will be an appropriate foreign policy in terms of what kind of society they want in America and what are the risks worth taking when trying to export that kind of society.

XII American Foreign Policy in the Middle East: Toward the Future

JOHN S. BADEAU

The task the United States faced in the Arab world after the 1967 debacle was not to rebuild its former position, but to work toward a new one. The collapse of American influence which accompanied the conflict made it clear that the position of the United States had not been as strong and solid as was assumed; in the hour of conflict, the persisting strains of the recurring encounters took command of the situation to wipe out many of the gains of earlier years. Not only was it impossible to return to what had been, but the former position had revealed inherent weaknesses that called into question its utility for the future.

Were the general approach and the tactical guidelines of the past still valid? The guidelines, which were never full-blown policies but only points of reference for policy formulation, had not lost their pertinency. The interests and realities out of which they arose still remained, although set in new positions and including new problems. Indeed, it was the failure more consistently to use them in approaching Arab problems which was one cause for the collapse of the American position in its hour of challenge. The decline and final cessation of significant aid to the U.A.R. after 1965 was a principal reason for President Nasser's conclusion that the United States had written off Egypt permanently as an element in its Arab policies, moving him both toward a confrontation with America and an increasing dependence on the U.S.S.R. Per-

In this edition, references to outdated events have been deleted and are indicated by ellipses. ED.

haps American aid to Egypt was unnecessarily generous from 1960 to 1964; certainly its cessation was unnecessarily drastic and did not serve American interests. Failure to be more impartial over a long period in the Arab-Israel dispute was paid for by a bitter price of broken diplomatic relations, interrupted petroleum production and transportation, and universal ill will throughout the Arab world. Directness and clarity in warning all states in the area (both the Arab states and Israel) where American interests lay, followed by appropriate action, would have averted some difficulties and given American diplomacy more weight as the 1967 crisis developed. Yet it must be remembered that the obstacles to this line of action were great and that the pressure of the Vietnam war made it increasingly unlikely that the United States would take any strong action until it was too late.

In facing the task of building a new position on the ruins of the old, the United States must begin by rejecting the temptation to grasp at dramatic panaceas. There is no conceivable policy which will set everything right in a few months, or even in a few years, rapidly restoring American influence throughout the Arab world and resolving the threat to American interests. Only a painstaking, sustained, and steady effort, in which each gain will be minor, is possible and useful. To try to re-enter the Arab world with a flurry of new activity would weaken whatever remnants of the American position remain (since no Arab state in the aftermath of conflict could afford to be the obvious target of an American drive) and would, in any case, be impossible while diplomatic relations remain broken. This is as true for policy toward Israel as toward the Arab states; in both cases the United States has little option but to "play it cool," not yielding to pressures from either side but proceeding with deliberation and a clear view of its interests quietly to seek new relations consonant with new conditions.

It is not the purpose of this essay to make detailed policy proposals for the specific issues of the day, but to point to the major problems in the large and to indicate the necessary approach to them. Of the many problems involved, three are central. The first is the future American attitude toward the revolutionary regimes of the Arab world. The traditional states have economic interests in a continued American and Western connection that are an asset in restoring some measure of the American position. Furthermore, most of these states were less directly involved in the 1967 conflict to the extent that they did not take leadership in formulating the Arab challenge to Israel but joined the fray when it became impossible for any self-respecting Arab to keep out of it. Additionally, their regimes on the whole weathered the immediate crisis better than those of some of the radical states, so that it could be argued that assisting them would further the American objective of area stability. Such considerations, backed by domestic American opinion, could easily lead to a policy of ignoring the more radical regimes and confining American attentions to the traditional states, in effect making them the "chosen instruments" of policy in the future.

For many reasons . . . such a course would be disastrous to any hope of building a new and significant American position in the Arab world. The U.A.R. and Syria will continue to be centers of political activity, and Egyptian influence, while severely damaged, cannot be written off as a factor in future Arab affairs. One result of defeat may well be the heightening of demands for more rapid change in traditional Arab societies; the leaders and centers of radical change thus may play a larger role in the future than they have in the past. Moreover, it is in the radical states that the Soviets will try to capitalize on their gains—and where they will face their most serious dilemmas. Consequently, dealing with the entire spectrum of Arab systems . . . is the only alternative to becoming so boxed in by identification with the conservative order that its future difficulties and possibly waning influence in Arab affairs would cut the United States off from the most significant developments of the future. Less than ever can the United States afford to polarize its position in the Arab world, becoming the champion of traditionalism (even when this is renamed "moderation") while the U.S.S.R. and radical Arab nationalists play the role of innovators and modernizers.

The second problem lies in the future relations of the United States to the Arab-Israel dispute, which is likely to continue indefinitely. Should this dispute somehow be resolved by a settlement stemming from Israel's victory or be moved by the Arabs toward a working accommodation with Israel, the problem would be less urgent—although the United States cannot expect that the Arabs will forget its role in the past. But even if resolution or accommodation can take place, it will be over an extended period and not by a dramatic denouement, as Arab attitudes after the war have indicated. During the process both Israel and the Arabs will be preoccupied with what American policies will be in regard to their mutual relations and to the ultimate goal toward which the dispute may move. This means that policy toward Israel will play an even greater role in the American approach to the Arab world than it did before 1966–67, when it was possible in some cases to adopt the "ice box" policy since a conflict did not appear in the making either to American or Arab eyes.

Here the problem is the willingness and ability of the United States to resist pressure to tie it even more closely to Israel. That pressure will probably seek three objectives: more concrete commitments to Israel's defense, a renewed supply of armaments, and support for the postwar Israeli position in regard to occupied Arab territories, both on the grounds of security and as an instrument for forcing peace on the Arabs. From Israel's standpoint these objectives are in keeping with its national interests, but they are not all in keeping with the interests of the United States. More than ever it is clear that the major premise of American policy in the Middle East cannot be the protection of Israel, but must be the protection of American interests, even when this may adversely affect Israel and Arab states. In the light of the past two decades, and especially in the aftermath of the 1967 conflict, it is impossible to escape the conclusion that the special relation of the United States to Israel has served neither the specific interests of the United States in Arab countries nor the long-range objectives of American policy in the Middle East.

This is not to say that the United States should switch to a pro-Arab policy. The only valid "pro" is a "pro-American" policy, which necessarily will involve relations with both Israel and the Arab world. But these relations cannot simply be a repetition of the past. . . . It would be unrealistic to assume that the United States can take any action which will permanently secure Israel against renewed Arab hostility, or guarantee to the Arabs that further Israeli expansion will not take place. Some supporters of Israel argue that firm American support for Israel's continued occupation of Arab territory until direct peace negotiations are held, backed by a new commitment to the defense of Israel and an unstinted supply of arms, would bring Arab leaders to a moment of truth and force them to capitulate. There yet may be some Arabs who think that the United States has such control over Israel that it could force withdrawal of Israeli troops from Arab territory and return the situation to its *status quo ante bellum*.

Both attitudes are wishful thinking, however desirable their intended results may be. The Arabs were indeed overwhelmingly defeated in 1967, but that defeat has given no evidence of breaking the Arab will or creating the conditions for a significant Arab-Israel rapprochement. Of all people, Israelis and the world Jewish community, in view of their own history, should appreciate the dogged determination of a community to sustain hope through the centuries. The Jewish community did not forget Palestine through its long years of exile; they should not be surprised that the Arabs display a similar tenacity of memory and purpose. Two decades of Israeli existence is but a minute in the thirteen hundred years of Arab and Islamic political consciousness; other foreign kingdoms have come and gone in Palestine, and many Arabs are willing to struggle on in the conviction that Israel will go as they did.

This set of the Arab mind is encouraged by the imbalance between the resources of Israel and the Arab world. While Israel has had an advantage in effective manpower (army, technicians, administrators) during its first two decades, its population is but a tiny fraction of that of the Arab world, in which training and technical skills are steadily increasing. Moreover, in 1966 the gross national product of the Arab world was approximately nine times that of Israel. The imbalance can be expected to grow in the future as the Arab world modernizes and progresses. Arabs are thus not yet of a mind to end the struggle in a moment of temporary defeat.

On the other hand, the Arab has never understood nor truly appreciated the deep convictions on which Israel was founded, nor the determination of the Israeli to exist by right in the land of his destiny. By viewing Israel as an "imperialist" and "neo-colonial" creation, the Arab has blinded himself to its true character and underestimated the forces which make for its continued existence. Israel's hope was that an overwhelming defeat would so bring this truth home in catastrophic terms that Arab leaders would give up the struggle rather than continue a fruitless adventure. But the hope was not realized; whatever Arab accommodation might come out of the conflict, permanent peace and renunciation of future moves against Israel appear the least likely.

In this situation the United States cannot afford to take a position of irrevocable commitment to either side. It does not have the capacity to change either Arab or Israeli attitudes, or permanently to guarantee one side against the other. Commitments made in such open-end situations, where future developments are unpredictable and the risk of war ever present, can only lead to a growing and frustrating involvement, as has so clearly been demonstrated in the case of Vietnam. Such a course would not serve American interests; the United States cannot surrender its options of action or commit its resources to the aims and policies of another state, especially a small one intent on pursuing its own aims regardless of global considerations.

It is thus not in the interest of the United States to follow a course in the future which commits it more deeply to either the Israeli or the Arab side of the dispute. To moderate the conflict and foster those influences working toward ultimate abatement is obviously in the American interest, but must be set in the framework of basic American objectives—stability, containment of Soviet influence, and protection of interests in the Arab world. This is to say that the tactical guideline of nonalignment in Middle East disputes becomes more essential than ever for approaching the problems of the Arab world.

What can the United States do? In the immediate aftermath of conflict it did not have much leverage on either Israel or the Arab states. Having confronted each other on mutually exclusive terms, the Arabs (especially the U.A.R., Jordan, and Syria) and the Israelis will have to come to their own moment of reality when each party discovers that its immediate objectives cannot be realized—that the Arabs will not enter into direct negotiations, or the Israelis unconditionally withdraw. When that moment comes, the United States should support an intermediary effort, probably under international auspices. . . . With all its difficulties, a stronger United Nations presence on a much larger scale, with extensive demilitarized buffer zones adequately policed by observers, seems the most useful solution. This is the one answer to Israel's border-security problems which the Arabs could accept . . . which could become the basis for a better adjustment to Israel in the future.

Such a solution will not please Israel, which will bitterly oppose it. But the United States has little option if it is to make the security of its own interests the primary concern of its policy. Israel must be told that its desires with respect to occupied Arab territory are secondary, so far as the United States is concerned, to the problem of coping with the new Soviet position in Arab lands. Israel cannot expect the United States to act on Israeli terms in formulating policy; America must act on American terms, even though both Israel and the Arab world will dislike it. At the same time the Arabs must have the lesson of 1967 kept before them—that the United States and other great powers will not rescue them from the results of ill-advised adventures against Israel. President Nasser maintained after his defeat that the United States had deliberately misled him by giving assurances that it would provide a peaceful solution to the dangerous impasse into which he had gotten himself. Certainly the United States tried to find a solution short of war, but it was in no position to give any binding assurances and cannot do so in the future. Both the Arabs and Israel must understand that the United States will not be a shield behind which either can machinate renewed conflict.

In the Arab world the problem of the United States is to

find means to identify itself afresh with Arab development and progress. Some will say that any assistance given to an Arab government will increase its capacity to turn on Israel again, and that a public renunciation of belligerency should be the precondition of American aid. But this approach is unrealistic and would only result in keeping the door closed to possibilities of renewed American influence in Arab affairs. What the United States should seek is a new and mutually profitable relationship with Arab states, involving America in their national development and economic progress while resisting any contribution to the growth of their military capacity.

American arms sales to Arab states should be greatly restricted, if made at all. One lesson the 1967 war would appear to have taught the Arabs is that a weak society cannot successfully risk a military confrontation with a thoroughly modern one. The urge to modernize which this lesson may heighten should be used by the United States to identify itself with sound, general nonmilitary developments wherever this is possible. The course of such a policy will be painfully slow at first, but the continued utility of a Western connection . . . makes the task at least feasible. Arms sales to Israel, as to the Arab world, should cease so far as possible. Adding more arms either to Israeli or Arab arsenals will neither moderate nor resolve Arab-Israel hostility, and the United States cannot expect to regain influence in the area or to be effective as a mediator if it becomes a major arms dealer to either or both sides.

The pressure for arms sales to Israel arises from the conviction of many that the Soviets have committed themselves to rearming Arab states as a prelude to a fourth round of conflict. This raises the third postwar problem of American policy —its attitude and actions toward the new Soviet position in the Arab world. Some of the potentials of that position have already been indicated, but they are only potentials, and the full audit of debits and credits must await future developments. . . .

Soviet policy may be determined by two factors. One is the Soviet Union's own reappraisal of its interests and policies in the Arab world in the light of the lessons of the 1967 crisis and of its general strategy as a great power. The other is the inherent resistance of Arab nationalism to foreign control, which in the past has prevented the Russians from penetrating deeply into the political systems of their clients. Both factors will limit the extent to which an unlimited flood of arms would serve Soviet purposes. . . .

These considerations do not rob the flow of Soviet weapons of its danger, but they do cut the edge of the argument that the objective is to prepare the Arabs for another attack upon Israel. The Soviets can be counted upon to capitalize on the weakened American position and to utilize the tensions of the Arab world for their own benefit. But Soviet policy is above all one of *Realpolitik*—which means that its freedom of action in the Arab world is limited by commitments and interests elsewhere and must stop short of a point where it would become captive to the clients it seeks to support.

The most satisfactory answer to the arms problem would be some sort of agreement between the U.S.S.R. and the West limiting the supply of weaponry to the Arab world. This possibility was apparently raised at the Johnson-Kosygin meeting in June 1967, but without positive result. Yet it should not be assumed that the door to an arms agreement is closed for all time. It is remarkable that in the face of the Vietnam situation and the Middle East crisis, American-Soviet relations have remained as good as they have. There is a much larger core of mutual interests in world stability than one would conclude from the public utterances of Soviet leaders. So long as the Vietnam war continues it will be impossible for the Soviets to come to an agreement on Middle East arms; but once that conflict is resolved (or as an element in its resolution), it would not be impossible for them to consider an arrangement which would lighten their burdens in the Arab world. The United States should continue to press this possibility, recognizing that to do so involves self-restraint on its own part in not recreating the Arab-Israel arms race by immediately supplying weapons to one or both sides. . . .

The United States can and should change the focus of its policy from a negative checkmating of Soviet influence to a positive concern for furthering the development of Arab lands. The record makes clear that the basic danger in the Arab world has not lain so much in Soviet capabilities as in Arab weakness and disarray. Arab development (whether in its traditional or radical form), if steadily supported, will do more to assure the independence and stability of Arab states than constant American counterattacks on the Soviet position. The basic policy objective must be to secure the health of the patient, not to outdo the rival physician in prescribing nostrums until he abandons the case. The Soviets have sufficient problems inherent in their own position, and Arab nationalism is sufficiently resistant to foreign control, to warrant the United States' turning away from anti-Sovietism as the beginning and end of its approach to the Arab world. In the aftermath of 1967, the American image in Arab eyes has been that of an anti-Arab, anti-Soviet, pro-traditional force. It will take a long time to erase this image, but the United States cannot afford to neglect the effort. Whatever success foreign powers can have in the Arab world in the future will be determined largely by their identification with the modernization and development of the area as an end in itself, and not simply as an instrument in a world power struggle.

This approach may be realistic so far as the Soviet position is concerned, but is it equally so in relation to the possible spread of communism in the Arab world? This question cannot be answered fully without a detailed assessment of the situation in each country, but several legitimate general observations can be made. One is that in no current system of Arab radical reform have Marxists or Communist institutions been made central. Some Soviet methods of government and economics have been adopted, but these were selected chiefly on a pragmatic basis and not because of an ideological imperative. Arab radicalism has been both nationalistic and pragmatic, more interested in solving the problems of development than adhering to a rigid and completely logical political or economic system.

Another consideration is that it is hardly possible to predict what a future "Communist" Arab state might be like. The particular mix of Arab nationalism, social radicalism, and communism which might emerge in some future state would

cause problems for the United States, but they would not be
the problems of dealing with an extension of the Communist
system of the Soviet Union, as the growing freedom of the
East European Communist states and the development of their
own domestic systems and policies in world affairs suggests.
A Communist-tinged Arab state would be more independent
of control from Moscow than many have assumed.

Moreover, the danger of the establishment of a Communist
system in an Arab country would not come so much from a
free choice on the part of current leaders as from a situation
in which a country's dependence on the Soviet Union would
be so overwhelming and irreversible as to give local Communists and their sympathizers increasing positions of power.
Some observers dispute this judgment, believing that the
radical leaders of the Arab world are either conscious tools
or unwilling instruments of the Communist system. But to believe this is to misread the character of Arab nationalism,
especially in its revolutionary phase. The revolutions of the
Arab world have been expressions of an extreme stage of
nationalist feeling, dedicated to complete independence from
all foreign control and ending the domination of the traditional, foreign-oriented elite. The danger does not appear to
lie so much in the original leaders of the Arab revolutions as
in those who might come to power if their regimes and the
systems of reform they instituted calamitously collapsed. Then
an organized Communist minority, supported by the Soviets,
might be able to seize power, owing to the chaotic state of
affairs and the conviction that with the failure of "bourgeois"
reform efforts the only alternative would be the full Communist system. . . .

A NEW MOOD

None of these suggested policy developments will work a
quick and radical change in the American position in the Arab
world. It must be said again that the problems are too deep
and . . . too pervasive to make possible a rapid return of
American influence. And none of the suggestions is a radical
departure from the tactical guidelines of the American ap-

proach which have been used spasmodically during the last decade. What they call for is a more sustained use of the guidelines as a basis for American policy. The nature of American interests, the characteristics of the Arab world, and the instruments of diplomacy available to the United States continue their essential character, despite the new circumstances. When American policy has gone astray, it has been because it undertook commitments not related to its interests, became partisan where it should have been even-handed, and failed to sustain its long-range objectives through the stresses of immediate situations. To avoid such actions in the future is an essential ingredient for success in the task of creating a new American position.

It is the mood in which policies toward the Arab world have been made that must change. The attitudes toward Arab affairs built up in the past deeply infect the atmosphere in which the policy maker weighs the problems of the future. Unencumbered by these, able to survey the scene for what it is rather than for what it was, he must approach the challenge of the future with a freshness of outlook which too often has been absent. This is what the American approach to the Arab world most needs—an open mind and a more confident spirit, less irritation, and more disposition to work steadily toward ultimate goals. The momentum of the past too easily dominates the direction of the future; new problems are faced as though they were old, old solutions offered as though they were new. A change in mood to fit the change in times is the most essential requirement for the United States in dealing successfully with Arab affairs.

What should this new mood be? Its first element is a more deliberate patience—steadily pursued effort with eyes fixed on ultimate objectives rather than always distracted by immediate problems. Steadiness is particularly needed in dealing with the Middle East, where change is rapid and continuous, stability tenuous, political leadership uncertain, and national policies compounded more of emotion than of rationality. In such a situation quick returns on a policy investment are few. It is only by sustaining a judicious course of action through an extended period that it can be effective. Neither revolutionary nor traditional governments are apt to respond to a foreign initiative as quickly as Americans expect. The first are changing too rapidly, the second too slowly, to move in the desired direction at a pace which immediately justifies the policy being used. Only persistent and sustained effort, undeflected by the vagaries of daily developments, can possibly result in lasting influence.

Too frequently in the past American policies have been characterized by the same headlong expediency of which President Nasser was often accused—reaction rather than action. Problems in the Arab world have been constant and numerous, but they cannot be dealt with successfully by alternate waves of activity and impatience, or simply by saying: "Go see what the Arabs are doing and tell them to stop it." . . .

The second element in the new mood is that of realism—estimating conditions for what they are, differentiating between interests and desiderata, appraising accurately the forces in the Arab world and not viewing them simply in the light of a popular or traditional image. A fresh evaluation of the capacity of the various centers of power is constantly needed. In the aftermath of the 1967 crisis, all the power factors of the Middle East underwent some change. The Soviets had new opportunities opened to them, which some observers wishfully devalued, yet at the same time they faced new problems which could inhibit their ability to make further permanent gains. American policy cannot be based either on underestimating the strength of the new Soviet position, or on overestimating the ease with which they may capitalize on it.

Nor is it possible . . . to maintain that the U.A.R. and its radical regime can dominate the Arab world. The capacity of revolutionary Egypt to gather the other Arab states under its wing has always been less than many have assumed, and the vision of an Egyptian empire stretching from the Valley of the Nile to the Persian Gulf was generated more by the fears of the West than the realities of the Middle East. Even before the 1967 defeat, it was clear that Egypt had neither the resources nor the capacity permanently to dominate the area. After defeat, with its economy shattered, its army proved wanting, its military leadership of Arab forces revealed as ineffective, and its relations with sister Arab states again thrown in turmoil, it faced a bleak future. Yet it would be unrealistic to write off the U.A.R. as of little importance in future Arab affairs. Its activism, although possibly curtailed by the experience of defeat, will continue to make it an influence in Arab affairs while its revolutionary goals will persist in their appeal to the discontented in neighboring Arab states. But the problem must be seen for what it is—a matter of intermittent interference and influence rather than of growing expansion likely to result in permanent control of the Arab world. . . .

Realism demands that the United States be more honest with itself in recognizing the problems for American interests in Arab lands caused by its history of special relationship to Israel. Whether it is possible to change the relationship . . . will depend partly on Israel's supporters in the United States, who can no longer assume that American and Israeli interests are inevitably parallel, partly on elected officials who are willing to make American interests take precedence over a popular election issue, and partly on the Administration's determination to pursue American interests in the Arab world in the face of recurring public pressure.

Above all, realism demands that the United States shall more accurately estimate the limitations of its power to control Arab affairs. Every time a new crisis breaks out there will be those who take it as a confirmation of passivity in American policy, or timidity in the use of American power. Less than ever . . . can any foreign power assume it has the power to police the Middle East or even to control its own clients there. The United States cannot expect more of its foreign policy than the instruments of diplomacy at its command make possible. . . .

The mood compounded of patience and realism is, in effect, a mood of sophistication in formulating and conducting foreign policy. To many Americans, sophistication is suspect; it suggests deception, specious argument, a wily course of action without principle or consistency. But this is an unwarranted connotation identifying the word with "sophistry" rather than with "wisdom," which is what the Greek root means. A sophisticated foreign policy is one which deals with things as they are, which accepts the necessity of diverse courses of action at different times (or at the same time) without belaboring every supposed departure from consistency, and which understands and makes place for the attitudes and responses of other nations even when we do not approve of them. Thus, a sophisticated policy need be neither devoid of principles nor in contradiction to them, but it must be one which recognizes that rarely in the Middle East is the balance of factors in a situation so overwhelming that one side can be fully supported and the other completely neglected.

This kind of approach has not been the hallmark of many American policies toward the Arab world. Too often problems have been approached in simple, moralistic terms, as when Secretary Dulles predicted that the nationalization of the Suez Canal would fail because he believed that the moral forces of the world would rally against it.

This may seem an exaggerated view of the American position or, more accurately, of the mood in which many American positions have been taken. Yet a senior official in the Department of State mentioned to a group discussing Middle Eastern affairs the near hopelessness of obtaining public or congressional support for sophisticated policies in that area. To accept that limitation on American policy is to say in effect that American interests in the Middle East cannot adequately be protected. No one knowing the area can be under the delusion that there are simple answers to its problems. The inner contradictions of Arab politics are too deep, the tempo of change too rapid, the disparity of interests between individual states too great, to be encompassed by anything but a flexible and sophisticated approach.

Under the Kennedy administration, the American approach to the Arab world began to develop a greater degree of sophistication. The guidelines reviewed in this study reflected a fresh appreciation of Arab affairs and the courses of action which could be applied to them. Some of the dilemmas involved could be faced with equanimity because they were only incidental to the long-range objectives of American policy. But it has been hard to maintain this sophistication: Weariness on the part of policy makers, pressure of other issues, and renewed disorder in the Arab world changed the mood to one of sharpened reaction and growing impatience. The problem for the future is whether the United States can rise above the irritations and frustrations which came to a head in the 1967 crisis to pursue more calmly, deliberately, and maturely its objectives in the Arab world.

XIII   Suez Is the Front to Watch

GEORGE W. BALL

A recurrent nightmare for many Americans is that our national preoccupation with Indochina and the resultant turmoil on our home front may induce us to sit paralyzed while the power balance shifts drastically against us. That nightmare came close to reality when Soviet personnel manned surface-to-air missiles and Soviet pilots flew combat missions in the Middle East as we dug ourselves deeper into Indochina—complaisantly permitting our South Vietnamese allies to double the area of the combat theater by deploying their already thin forces in Cambodia.

The Russians are inevitably factoring our Cambodian intervention into their continuing appraisal of America's capabilities—an appraisal that will go far to shape their planning. How do the leaders of the Kremlin view us today? To them we almost certainly appear as an angry nation, obsessed with troubles at home and a war 5000 miles from our borders, deeply divided as to the usefulness, or even the morality, of that war—and therefore incapable of focusing prime attention on events elsewhere in the world. Only by assuming such an appraisal can one explain the quantum jump in Soviet adventurism in the Middle East.

Up to now the conventional wisdom has been that the Soviet Union would continue to find it useful to keep the Middle East off balance, frustrating any final settlement in order to fish in troubled waters, but always seeking to avoid another military explosion that could bring it into confrontation with the United States. So why worry?

But taking account of our own relative disablement and the Russians' bold and provocative actions, one should no longer swallow this soothing doctrine without second thoughts. That most Americans still do swallow it is cause for disquiet. Boredom is no doubt largely responsible, since most of us have learned to take the daily news of Arab-Israeli conflict as routine, assuming—without giving the matter much reflection—that if affairs should again come to a showdown, the Israelis would win another quick victory, thus saving America from the hard decision of involvement.

Yet experts on both sides of the Atlantic no longer take such an outcome for granted. NATO military officials increasingly believe that recent Soviet activities in Egypt have so altered the military situation that Israel may not much longer be sure of defending all of her frontiers, while certain American military experts see a serious possibility that the Soviet Union may seek to—and indeed be able to—neutralize the Israeli Air Force, which is the indispensable instrument by which 2.5 million Israelis have so far defended themselves against 90 million Arabs.

Nor are these anxieties without foundation. There are indications that the Russians may try to push the line of their surface-to-air missiles (SAM-3s) progressively nearer the Suez Canal, in which case they will almost certainly move forward their MIG-21s to protect the missile installations. Once the air over the canal is within the cone of fire of the SAMs and the interception range of the MIGs, Israel's ability to keep Soviet-directed Egyptian artillery fire within acceptable limits will be critically impaired, and the attrition of Israeli fighting power can go forward at an accelerating rate.

No one can construct the scenario with precision; yet it is not impossible that such developments might be followed by a unilateral Soviet effort to reopen the canal. It has been widely recognized that ever since the war in June 1967, the Soviet Union has been more anxious than other nations to have the canal operational again. Unlike Britain and continental European powers, whose declining interest in the canal has been mainly economic, the Russians have seen it as an essential aid to their political strategy.

So long as the canal remains closed, the Soviets are hampered in their efforts to establish an effective presence and influence at the mouth of the Red Sea, where they can stir up greater trouble in such areas of discontent as the Yemen and Southern Yemen. By creating such a presence they could not only command the Israeli supply route through the Gulf of Aqaba, but would have available a land bridge to the horn of Africa and—even more important—a passage around the Arabian peninsula to Muscat and Oman and the oil-rich sheikdoms on the Persian Gulf. By subverting those territories, the Soviet Union could achieve the encirclement of Saudi Arabia and enhance Iran's claustrophobia. In addition, a reopened canal would facilitate Russian efforts to establish a more powerful position in the Indian Ocean, where Moscow could work mischief with a weakening India and a post-Ayub Pakistan.

But even if the Soviet Union does not try to reopen the canal, the advancement of MIG deployment and of the SAM line would greatly worsen the Israeli position. By stopping further deep air strikes into Egyptian territory it would enable the 10,000 to 12,000 Soviet military and technical personnel in the United Arab Republic to carry out the careful and systematic conversion of the Egyptian armed forces into something resembling a modern fighting machine. Meanwhile, Israeli planes attacking Egyptian artillery emplacements on the west bank of the canal would find themselves in regular conflict with Soviet-flown MIGs, and Israel's limited supply of planes and pilots would eventually be worn down.

Nor is there reason to believe that, without some affirmative act on our part, the Middle East can remain in a permanent state of half war, half peace, or that the Soviets will stop with the commitment of limited forces pursuing a purely defensive role. Unless Israel halts all attacks on the U.A.R., not even responding to Egyptian harassment of her canal positions —which is, of course, out of the question—the Russians will be under increasing pressure to expand the scope of their missions, particularly if they think the United States is looking the other way, as we are. The moment they feel they have worn down the Israeli Air Force enough to secure command of the air, they may well be tempted to trigger a major offensive.

Such an offensive would pose totally new problems for Israel, for this time a quick knockout blow would be precluded. In 1967, Israel was able to play David to the Arab Goliath because she could take out Egyptian planes and air defenses and send armor slashing across the Sinai Desert in a lightning blitz; but now her troops are already at the canal and Soviet-flown fighters and Soviet-directed artillery are denying her access to the areas around Cairo that are the profitable targets for such a strategy.

So, with the reversal of the balance of forces now taking place, America must wake up to the fact that a renewed Middle-Eastern war could result in the destruction of Israel, the passionate objective of millions of Arabs. Before that took place, however—and the scenario becomes blurred at this point —a desperate Israel might understandably be driven to announce her intention to use an atomic weapon as a last resort against the U.A.R. That she has some kind of nuclear device and the ability to deliver it is not officially established, but it is the probable inference from several bits of evidence: the known capabilities of the Dimona reactor, Israel's high level of scientific and industrial competence, and her steadfast refusal to sign the nuclear nonproliferation treaty.

The Israeli announcement of a plan to use nuclear weapons would—to use a bit of understatement—set off unpredictable forces. At the very least, the international temperature would soar to the boiling point while Arab hysteria and Soviet threats of a preventive strike would incalculably damage the whole structure of nuclear restraint.

But apart from that Dr. Strangelove possibility, the destruction of Israel with the help of an active Soviet military effort would be a disaster the West could never accept, for it would establish effective dominion of the Soviet Union over most, if not all, of the Arab world.

In assessing the degree of that dominion, one must, of course, distinguish between the mere furnishing of arms and equipment to the Arab states and the participation of Soviet military units in combat operations. So far the Russians have advanced from sending "military advisers" to putting their pilots in Egyptian MIGs (that Soviet-flown MIGs seem always to be in the air when Israeli planes threaten to penetrate to interior targets is obviously more than coincidence); though such antics can still be palmed off as "defensive" in character, they are clearly only the beginning. The Soviet Union has almost as many "advisers" in the Arab world as the United States had in South Vietnam when President Kennedy was shot, and—as we should have learned from our own experience—the progress from "advisers" to participation in "defensive" missions to carrying the brunt of the offense is an easy slide for a great power, particularly when the local military material is so indifferent in quality as the Vietnamese or Egyptians.

Certainly there is nothing in postwar Soviet history to suggest that once their forces were engaged the Russians would tractably withdraw when victory was won. On the contrary, there is every reason to expect them to exploit to the fullest their position of advantage, exacting from their Arab clients the maximum *quid pro quo*.

Ever since World War II our country has designed its foreign policy to achieve a central objective: to preserve the peace by maintaining a precarious balance of power with the Soviet Union and, more recently, with Communist China as well. To maintain such a balance we have repeatedly felt compelled, with the help of our allies, to use military means or at least the threat of military action to prevent the fracturing of the *de facto* lines established during the early postwar period. For the Russians to gain dominion over the Middle East would clearly mean a breach of a vital line at a vital point.

Why should the Soviet domination of the Middle East affect the power balance more decisively than a North Vietnamese victory over Saigon? The answer is twofold: because the nature of the antagonists is widely different and because there is a disparity in the significance of the two areas.

Few people any longer believe that the defeat of South Vietnam would mean the direct extension of the power of either Moscow or Peking. North Vietnam is a small, primitive country, not remotely in the same league with the Soviet Union or Communist China, and she has so far succeeded by the tenacity of her own soldiers. She has invited neither Moscow nor Peking to commit combat forces to the Indochinese struggle, but has held both powers at arm's length, successfully playing one off against the other to preserve freedom of action and maneuver. To think that the North Vietnamese would give up that effort once victory was won is to ignore their history and misconceive the deeply nationalist nature of their objective. What some Americans once confused with Chinese expansionism has now clearly been revealed as Tonkinese ambition.

Yet even if Russia or Red China were to reverse course and actively engage their forces in the defeat of South Vietnam, the effect would be only marginally important to the power balance; in fact, proponents of the war have had to devise the dubious argument of the "domino theory" to establish any serious importance at all. South Vietnam has little significance for either economic or geographic reasons; it neither produces any strategic commodity nor lies near the center of industrial power, which is, in this modern age, the heart of danger for world peace.

The Middle East, on the other hand, is an economic prize of extraordinary value. Supplying a substantial part of the energy requirements of Western Europe and even Japan, it is an area of concentrated American investment providing a major source of our foreign-exchange earnings. Nevertheless, it is not these facts that make the Middle East worth a dangerous clash with Moscow. What vitally relates to the power balance and thus to the maintenance of world peace is the strategic location of the area and the effect on world politics of its inclusion in a Soviet sphere of influence. In marked contrast to Vietnam, the Middle East *does* lie near the center of world power—just below Central and Western Europe—and what happens in the U.A.R. and Israel would have a profound effect on millions of people in the industrially advanced countries.

For the people in Central and Eastern Europe Soviet domination of the Mideast would mean one more chain on the door to freedom, breeding further despair and resignation.

For Western Europeans, it would come as a brutal disillusionment, further discrediting American diplomacy, which has played a principal role in the area. It would call into question the reliability of the United States, which had failed to defend a country obviously important to Western interests and which had long appeared to be that country's political champion. The loss of the Middle East to Soviet influence would also inspire many to re-examine the belief—discredited in recent years—that Russia may still represent the wave of the future.

Admittedly, maps are no longer read in terms of sea power, and no one speaks any more of the "lifeline of empire." Both Kipling and Admiral Mahan are dead, and jet planes make nonsense of old strategic concepts. Yet the south and east coasts of the Mediterranean remain critical to Western survival, and a dominant Soviet position throughout the Arab world would threaten our most vital interests—challenging the ancient concept of the Mediterranean as a safe inland sea; shattering NATO's right-flank defenses by threatening the independence of Turkey and Greece; driving Yugoslavia toward Soviet dependency; stirring the huge Communist parties in Italy and France to new activity; isolating Iran, and imperiling the air passage to India and Pakistan. These are only some of the possible consequences; sooner or later one could, for example, expect the downfall of the moderate Arab states, erecting a barrier between Europe and Africa, and the impact on the great non-Arab nations of Islam—particularly Pakistan—would be profound.

It is this situation that poses the real danger to the interests of the United States and the West, and we would do well to consider how our nation would face such a prospect.

As a veteran of the coordinating committee that advised President Kennedy during the tense days of the Cuban missile crisis in October 1962, I am alarmed by the recent spate of well-orchestrated leaks from Eastern European embassies to the effect that Soviet activities in the Middle East will soon confront the Americans with the equivalent of another Cuban crisis, and that this time the United States will be the one to back down.

Viewed from the Kremlin, such a prospect is both tempting and plausible. If our Cambodian decision is seen—and the Soviet Union is likely to see it this way—as broadening the combat theater while implicitly extending the geographical scope of our commitments and widening the fissures in our national life, the Russians may well conclude that no United States government could command the national attention and will to intervene in the Middle East, even though the continued existence of Israel were threatened.

Whether Moscow would be correct in assuming our impotence to respond effectively would depend on how the American people viewed their predicament. That, in turn, would depend on education and leadership the President alone can provide—how inspiringly he alerts America to the danger and how clearly he defines the issue for popular understanding.

It is the question of definition that seems to me of the greatest importance, since Soviet skepticism would probably be justified if we were to view the problem solely as a question of coming to the defense of an Israel threatened by destruction at Arab hands. To be sure, our national feeling for Israel is deep and strong, and for more than two decades we have supported her efforts to realize for the Jewish people their ancient dream of a national home. Yet the suggestion that Americans should risk another foreign war to preserve that national home could not arise at a worse time. Not only has disenchantment over Vietnam been translated into suspicion of all military commitments overseas, it has led us dangerously close to pacifism and isolationism. Frustrating rational argument would be vicious expressions of anti-Semitism, the ugly reflex of a frightened people, no doubt with lunatic charges that we were being led into the danger of world conflict by the Jewish publishers of our Eastern press. This sort of charge is already foreshadowed in right-wing fringe literature.

But in terms of the events I am positing it would be neither necessary nor right to define the issue in the narrow framework of Arab-Israeli conflict. What must be made clear is the essential distinction between action to defend Israel from destruction at Arab hands and action to prevent the Soviet

Union from using Arab surrogate armies to extend its dominion over the Middle East.

Obviously, to refocus public attention from the paddies and jungles of Indochina, with their merely peripheral relation to United States interests, onto a new threat in a vital area that could destroy the world power balance and gravely weaken our security would require convinced and incisive leadership. Yet I do not believe it would be impossible. Americans have many times shown their capacity to respond with valor and energy to threats, once the threats were clearly understood, and it is questionable whether the nation is much more divided over Vietnam than it was over the issue of intervention in the months before Pearl Harbor. Yet once the danger was made clear by the Japanese attack and Hitler's fatuous declaration of war, we reacted with strength and unity. So in spite of our current divisions I have faith that America would once again hearken to a reasonable voice clearly articulating the critical danger with which we are confronted. In fact, many Americans might almost welcome a change of subject and the chance to put the world back into perspective.

With the President inspiring a sense of urgency and danger, we should stand a good chance both of forcing the withdrawal —or at least the severe restriction—of Soviet military elements and of transforming the current hazardous situation into a move toward stability. In fact, there is grave doubt that we could achieve one without the other.

For the last four years, affairs in the Middle East have undergone a pernicious deterioration. The increasing scale and intensity of violence on both sides; Israel's continued occupation of the territory overrun during the 1967 war, and Arab resentment, hopelessness and irrationality have created a state of indeterminate war. To counter raids across the canal, as well as the depredations of the Al Fatah and other insurrectionary groups, Israel has progressively extended her bombing penetrations of the U.A.R., hoping to keep Egypt off balance while giving notice to the whole Arab world that the Israelis would react to any attack with stiffer reprisal.

Unhappily, an operational policy of two eyes for an eye is the essence of escalation, and since this modified form of the Mosaic law has been followed by both sides, it has—rather than deterring violence—tended to make it competitive. It has been clear for a long time that sooner or later progressively more daring Israeli attacks on Egypt's air force and on her interior defenses would reach a point where the Soviet Union could no longer passively accept the wastage of the expensive hardware it had given Egypt or the humiliation being imposed on a client state, a humiliation that could not help but discourage other nations from relying on the Soviet Union for defense.

Against this background the decision of the Soviet Union to deploy its own personnel to man SAM sites and fly Egyptian aircraft was, though reckless, understandable in spite of the fact that it meant a sharp break with past policy.

Throughout history, astute diplomats have sought to utilize the strains and tensions leading to conflict as a motive force to resolve conflict, and this principle has relevance to the Middle East. Is it, then, too much to hope that the Russians' more adventurous role in that area may, by creating a situation that brings into sharp relief the dangers of great-power collision, provide us the lever to restore the Middle East to equilibrium?

Here again, we may extract some wisdom from our experience in the Cuban missile crisis. In the popular interpretation of that harrowing incident, the United States faced down the Soviet Union by declaring a Cuban embargo that forced Soviet ships to turn around. What is often forgotten, however, is that, in confronting the Soviet Union with an ultimatum, President Kennedy was careful to eliminate the ostensible Soviet excuse for implanting the missiles—the fear that the United States might invade Cuba. Thus, in the now-celebrated "pen pal" letters between Kennedy and Khrushchev, the President quite clearly made the point that the United States would not attack or invade Cuba.

Applying this tactic to the Middle East is an instructive exercise. In any approach to a confrontation with Moscow, the President must, at least by implication, take account of the fact that in the eyes of the world the Russian hand was in part forced by an excess of Israeli zeal; thus any American demand that the Soviet Union remove its forces from Egypt should be accompanied by steps to assure that the humiliation of Egypt—and, in fact, the conflict that has caused it—will be halted permanently.

The beginning of wisdom regarding the Middle East is the recognition that the immediate parties to the struggle—Israel and the Arab states (which in practice means the U.A.R.)—are quite incapable of reaching a settlement. At the same time—except for the refugees and, perhaps even more critical, the problem of Jerusalem, which for both sides is encysted in multiple layers of history and religion and sentiment—the basic lines of a reasonable settlement are not difficult to delineate. Yet passion, mistrust and internal differences within each camp preclude progress.

So each side, for its own reasons, has proved unwilling to yield on procedural conditions that foreclose even the beginning of a discussion of substantive issues. There is no need to try to assess the blame for this impasse; it is enough to recognize it as a fact too formidable for the parties to dispose of by themselves. For their own good as well as for the peace of the world, some outside agency must be found to make the peace.

Given the realities of world politics—including the bloc politics of the U.N. General Assembly—the only competent agency is the kind of great-power consortium contemplated by the drafters of the United Nations Charter, who in designing the Security Council sought consciously to institutionalize the basic concept of the Concert of Europe. In recognition of this, the Nixon administration, acting primarily through a skilled diplomat, Joseph Sisco, the Assistant Secretary of State for Near Eastern and South Asian Affairs, in 1969 initiated serious negotiations with the Soviet Union (parallel to a four-power effort that included two other permanent members of the council, France and Britain). What was sought was an agreement on the fundamental elements of a Middle-Eastern settlement. That initiative, which marked a commendable departure from the passive role pursued by previous administrations, appeared for a time to hold promise. As expected, however, the effort was viewed with suspicion by both the Egyptians and the Israelis, who raised the old bugaboo of an "imposed peace"; at the end of the day, the Kremlin drew back under pressure from the United Arab Republic.

So long as the United States continues to watch the evolution of events in the Middle East with her thoughts largely elsewhere, the chances of reviving serious discussions looking toward an overall settlement seem quite remote. But now the deployment of Soviet pilots has added a new element of urgency, and—provided we have the realism and incisiveness to react to the danger—effective common action may be possible this time.

If we do face up to the problem and the President gains the understanding and support of the American people, we should be in a position to demand, on threat of direct American military involvement, that the Soviets remove most if not all of their military personnel from Egypt. At the same time we should insist on urgent action to develop an agreed-upon blueprint for the settlement of the Middle-Eastern problem, including necessary guarantees for both sides.

To be effective, such a *démarche* would require as a prelude a clear presidential message to the American people and full and urgent consultations with key members of the Congress, for the President must make it clear to the leaders of the Kremlin not only that he is determined to bring matters to a showdown, but that he carries with him the support of the nation and is thus able to translate his words into action.

At the same time we should impress upon our Western allies the fact that Soviet military activities in the Middle East gravely endanger their security and that of the entire West, and that their help is needed in the search for a definitive Middle-Eastern settlement. In the process, we should make the Europeans emphatically understand that the time is long past when the Western nations can afford to indulge in such disruptive games as the French action in supplying Mirage jets to Libya.

The signals that echo loudest in Moscow are, of course, not words but acts (for instance, our reinforcement of our garrisons in Europe at the time of the Berlin crisis and in October 1962, when our preparations for an air attack on

Cuba brought home to Moscow the deadly seriousness of our intentions). Our voice would therefore have gained resonance in the Kremlin if we had quietly increased Polaris deployment with the Sixth Fleet. The President might have sent a message to Congress emphasizing the impossibility of reducing United States forces in Europe so long as Soviet military personnel continued to fly combat missions in Egypt.

Proposals of this kind are merely suggestive of the types of action that might have been taken to signal to Moscow the solemnity of our purpose and given credence and urgency to the showdown Soviet military intervention is precipitating.

But if we follow a clear, unequivocal policy of strength in confronting the Soviet Union, what are the chances of a successful outcome? For anyone familiar with the first messages over the Hot Line on the outbreak of the Mideast war in June 1967, the answer is likely to be affirmative, since the initial Soviet reaction when the balloon went up over the Sinai Desert was one of almost frantic anxiety. What the Russians emphatically did not want—as they made abundantly clear—was an unmanageable escalation that could lead them to a collision with America.

To be sure, the situation has changed drastically since then, and our preoccupations elsewhere and malaise at home have cast grave doubts on our capability for effective intervention. Yet all that can be changed by wise action, taken at once, before "things get in the saddle," the Soviets involve themselves irretrievably, and both sides lose control over the escalator.

It will undoubtedly be noted that in this recital of possible measures no mention has been made of the provision of additional Phantom jets to Israel. This omission does not suggest that the Phantoms may not be needed or should not be supplied, but rather that, with the direct injection of Soviet air strength, the Phantoms would represent at best only a momentary barrier to Soviet ambitions. Certainly the Israelis by themselves could never withstand the almost unlimited Soviet resources of men and matériel—that is not a question of valor but of mathematics—and it seems likely that supplying the Phantoms (rather than deterring Soviet action) would stimulate a greater involvement.

Nor should we under any circumstances permit Israeli units to be reinforced with American volunteers. The precedent of the Spanish Civil War is not one that either side can afford to follow in this atomic age.

Instead, let us concentrate on facing the realities of an American-Soviet showdown, recognizing the special difficulties it presents for our country at a time of great national disarray. To transform the public mood, equipping America to face up to the Middle East crisis, will require a great deal of clear thinking and straight talking. Certainly we could not impress the Kremlin with our seriousness in the Middle East by escalating the violence in Southeast Asia; the Russians would read that simply as one more evidence of our Indo-chinese obsession, which is making us a paper tiger elsewhere in the world.

Nor can we make our point simply by speeches or congressional resolutions or even formal *démarches*. For one thing, we must be quite clear that we demand no more than the possible. To ask that the Soviets withdraw entirely from the Middle East or that they remove their navy from the West's *mare nostrum* would be utter futility. Russia has, after centuries of yearning, become a Mediterranean power, and —short of nuclear war—we cannot totally dislodge her. What we can do is require strict limits and ground rules for her military personnel and insist that together we find the key to peace in the Middle East.

To achieve this, incisive and necessarily risky action will be required—which is admittedly a tough prescription for a government already facing harassing problems both on the home front and abroad. But that is the only course open to the United States if we are to avoid the implacable evolution of forces that could—almost before we knew it—put the values we love in grave jeopardy.

XIV The United Nations, the United States, and the Maintenance of Peace

INIS L. CLAUDE, JR.

This essay is addressed to the issue of the extent to which and the ways in which the United Nations may serve the interest of the United States in the maintenance of world peace during the decade that lies ahead. It rests upon two assumptions, both of which require careful qualification: first, the assumption that the United States has, and recognizes that it has, a fundamental interest in international peace; second, the assumption that the United Nations is in principle an organization dedicated to the promotion of international peace.

The first assumption must be qualified by the acknowledgment that the United States does not regard every outbreak of violence in the international realm as equally threatening to its interests; it does not take the doctrine of the indivisibility of peace as literal and absolute truth. Moreover, the enthusiasm of the United States for the condemnation and repression of international violence is limited by the conviction that resort to force in some circumstances may be necessary and salutary. The United States has in recent years encountered situations which it has interpreted as justifying and requiring military action, and it must contemplate the possibility that similar situations may arise in the future. "Peace at any price" is not the American theme, nor is total renunciation of the national right to decide upon and undertake acts of coercion a feature of American foreign policy.

These two positions—that some disruptions of the peace may be tolerated and that some circumstances may demand even unilateral resort to violence—may be regarded by some as evidence of American cynicism, of commitment to the goal of world domination by the United States, achieved by force if necessary, rather than to the ideal of world peace. In the more orthodox American view of the matter, which I share, these positions reflect sophistication rather than cynicism. Far from indicating callous disregard for global order, they reflect an awareness of the cruel complexities of the international system and a rejection of the view that a simple "Thou shalt not fight" formula can cut through all the difficulties. Indeed, a strong case can be made for the proposition that these qualifications of the commitment to nonviolence do not qualify but rather serve to define and to implement the basic American commitment to world peace. The commitment is to the *general* stability of the international order, and it may be argued that the maintenance of this stability permits and even requires a hands-off attitude toward certain conflicts that appear to be not only isolated but isolable. In other situations national willingness or determination to fight may, while possibly producing some bloodshed, prove indispensable to the avoidance of general international conflict. In short, commitments to world peace and to nonviolence are not necessarily identical. This is not to argue that the United States has mastered the art of maintaining world peace, nor is it to deny that the actual behavior of the United States may on occasion contradict rather than serve the objective of world peace. It is simply to insist that the qualifications imposed by the United States upon its commitment to nonviolence do not invalidate its proclaimed devotion to the ideal of world peace; it is to defend the assumption that the United States has, and recognizes that it has, a fundamental interest in international peace.

The second assumption, pertaining to the dedication of the United Nations to global pacification, is subject to the observation that the stated purposes of an organization are not necessarily its operative purposes. Constitutional dedication is less decisive than political determination; examination of the politics of the United Nations is superior to perusal of its Charter as a means of identifying the organization's actual objectives. The Charter's affirmation of the aim of promoting and maintaining peace is not irrelevant. It provides a standard against which the propriety of various purposes that the organization may be made to serve can be judged, and it establishes the orthodoxy into which all heresies must be squeezed by whatever ingenious methods their proponents can devise. It cannot, however, provide a guarantee that the uses to which the United Nations is put will invariably be conducive to or even compatible with world peace. Given the facts that the primary participants in the shaping of United Nations policy are the member states, that these include virtually all the states of the world, and that their membership carries with it no automatic transformation of their attitudes and objectives, it would be surprising indeed if United Nations policy were characterized by single-minded and undeviating devotion to the cause of international peace and order.

If we approach the record of the United Nations in the mood of one who seeks to analyze the working of a political institution rather than that of one who is concerned with the advancement of a sacred cause, we find ample evidence of the variety of uses for which the organization may be available. These range from efforts to develop a durable system of peace, through programs only tenuously related, if at all, to the problem of peace, to activities in support of attacks upon the status quo which, whatever their justification, tend to be disruptive of the peace. While we cannot take it for granted that the United Nations will function consistently as an agency of pacification, we can assert that its constitutional mandate defines the organization's proper role in these terms and assume the possibility that the organization may be directed and controlled by those who give priority to its actual and potential capability for contributing to peace.

I return to the original issue: Assuming that the United States has a fundamental commitment to world peace, though it be a commitment qualified by denial that every conflict must be treated as a threat to the general order and by refusal to renounce the possibility of unilateral military action, and assuming that the United Nations is properly conceived as an agency to be used for the maintenance of peace without forgetting that it may be directed toward other and possibly contradictory objectives, to what degree should the United States rely upon the United Nations for the keeping of the peace in the years immediately ahead? What role can the United States reasonably expect the United Nations to play in the furtherance of world order? What potentialities inhere in the organization which the United States and like-minded states might develop and exploit in the interest of peace? How, in other words, should the United Nations figure in the American approach to the problem of world peace?

The first essential step in the approach to the issue that these questions elaborate is to develop a sensible reaction to the prevailing ideology of multilateralism in international relations. I refer to the point of view according to which collective or multilateral decisions, actions, and programs are regarded as intrinsically preferable to those deriving from the policy processes of a single state.[1] Resting upon the assumption that multilateralism guarantees policy that is uniquely effective, wise, and virtuous, this ideology tends to inspire a mood of doctrinaire antiunilateralism; emanations from Foggy Bottom are automatically to be disparaged and deplored while Turtle Bay is to be regarded as the authentic source of whatever is constructive, decent, and desirable in international relations.

There is evident merit in this emphasis upon the importance of developing and the value of using the collective instrumentalities of the international system. The establishment of international organizations and the systematic development of multilateral processes are among the most promising phenomena of international relations in the twentieth century, and states, particularly powers great enough to consider thoroughgoing independence of operation an alternative plausibly open to them, may profit from the reminder that they have a stake in the ordering of the global system which can be promoted only by flourishing international organizations. Moreover, there *is* strength—moral and political if not military—in numbers, and many national heads *may* be wiser than one; to give earnest consideration to the will and judgment of the community of states, whether expressed by consensus or by majority vote, is an act of prudence and conceivably of virtue.

[1] I have attempted a critical analysis of this doctrine in "The Vogue of Collectivism in International Relations," *Interstate* (University College of Wales, Aberystwyth), November 1968 (No. 1, 68'69), pp. 14–18.

Nevertheless, it seems that the doctrine of multilateralism should inspire pragmatic consideration rather than dogmatic acceptance. The relative effectiveness of unilateral and multilateral activities is an issue to be examined in the concrete case, not to be settled by reference to an abstract formula. The quality of policy—its wisdom and propriety—is not a function of its unilateral or its multilateral origins. Since international unpopularity may prejudice the results of a national foreign policy, statesmen are well advised to pay careful attention to the multilateral reception of national behavior but not to pay it automatic deference. Sound and necessary policy is no more so for its having emerged from an international organization and no less so for its having been produced and carried out by a single government. Intelligent foreign policy is a sufficiently rare commodity that it should be welcomed wherever it can be found.

One should also deal cautiously with the advice to treat the making of foreign policy as an occasion for conferring authority and prestige upon the United Nations, as if the latter were a muscular organism that requires exercise to grow strong and avoid atrophy. Quite aside from the fact that overburdening is as great a peril to the world organization as inactivity there is the central consideration that the United Nations is a means and not an end. Strengthening the United Nations is important, but it deserves a lower priority than dealing successfully with the problems that literally involve the destiny of man. The responsible statesman faces a dilemma that entitles him to something better than ritualistic advice—namely, to sensitive and sympathetic understanding of his predicament. He *ought* to be concerned with the long-term development of an effective system of world order; he *must* be concerned with the short-term solution of pressing problems. He is fortunate when there is no difficulty in reconciling these two concerns. He begins to earn his pay when he grapples with situations involving a conflict and requiring a choice between system building for the long run and problem solving for the short run. This, I suggest, is the nature of the dilemma that American policy makers can expect to confront with some frequency as they consider the relevance of the United Nations to the problem of maintaining world peace in the forthcoming decade. In such situations the doctrinaire insistence that their correct course is to turn to and defer to the United Nations is unconvincing, just as the easy assertion that they should follow the national interest is unrevealing; their responsibility cannot be intelligently discharged by the application of a formula.

A fascinating and significant shift is now occurring in the political symbolism of the United Nations as it relates to American foreign policy. Until recently participation in and support of the United Nations by the United States was above all a symbol of America's new internationalism, its abandonment of the isolationist tradition, and its commitment to the steady and dependable performance of an active role in world affairs. It can be argued that this is what the formation of the League of Nations and subsequently the United Nations was primarily aimed at achieving; the organizations were designed to entice the United States into a leading role in international relations. The American decision to abstain from the League amounted to a rejection of that new role, and the decision to join the United Nations reflected the reconsideration that had been stimulated by World War II and symbolized the reversal of the earlier decision. For many of the founders of the United Nations this transformation of the American position provided the basis for whatever optimism they felt concerning the stability of the postwar international order. They rejoiced at the return of the prodigal Great Power, served up a fatted calf in the form of the veto privilege, and contrived to place the United Nations in the United States in the hope that this would make it easier to keep the United States in the United Nations. American internationalists similarly treated ratification of the Charter as the symbol of belatedly triumphant Wilsonianism in the struggle over United States foreign policy, and they have regarded attentiveness to the United Nations as the essential manifestation of the American resolution to continue in the new role, an earnest of the sincerity of the American conversion to internationalism. Passionate warnings about the danger of neglecting or bypassing the United Nations have come largely from nervous internationalists seeking reiterated assurances as to the solidity of the American commitment.

Considering this background there is a certain irony in the fact that American political leaders today are tending to use the United Nations as a symbol of the possibility of the substantial reduction of the international responsibilities of the United States. The bitter controversy over Vietnam has produced massive pressure against the continued performance of the role of "world policeman" by the United States. Protest against the American military action in Vietnam is doubtless strengthened by the fact that this action does not enjoy the official endorsement of the United Nations and has indeed incurred widespread censure within the organization. If the American action had been launched in conformity with a United Nations mandate or had been granted formal support by the United Nations, it would presumably have engendered less criticism. However, most of the substantive arguments advanced in condemnation of the American engagement in Vietnam would apply even if the United States were acting for, with, or through the United Nations; in that case it would be logical for those who accept these arguments to denounce the United States for having perverted the United Nations, for having twisted arms to secure endorsement or sponsorship of the organization for what might still appear to them an unjustified and unwise policy. In short, those who have argued most vociferously that Vietnam should have been left to the United Nations have not, in my judgment, been motivated so much by the conviction that the United Nations should have intervened in that unhappy country as by the conviction that the United States should not have intervened there. Nevertheless, the reaction against Vietnam in the United States is increasingly finding expression in assertions of the proposition that international organizations, not the United States, should engage in the messy business of keeping order where chaos threatens. There is a strong and understandable urge—though it may not be a realistic one—to shift to other shoulders, usually identified vaguely as those of the United Nations, the burdens, the costs, the risks, and the blame that this business entails. Political leaders, bowing to the necessity of making concessions to the Vietnam-generated demand for American retrenchment, develop the theme that the

United States should abdicate the policeman's role to the United Nations.

In his 1968 presidential campaign speeches Hubert Humphrey accepted the proposition that the United States has burdened itself with excessive commitments in international affairs and promised careful trimming of those commitments with a view toward shifting greater emphasis to domestic problems:

> The lesson [that we have learned from Vietnam] is . . . that we should carefully define our goals and priorities. . . .
> . . . I would insist as President that we review other commitments made in other times . . . that we carefully decide what is, and is not, in our national interest.
>
> . . . .
>
> . . . if I am President, I owe it to this nation to bring our men and resources in Vietnam back to America where we need them so badly . . . and to be sure we put first things first in the future.[2]
> Our world role in the next ten years will be different from that in the last. There are pressing problems at home, which cause us to place careful priorities on allocation of resources abroad.[3]

From this point he moved directly to the position that primary responsibility for the maintenance of peace should be transferred to the United Nations:

> I pledge to you . . . that one of the high priorities of my Presidency will be to strengthen the peacekeeping and peacemaking capacity of the United Nations.
> This is our third step toward a new strategy for peace: To make the U. N. the instrument for controlling conflict it has so far failed to be.
> The United States cannot play the role of global gendarme. The American people don't want it, and the rest of

[2] The passage is from the text of a television address, published in *The Washington Post*, October 1, 1968, p. A 6.
[3] From a speech delivered in San Francisco on September 26, 1968. *Ibid.*, September 27, 1968, p. A 6.

the world won't accept it. We know better today than yesterday that "the illusion of American omnipotence"—in D. W. Brogan's phrase, "is an illusion."

But the alternative to American peacekeeping cannot be no peacekeeping. It must be peacekeeping by the United Nations or by regional agencies.[4]

Humphrey was not advocating a return to isolationism. In the speeches that I have cited and in others he was explicit and emphatic in his insistence that the United States should not draw back within itself and abandon its active role in world affairs. Moreover, he did not suggest that this country could or should simply delegate its responsibilities to the United Nations, but recognizing the existing limitations of that organization, he asserted that the United States should promote and support the development of the capacity of the United Nations to assume the major burden of coping with threats to the peace. He stressed leadership and partnership; the United States should work with other states and through international agencies to maximize the possibility of multilateral action and thereby to minimize the necessity for unilateral American action in keeping the peace.

Nevertheless, it is clear that Humphrey was making an effort to assure the electorate that if he became President he would act in accordance with the widespread demand for reducing the commitments of the United States, and it is significant that he treated the United Nations as a vehicle for realizing this objective, an agency potentially capable of providing an "alternative to American peacekeeping." His references to the limitations of the United States, the need to turn primary attention to domestic problems, and the consequent

---

[4] *Ibid.* Cf. this comment concerning the mood of the new administration of Richard Nixon: "There is a disposition . . . to be chary of any more Vietnams—to shy from unilateral entanglements and rely more on international organizations to police the peace and good order of the world." (" 'Let Us . . . Go Forward Together,' " *Newsweek*, January 27, 1969, p. 19.) Whether or not this is an accurate appraisal of the Nixon administration's attitude it is a striking example of the widespread tendency to regard action by multilateral agencies as an alternative to American involvements.

urgency of reducing our foreign involvements underlay his proposal to place greater reliance upon the United Nations and other multilateral agencies. As he presented the matter, American retrenchment was to be facilitated rather than inhibited by the membership of the United States in these organizations. Despite his reminder that this country would have to exert itself to expand the capacity of the United Nations and other agencies for undertaking heavier responsibilities the central theme of his remarks was that international organizations might in some measure relieve the United States of its international burdens.

The significant point of this analysis is that Humphrey's position represents the reversal of the conventional symbolism according to which the United Nations is conceived as a means of calling in the United States to redress the balance of forces in the world. It calls in the United Nations to cover the partial retreat of the United States, to help this country get itself off the international hook. The world organization is invoked to symbolize and legitimize not the American commitment to internationalism but an American shift toward a more limited global role.

Humphrey lost the election, but I see no evidence that his defeat should be construed as a repudiation of the position discussed above. On the contrary, it may be argued that his electoral failure is at least partly attributable to the fact that his movement in the indicated direction was too little, too late, and insufficiently convincing to many of those who have traditionally provided the major support for American commitment and involvement in world affairs. The dominant mood in the United States is one which favors the deflation of foreign policy, as Walter Lippmann has described it,[5] and which is no longer so concerned about the danger of bypassing the United Nations as about the possibility of buck-passing to the United Nations.

As we consider the potentialities of the United Nations for contributing to the maintenance of peace and order in the next decade, we must confront the question of the impact

[5] See his column in *The Washington Post*, February 9, 1969, p. B 1.

upon the organization of this American mood and the trend in American foreign policy that it foreshadows. Generally, the record suggests that American retrenchment will, while creating a need for the United Nations to expand its role in world politics, reduce rather than increase the probability that it will and the possibility that it can do so. In most areas of activity the rule of thumb has been that the less the United States is willing to do, the less the United Nations can be expected to do—and vice versa. It is open to question whether that relationship can be reversed, whether the objective of increasing the activity of the United Nations to permit and compensate for the diminution of the activity of the United States can be achieved. How capable a buck receiver can we realistically expect the United Nations to become?

I suggest that the conception of the United Nations as a possible substitute for the United States in carrying out some of the tasks that may be required for the maintenance of world peace provides too limited a basis for the consideration of the relationship that should prevail between the global organization and its most powerful and influential member. The nature and identity of the United Nations can be conceived in several ways with varying implications for the functional relationship between the organization and the United States.

The United Nations may be conceived first of all as an entity in itself, a synthetic but separate actor on the international stage, created by states and dependent upon them for its survival but capable of acting in its own right. This conception focuses upon the Secretariat and in particular upon the Secretary-General—those who in a special sense constitute the organization. This bureaucratic entity is largely controlled and directed by states, but states do not compose it; it is for every state an "other," an agency external to itself.

Second, the United Nations may be regarded by the United States or any other member as a vehicle for other states, a mechanism for the registration of their judgments, the rendering of their decisions, and the facilitation of their joint action. Looking at it in this way, a particular state sets aside its own membership and involvement and envisages the organization as a collective "them" distinguished from the national "us." Thus, it becomes possible to speak of the United

Nations as assisting in our economic development, improperly meddling in our affairs, or approving our policy.

A third conception of the organization brings one's own state back into the picture along with the other states and the supporting staff. The United Nations becomes a combination of "them" and "us," a setting within which "we" interact with the massive "them" and its component parts, competing and cooperating, winning and losing, persuading and conceding.

These three versions of the United Nations may be tagged as "it," "they" (or "them"), and "we and they" (or "us and them"). Clearly, these are alternative conceptions that do not require a definitive choice but are available for periodic selection. No one of them expresses the exclusively correct perception of the United Nations, and resort to all of them poses no problem if we keep clearly in mind which of them we are dealing with at any given time.

As "it" or "they" the United Nations is theoretically eligible to substitute for the United States in the performance of tasks that may be regarded as conducive to peace. The United States can conceivably reduce its involvement by standing aside in favor of "it" or "them." We should be very clear that what this means is that the buck is passed to the United Nations Secretariat, to an indeterminate group of other states, or to some combination of the two. The questions of what functions should be handed over in this fashion and of what burdens the United States might wish to dispose of in this way must be considered in relation to a third question: What tasks can "it" and "they" reasonably be expected to be willing and able to undertake?

The "we and they" conception of the United Nations, on the other hand, provides no scheme for American disengagement. It involves action by the United States in combination with other states through, or under the auspices of, or with the sanction of, the United Nations. Unless the record of the past misleads us as to prospects for the future, the contributions of other states will vary directly, not inversely, with the contributions of the United States. In matters ranging from the defense of the Republic of Korea (South Korea) to the funding of multilateral economic aid and technical assistance programs major American commitments have been the key to the involvement of other states; if the United States had done less, it seems unlikely that others would have done more. In the area appropriate to action by "us and them" American retrenchment can be expected to spell United Nations retrenchment; and if the United Nations is to be made a more adequate and vigorous organization, this will mean more, not less, responsibility and involvement for the United States.

The classical notion of the potential and desirable contributions of general international organizations to the maintenance of peace assigns primacy, in importance if not in sequence, to the peace-enforcement function, the mobilization of collective pressure and action—by military means if necessary—to control states breaking or threatening to break the peace. This originally implied the operation of a reliable and generally applicable system of collective security, promising quasi-automatic action by a quasi-universal body of states to squelch any aggression that might occur. While the idea of such a system is no longer taken seriously, the basic objective that the theory of collective security was designed to serve, the development of a systematic means for compelling states to refrain from disruptive international behavior, remains central to contemporary thought and aspiration concerning world order. The question of United Nations peace enforcement figures prominently in the standard agenda of those who ponder the future role of the United Nations in the maintenance of peace.

I submit that if the United Nations has a peace-enforcement system in its future, that system will be a function of "us and them," not of "it" or "them." To discuss the repression by the United Nations of aggression or other disruptive behavior is to talk not about how to reduce the commitments of the United States but about how to maintain and increase them. Considering the United Nations apart from the United States, I see no evidence that it has, and no prospect that it will develop, either the power or the political will requisite for the coercive restraint of peacebreakers. Any conceivable United Nations function in this vein would seem to involve the organization's serving as a vehicle for action led by and heavily dependent upon the participation of the United States rather than as a replacement for the weary, frustrated, and disillusioned American "world policeman."

To view the matter in this light is to regard the enhancement of the role of the United Nations in peace enforcement as a very unlikely prospect at least for the next few years. At most the organization can be expected to carry out the function of authorizing and encouraging member states to undertake joint resistance to breaches of the peace. Such joint actions are improbable except as enterprises under American leadership, and the facts that few states are disposed to follow the United States and that the latter is increasingly indisposed to take the lead in enterprises of this kind militate against their occurring. If situations develop which the United States regards as sufficiently threatening to the stability of the global order to require an effective military response, this country will have to choose between acting and not acting; the choice of leaving it to the amorphous "them" of the United Nations will not be available. If it decides to act, the United States will and should welcome the legitimizing endorsement of the United Nations, to be sought in the "we and they" forum of that organization, but in most circumstances it will be unlikely to find that endorsement obtainable. Failing that, the United States will have to decide whether the case justifies or demands that it proceed without United Nations support. Many of the states that are least likely to give their approval to American action in cases such as these can be expected to appeal for coercive measures in situations involving residual colonialism and recalcitrant racialism, cases in which the United States tends to regard coercion as having peacebreaking rather than peace-maintaining consequences. Thus, it may well be that United Nations policy will be supportive of ventures to which the United States will be unwilling to commit its power and that the United States will think it essential to invest its power in ventures to which the United Nations will be unwilling to lend the support of its policy. The combination of United Nations policy and United States power in a mutually supportive relationship may be difficult to achieve in the years that lie ahead; that is to say that the United Nations is unlikely to play a prominent role in the enforcement of peace against determined trouble-makers.

Peace enforcement is not, however, the sole or necessarily the most important function in the realm of peace mainte-nance. Perhaps the most significant development in the thinking of scholars and statesmen about international organi-zation in the postwar period has been their gradual emancipa-tion from the collective security fixation, their breaking out of the intellectual rut in which it was taken for granted that the suppression of aggression was so crucial a function of general international organizations that if this function could not be exercised, the only issue worth thinking about was how to make its exercise possible. Dag Hammarskjöld gave dra-matic and forceful expression to the new and less constricted approach to international organization when he put the ques-tion of how the United Nations could contribute directly to keeping the peace when it could not enforce the peace and answered the question by formulating the theory of preven-tive diplomacy, now generally known as peacekeeping.[6]

The provision and the management of peacekeeping oper-ations constitute the primary function which from the Amer-ican perspective lies essentially within the province of the United Nations understood as "it" and "them." This func-tion, designed to induce and facilitate the standing off of the superpowers at a safe distance from the scene of potentially spreading trouble, is the major exception to the general rule that American inactivity tends to promote the reduction rather than to stimulate the increase of United Nations activity. In this instance the willingness of the major powers to become or to remain disengaged from the situation is a basic require-ment for successful action by the United Nations. Moreover, the disposition of the United States and the Union of Soviet Socialist Republics to regard and treat the United Nations in third-person terms enhances the prospect that each of them will consider the organization sufficiently impartial to be

[6] See his *Introduction to the Annual Report of the Secretary-General on the Work of the Organization, 16 June 1959—15 June 1960* (General Assembly *Official Records* [15th session], Supple-ment No. 1A).

trusted with the carrying out of the peacekeeping function. This is preeminently the functional sector in which United Nations action may be conceived as a substitute for American action, where "leave it to the United Nations" can be regarded as the invocation of a meaningful and preferable alternative rather than as a slogan designed to excuse inaction.

There is a limit, however, to the necessity for and the virtue of the American treatment of the United Nations in its peacekeeping role as a third party rather than a "we and they" grouping. While emphasis upon the "otherness" of the United Nations is conducive to its political eligibility to serve the Great Powers by ministering to their need for avoidance of confrontations, it does nothing to remedy the deficiency of the organization in the resources required for meeting the practical problems involved in rendering such service. To put the matter bluntly, the United Nations has encountered such formidable difficulties in peacekeeping operations, ranging from the threat of bankruptcy to the development of political discord threatening to disrupt the organization, that the will of "it and them" to continue this kind of service has been placed in question. There is an unpleasant analogy between the effects of Vietnam upon the United States and the effects of peacekeeping ventures, notably the Congo operation, upon the United Nations; the American "policeman," embroiled in what he regards as peace enforcement, is no more sourly convinced of the truth of the Gilbertian maxim concerning the unhappiness of the policeman's lot than is the United Nations "policeman," recently experienced in the perils of peacekeeping.

A major task for the United States in the next few years is to promote the development of the capacity of the United Nations to conduct peacekeeping operations without thereby jeopardizing its survival. Such enterprises may always present more than routine problems, but it should be possible to remove them from the category of traumatic experiences for the organization. While the conduct of peacekeeping operations requires that the United States stand aside and defer to "it and them," the creation of adequate United Nations potential for exercise of this function demands a "we and they" approach on the part of the United States. This country cannot perform the task alone. Some of the most critical contributions—the provision of the appropriate personnel for operations in the field, for instance—are dependent upon the will of states far removed from American influence. Nevertheless, American leadership is vital. The truth is quite simply that unless the United States takes the lead in promoting the solution of problems relating to the authorization, management, and financing of peacekeeping, those problems will remain unsolved and will spoil the future of this new and promising function of the United Nations.

In any case, United Nations peacekeeping has a limited range of application. It is not, even in theory, a technique suitable for dealing with the great bulk of the situations and events that may endanger the peace. It is certainly not applicable to situations of the kind that most explicitly and directly threaten the peace: those which involve a belligerent so determined and powerful that forcible resistance on a substantial scale is indispensable. We must be very clear about the point that it is as unrealistic to consider the United Nations a potential substitute for the United States in cases of that type as it is inappropriate to regard the United States as a substitute for the United Nations in cases where the interested parties are willing to accept the interposition of a politically disinterested force to calm an explosive situation. One may legitimately argue that the United States should not have intervened in Vietnam to deal with what it regarded as a case of indirect or covert aggression, but one cannot realistically suggest that the United Nations might have acted in lieu of the United States to carry out the mission that the United States attempted; the alternative was that the task would not be undertaken, not that the United Nations would undertake it. The essential point is that there are basic differences between peace enforcement and peacekeeping that indicate the ineligibility of the United Nations for the former and its eligibility for the latter. Peace enforcement requires power that the United States has and policy that the United Nations is unlikely to engender or even to support. Peacekeeping requires a political stance that is conceivable for an international organization but not for a Great Power and agents whose effectiveness depends not upon the power but upon the presumed impartiality of their states.

To say that the potential scope of peacekeeping is limited and uncertain is not to minimize its potential importance and value. The cases appropriate for its exercise may be few, but their significance may be critical; it takes only one uncontrolled fire to develop into an uncontrollable conflagration. A situation that causes both the United States and the Soviet Union to sense and acknowledge the need for a buffer to forestall their competitive involvement is by definition a dangerous one. If it inspires them also to welcome and support the initiation of a United Nations peacekeeping operation, it becomes a hopeful situation. Working imaginatively and persistently at the task of achieving the solution of the problems that inhibit the continuation and further development of the world organization's peacekeeping role is the most important way in which the United States can promote the usefulness of the United Nations in the maintenance of peace.

Beyond the realm of peace enforcement and peacekeeping there obviously lies a broad functional terrain upon which the United Nations can operate to promote world peace and order. Major challenges to the wisdom and ingenuity of those who put the mechanisms of the United Nations to use are posed by the problems of promoting peaceful settlement of disputes and peaceful toleration of unsettled disputes, peaceful change and peaceful resistance to change. The United Nations will presumably continue to provide the setting for a considerable portion of the rapidly expanding business of international relations in future years—for much of the debate and the diplomacy, the conduct of negotiations and the registration of consensus, the declamation and the consultation that mark the interaction of states in an increasingly intimate but explosive world. Still farther from the edge of conflict the United Nations will have the opportunity to engage in peacebuilding activities no less important than operations bearing more directly upon specific areas of friction.

The United States has a stake in the development and use of the United Nations as a contributor to world order in all these respects, but for the short-term problem of dealing with threats to the peace its best hope of obtaining substantial assistance from the United Nations seems to lie in the possibility of strengthening the will and capacity of the organization—of "it" and "them"—to perform the peacekeeping function.

We live, and will continue for the foreseeable future to live, in an international system plagued by the actuality and the potentiality of conflicts between states, over states, and within states—conflicts which in varying degrees endanger or involve the possibility of endangering the general stability of world order. The variety of potential crises is enormous; the possibilities include direct clashes between the United States and the Soviet Union, between either of them and the People's Republic of China (Communist China), between either of them and a member of its own or of the other's system of alignment, and between states or groups of states outside these blocs. The range of dangerous action that must be anticipated extends from overt and clear-cut aggression to the most subtle and ambiguous forms of intrusion, from direct confrontation of hostile states at territorial boundaries to competitive involvement of external powers within the political life of third states.

How should the United States respond to the procession of crises that seems certain to bedevil the world in future years? I have contended that it can look to the United Nations as an agency of action for the maintenance of peace only in those instances where the parties involved and the potentially intrusive Great Powers value the avoidance of continuing and expanding conflict so highly that they are prepared to welcome or accept the intervention of a United Nations peacekeeping force. The ability of the United Nations to perform even this function will be precarious until and unless solutions are found for the grave problems, fundamentally political in nature, that previous performances have entailed. The United States will be well advised to do all that it can to enhance the general capacity and eligibility of the United Nations to engage in peacekeeping operations, to examine conflicts that arise for evidence of their susceptibility to management by such means, and to encourage and support peacekeeping by the world organization whenever this seems feasible.

Beyond this we encounter the range of cases where the consensual basis for United Nations peacekeeping is lacking and cannot readily be contrived, where one or more of the parties is more devoted to the conduct of a struggle than to the enlistment of assistance in calling off the struggle; in such instances the issue is not peacekeeping but peace enforcement, the threat or the use of force to counter the action being undertaken. The United States may find itself in any one of several situations: 1) It may be resolved to take action, with or without the collaboration of other states, at the behest of the United Nations or with the latter's approval; 2) it may be unwilling to participate in action endorsed or demanded by the United Nations; 3) it may be opposed to action undertaken by other states with the sanction of the United Nations; 4) it may think it necessary to take action, alone or with others, without the approval or even in the face of the disapproval of the United Nations; 5) it may abstain from involvement and urge other states to do likewise. In cases of this variety the potential function of the world organization has to do with the legitimization of action by states. The United Nations may endorse or condemn, encourage or discourage military intervention in situations of conflict; it offers no substitute for the power of states, but its machinery provides facilities for multilateral efforts to influence the policies of states.

I can conceive of no pat formula for determining the proper course of the United States in cases of the kind under consideration. Acting, or refraining from acting, in conformity with the resolutions of United Nations organs is highly desirable—though less because of the presumption that there is virtue in adherence to the "will of the United Nations" than because of the recognition that there is pragmatic advantage in concerting American policy to the fullest possible degree with that of other states. Similarly, congressional and public opinion and reaction within the United States must be considered and anticipated since the effectiveness of foreign policy is a function even more of domestic than of international acceptance and support. Ultimately, however, the task of statesmanship is to judge whether American involvement in a given situation is more likely to produce consequences that weaken or that strengthen the stability of the general international order. Such judgments can never be certain, but they must be made, with wisdom if possible and courage if necessary. Neither passivity nor active engagement on the part of the United States is in principle the key to the management of international crises. Responsible leaders of the United States can neither evade nor delegate the burden of deciding, case by case, how American policy and power are to be related to the objective of the maintenance of peace.

XV United States Policy Toward
Regional Organization

JOSEPH S. NYE, JR.

Regionalism has a long history as an important instrument of American foreign policy. Yet such a statement does not do justice to the variations in goals, means, and settings that have affected United States policy toward participation in and cooperation with regional organizations. These differences have been the cause of serious debate in the past and are becoming so again as we enter the 1970s.

REGIONALISM IN OUR PAST

One of the earliest strands of United States foreign policy, one that has persisted with varying strength to the present day, is the "Western Hemisphere idea," the notion of the uniqueness of the Western Hemisphere and its isolation from the rest of the world,[1] which was given form by James Monroe's disengagement of the Western Hemisphere republics from the Europe-centered international system. However, the United States did not demonstrate great interest in regional schemes such as the 1826 Panama conference proposed by Simón Bolívar. After 1890 the International Union of American Republics and its Commercial Bureau represented a pioneering example of a multipurpose regional organization, but it remained a weak and North American-dominated organization.[2]

[1] See Arthur P. Whitaker, *The Western Hemisphere Idea: Its Rise and Decline* (Ithaca, N.Y.: Cornell University Press, 1954).
[2] According to William Manger when the Commercial Bureau

It was not until the early twentieth century, in the aftermath of the United States intervention in response to the collapse of the European balance of power in World War I, that one finds in Woodrow Wilson's proposal of a policy of global collective security "the first instalment of the conflict between regionalist and globalist ideas."[3] It is ironic that the language of Article 21 of the Covenant of the League of Nations, stating that the global doctrine of collective security did not necessarily interfere with "regional arrangements" such as the Monroe Doctrine, was an insufficient bait to lure the United States Senate (for which it was written) into ratification of the Covenant but did become a convenient loophole for governments in the interwar period.[4] The United States, in any case, returned to its traditional policy of hemispheric regionalism as a counterpart to its isolationist European policy.

The major United States debate over policy toward regional organizations occurred during the latter part of World War II after the United States had been drawn once again out of "isolation" and beyond hemispheric regionalism. If the formal outcome of the debates as written into the United Nations Charter represented a globalist victory, it was in a large part because of the success of Secretary of State Cordell Hull who "represented a kind of residual Wilsonianism."[5] Arguments by writers like Walter Lippmann or statesmen like Winston Churchill abroad and Sumner Welles at home in favor of establishing organizations on the basis of explicit recognition of regional spheres of influence were rejected by Hull for fear that they "might lead to questions of balance of power" and provide a means for another retreat into isolationism.[6] Such

---

was under the United States Secretary of State, it was more like an American agency than an international organization. See *Pan America in Crisis: The Future of the OAS* (Washington: Public Affairs Press, 1961), p. 33.

[3] I. Claude, Jr., *European Organization in the Global Context* (Brussels: Institut d'Études Européennes, 1965), p. 8.

[4] See B. Boutros-Ghali, *Contribution á l'étude des ententes régionales* (Paris: A. Pédone, 1949), p. 8.

[5] Claude, p. 9.

[6] Cordell Hull, *The Memoirs of Cordell Hull* (2 vols; New York: Macmillan, 1948), Vol. II, p. 1646.

globalist idealism seemed hypocritical to leaders of the United Kingdom who saw Latin America as a United States sphere of influence even if the United States did not call it such. However, by the time of the Quebec Conference of 1943 Churchill had lost faith in the possibility of creating a strong European regional council and decided that henceforth "the United States, rather than a revived and reorganized Europe, would have to counterbalance Russian power."[7]

Ironically, Churchill's decision was a harbinger of a coming change in the international system from a multistate balance of power to a bipolar structure that made Hull's victory a hollow one and greatly diminished the importance of the subsequent debate at the 1945 United Nations Conference on International Organization at San Francisco. One of the effects of United States hemispheric policy in the 1930s had been an increase in Latin-American enthusiasm for hemispheric regional organization. Becoming aware of the high costs and low benefits of the past interventionist policy in Latin America and later faced by the threat of Axis powers' incursion into the area, the United States had gradually accommodated Latin pressures to use inter-American organization to introduce constraints on its freedom of action.[8] This experience of the 1930s and of close cooperation during the war, plus a reluctance on the part of some conservative Latin-American elites to become too tightly enmeshed in an organization which the Union of Soviet Socialist Republics could use against them, led to Latin pressures at the 1945 Inter-American Conference on Problems of War and Peace at Chapultepec for revision of the Dumbarton Oaks proposals to protect regional organizations.

Thus at San Francisco, while resisting Egyptian efforts to define acceptable regional organizations in such a way that they would resemble the recently formed Arab League, Sena-

[7] William Hardy McNeill, *America, Britain and Russia* (London: OUP, 1953), p. 323. Subsequently, when out of power Churchill called for European unity, but it was never completely clear what he meant by "unity" or how he saw Britain's relation to it. Nor did his actions upon his return to power clarify the issue.

[8] See Bryce Wood, *The Making of the Good Neighbour Policy* (New York: Columbia University Press, 1961).

tor Arthur Vandenberg and America's Latin allies succeeded in amending the proposed charter to ensure that inter-American organization would not be jeopardized by the global organization.[9] Vandenberg argued that they had "infinitely strengthened the world organization by thus enlisting, with its overall supervision, the dynamic resources of these regional affinities"[10] while critics deprecated the resulting ambiguity in the language of the Charter. In fact, however, the formal outcome of the debate was far less important than the changes in the setting of international organization. After the onset of the Cold War and in response to Soviet support for UN involvement in Western Hemisphere crises American statesmen reinterpreted the relatively precise language of the Charter on "enforcement" action by regional organization just as easily as they did the relatively ambiguous language on "priority" for regional organizations. As Inis Claude so aptly describes, the Cold War prevailed over the Charter.[11]

In the decade following San Francisco American disillusionment with the United Nations as a security system led to the creation of a series of military alliances and organizations which came to be called "regional" although in some cases the degree of geographical proximity involved was very slight.[12] The first of these "regional" security pacts was the Inter-American Treaty of Reciprocal Assistance (Rio Treaty) of 1947; but like the Charter of the Organization of American States (OAS) of the following year this is best understood in terms of traditional hemispheric regionalism as a sort of epilogue to the 1930s or, in Arthur Whitaker's analogy, as a

[9] See Ruth B. Russell, with Jeannette E. Muther, *A History of the United Nations Charter: The Role of the United States 1940–1945* (Washington: Brookings Institution, 1958), Chapter 27.

[10] Arthur H. Vandenberg, Jr., *The Private Papers of Senator Vandenberg* (Boston: Houghton-Mifflin, 1952).

[11] Inis L. Claude, Jr., "The OAS, the UN and the United States," *International Conciliation*, March 1964 (No. 547).

[12] For instance, the longest distance between the capitals of Southeast Asia Treaty Organization (SEATO) members (11,500 miles) is only slightly less than the longest distance between the capitals of UN Members (12,400 miles). We shall refer to such organizations as "quasi-regional."

glacier that continued to move long after the snows that caused it had stopped.[13] The Rio Treaty helped serve as a model for the North Atlantic Treaty of 1949. However, the impetus for the creation of the North Atlantic Treaty Organization (NATO) and later of the establishment of the Southeast Asia Treaty Organization (SEATO) and the Central Treaty Organization (CENTO) was not the traditional United States regional policy but a growing involvement in the global politics of containment in a bipolar world. Along with its direct participation in the quasi-regional military pacts the United States also supported the economic reconstruction and regional integration of Western Europe through the Organization of European Economic Cooperation (OEEC) and the European Coal and Steel Community (ECSC). The United States also encouraged, or at least sympathized with, the Colombo Plan and made abortive efforts at the 1955 Simla Conference to stimulate similar regional organization in what it called "the arc of free Asia." In the mid-1950s the United States was likened to "a switchboard for most of the regional and joint efforts in the free world."[14]

By the 1960s the setting for regional organization had changed. The process of decolonization had greatly increased the number of third-world countries whose existence dramatized the "development problem" and whose slogans frequently stressed regional aspirations. This change was reflected in United States policy. In Walt Rostow's words it was

> one of the most important, if unnoticed, transitions in policy under President Johnson . . . that we are now actively supporting the building of regional institutions and regional cooperation in Latin America, Asia, and Africa as well as Europe.[15]

[13] Whitaker, p. 155.

[14] Norman J. Padelford, "Regional Organizations and the United Nations," *International Organization*, May 1954 (Vol. 8, No. 2), p. 206.

[15] W. W. Rostow, "Regionalism and World Order," Department of State *Bulletin*, July 7, 1967 (Vol. 57, No. 1464), p. 69. (Originally a commencement address at Middlebury College, Middlebury, Vermont, June 12, 1967.)

At the same time the degree of détente between the United States and the Soviet Union following the Cuban missile crisis of 1962 both eased the direct security threat in Europe and created a certain distrust of direct American dealings with the Soviets at potential European expense. This situation provided leeway for policies, including those of General Charles de Gaulle, which were less "Atlantic-oriented." Perhaps even more important than the announcement by France in 1966 that it would withdraw its forces from NATO assignment and command was the beginning by the Federal Republic of Germany (West Germany) in the same year of a new policy of contacts with the East which Pierre Hassner calls "the hour, so often falsely predicted, of a search for alternatives to the policy of integration in the West and reliance on the United States."[16] At the same time United States European policy turned away from the "Atlanticist" schemes of the early 1960s, such as the creation of a multilateral force (MLF) for NATO, toward an emphasis on détente which sometimes appeared to Europeans to be at the expense of the Atlantic alliance. Whether the Soviet invasion of Czechoslovakia and the change of American administration have really altered these trends or, as seems more likely, have merely delayed them remains to be seen.

In any case, American policy toward regional organization was again under debate in the late 1960s. In the eyes of its critics the Administration of Lyndon Johnson was using the names of ephemeral Asian organizations to answer questions about its goals in Vietnam at the same time that it was neglecting regional organization in Europe. Thus critics charged that it had no overall policy toward regional organizations except at the declaratory level. Whatever the merit of this criticism, a number of critics, faintly echoing the debates of 1943, have advocated a more consistent policy of support for autonomous regional organizations without direct United States membership as a means to a new structure of world order.

---

[16] Pierre Hassner, *Change and Security in Europe.* Part I: *The Background* (Adelphi Paper, No. 46) (London: Institute for Strategic Studies, February 1968), p. 2.

COSTS AND BENEFITS OF CONTINUING PAST POLICIES

Before turning to the problems raised by the question of a policy of support for autonomous regional organization as a principle of world order, we must look in more detail at how the United States has used regional organizations in the past and at what the costs and benefits of extending such *"ad hoc"* policies into the 1970s would be. In general, one can identify four major clusters of interests that the United States has served through participation in and cooperation with regional organizations since World War II: 1) hemispheric influence; 2) containment; 3) economic development; and 4) conflict prevention and management.

Hemispheric Influence

One of the major United States policy interests that has been served through regional organization and certainly the most long-standing one has been the maintenance of a sphere of influence (exclusion of what *we* define as hostile external influence) in the Western Hemisphere, particularly in the Caribbean region. This is not to say that the only role of the OAS has been maintenance of a United States sphere of influence, but this has certainly been one of the roles as the United States use of the OAS in the cases of Guatemala in 1954, the Dominican Republic in 1965, and Cuba since Fidel Castro's takeover indicate.[17] It is instructive that at the time of the 1945 debates on the inclusion of a special clause in the UN Charter to protect the Pan-American arrangements Vandenberg quotes Leo Pasvolsky, a staunch "globalist" opposed to the inclusion of such a clause, as arguing that we would act despite a veto in a Pan-American dispute requiring force.[18]

A regional organization offers the dominant power a basis for signaling "hands off" to an external power and the means to achieve collective legitimization of actions it wishes to take

[17] See Claude, *International Conciliation*, No. 547.
[18] Vandenberg, p. 189.

in the region. A mistake by one superpower in its estimates of the other superpower's intentions is a potential source of nuclear holocaust. However, explicit agreements on spheres of influence that might prevent such a mistake are taboo in the current system.[19] In these circumstances regional organizations such as the OAS or the Warsaw Treaty Organization (WTO) can serve as salient points for tacit warnings between the superpowers. Second, in cases in which the United States feels that its security interests compel it to intervene to maintain its sphere of influence it can turn *post hoc* to the OAS for at least partial collective legitimization, and in the bargain over granting OAS approval the Latin states are given at least a minor degree of leverage over the actual continued conduct of the intervention.[20]

There are several possible costs of using a regional organization for maintaining a sphere of influence. First, as occurred in the Dominican Republic affair, intervention may appear to achieve legitimization primarily in the eyes of United States elites and publics rather than in the eyes of elites and publics abroad. If changing military technology in the 1970s reduces the military security value of a sphere of influence[21] and increased polycentrism further reduces the meaning of "communism" and thus the psychological or political loss we might incur from leftist revolutions in Latin America, the existence of the OAS may lead to a considerable lag in the evolution of United States domestic opinion behind the realities of the need for or the possibility of a sphere of influence.

[19] See *International Herald Tribune,* September 14–15, 1968. Secretary of State Dean Rusk said last night that the Soviet Union, through military force, had established and maintained a "sphere of dominance" in Eastern Europe. He made the statement in categorically denying again that the U.S. government ever had any "spheres of influence" agreement or understanding with Moscow.

[20] See Jerome Slater, "The Limits of Legitimization in International Organizations: The Organization of American States and the Dominican Crisis," *International Organization,* Winter 1969 (Vol. 23, No. 1), pp. 48–72.

[21] For an argument that spheres of influence are becoming obsolete see Albert Wohlstetter, "Illusions of Distance," *Foreign Affairs,* January 1968 (Vol. 46, No. 2), p. 250.

Second, spheres of influence tend to be unilateral impositions which may be resented by smaller countries and some elites at home as well as abroad. If the United States public believes in the legitimacy of OAS actions far more than the Latin Americans do, this may mislead United States decision makers and prevent them from making necessary responses and adjustments that might alleviate such resentment short of costly violence. As evidence of such asymmetrical perceptions of legitimacy one can cite the difficulty with which the OAS has treated cases of alleged Communist threat in the hemisphere and the refusal of the Latin states to allow the organization to develop any permanent or independent military capacity.[22] Nor is this situation likely to change in what will probably be a period of increasing nationalism as economic forces mobilize even greater proportions of the populations of Latin states in the 1970s.

Containment

A second major foreign policy objective which the United States has pursued through regional organizations has been the objective of "containment"—originally of Soviet power, later broadened to containment of "communism." Both economic and military organizations have been used. Among the latter the United States created and participated in NATO—first the Treaty in 1949, then the highly developed organization after the onset of the Korean war in 1950—as a means of establishing a credible commitment to defend Western Europe against the Soviet Union. With decolonization and increased focus on the power of the People's Republic of China (Communist China) in Asia Secretary of State John Foster Dulles promoted the quasi-regional Baghdad Pact (later CENTO) in which the United States was an observer and the quasi-regional SEATO of which the United States was a nonregional member as a means of completing the ring around "the Communists." It has been suggested that Dulles turned to these quasi-regional imitations of NATO because they were

[22] See John C. Dreier, "New Wine and Old Bottles: The Changing Inter-American System," *International Organization*, Spring 1968 (Vol. 22, No. 2), p. 485.

easy to sell to Congress, because they were expected to allow easier access to weak areas, and because they promised to limit American expense and responsibility.[23] In any event, the opposition of neutralist Asian countries and their refusal to join made the inadequacy of the quasi-regional pacts apparent even to Dulles who soon limited the United States commitment in SEATO.[24]

With the exception of NATO and the belated resurrection of SEATO for legitimization purposes after the United States had run into increasing criticism of its Vietnam policy, quasi-regional military "pactomania" proved to be a very brief phase in United States policy. On the other hand, the objectives of containment have been pursued through other forms of regional organization.

In Europe the United States supported the economic integration of the Six while being cool to the ideas of a European Free Trade Association (EFTA) in part at least because it was hoped that the former would lead to sufficient political integration to support a defense capability that could become an equal partner ("the other end of a dumbbell" in the image of the day) tied to the United States in the Atlantic alliance half of a bipolar world. In Asia after Dulles realized the failure of his pacts to attract neutral countries, which were then scheduled to meet at Bandung, the United States turned briefly to the idea of a regional economic organization supported by United States economic aid ("something like the OEEC") as a means of keeping Communist influence out of "the free arc of Asia." The regional organization aspect of the idea was dropped, however, after an unsuccessful conference in Simla, India, in May 1955 at which the smaller Asian states proved reluctant to accept a regional body interfering with their bilateral aid from the United States, particularly one that might be subject to Indian or Japanese leadership.[25]

[23] Edgar S. Furniss, Jr., "A Re-examination of Regional Arrangements," *Journal of International Affairs,* 1955 (Vol. 9, No. 2), pp. 80–81.

[24] See Louis Halle, *The Cold War as History* (London: Chatto and Windus, 1967), p. 304.

[25] See Lalita Prasad Singh, *The Politics of Economic Cooperation in Asia: A Study of Asian International Organizations* (Col-

More recently the Johnson administration has turned to Asian regional organizations ranging in scope from the Asian Ministers of Education to the Asian and Pacific Council (ASPAC) as means of creating a sufficient sense of unity and common interest among the countries bordering Communist China so that they would no longer present a "vacuum of power" into which the United States might be drawn but could become strong "partners" instead.[26] The United States hoped to reduce the burden of containment by finding

in regionalism a new relationship to the world community somewhere between the overwhelming responsibility we assumed in the early postwar years as we moved in to fill vacuums of power and to deal with war devastation and a return to isolationism.[27]

In assessing the benefits and costs of using regional organization as a tool for containment we cannot hope to settle differences of opinion over whether the goal of containing the power of Communist China, the Democratic People's Republic of Korea (North Korea), and the Democratic Republic of Vietnam (North Vietnam) in Asia and the goal of containing Soviet power in Europe are (or were) of equal (or any) merit. We can, however, discuss the suitability of regional organizations as means to those goals in the two settings.

The prime benefit of using military quasi-regional organizations for containment is that by institutionalizing and preparing defense projects in advance the credibility of the American commitment to the protection of an area is underlined or enhanced and thus so is the ultimate deterrent effect. However, United States membership in an organization alone is not a sufficient guarantee of credibility. The quasi-regional and poorly organized SEATO seems to have lacked credibility. Even in the highly organized NATO, however, doubts

umbia: University of Missouri Press, 1966), pp. 9–11. I am also indebted to Robert Denham for the research on this point.

[26] See Bruce M. Russett, "The Asia Rimland as a 'Region' for Containing China," in *Public Policy*, ed. by John D. Montgomery and Albert O. Hirschman, Vol. 16 (1967), pp. 226–249.

[27] Rostow, Department of State *Bulletin*, Vol. 57, No. 1464, p. 69.

about the credibility of the United States commitment, even reinforced by the stationing of American troops, arose in some circles in Europe, particularly after the Soviets obtained ballistic missiles capable of devastating American cities while (despite various efforts at institutional engineering) NATO's important nuclear retaliation capacity remained firmly in unilateral American hands. A second benefit of using the regional organization instrument is the creation of improved channels of communication both through regular conferences and through personal contacts that lead to "interpenetration of bureaucracies." A third benefit of the regional military alliance is the legitimization of "leverage" over partners' defense policies. Although this leverage has always been imperfect and depends on the need to control German power (independent of the Soviet threat) it also tends to vary with the degree of agreement in perception of the imminence and nature of the external threat. Consequently, to the extent that it does vary with the external threat and to the extent that détente progresses and the international system becomes less bipolar in the 1970s the benefits sought through regional military organization are less likely to be available.

The costs of the regional organization instrument are the obverse of its benefits. Influence is a double-edged weapon and the need to work through an organization may constrain America's freedom of policy. According to William and Annette Fox, United States membership in regional alliances

has somewhat inhibited its policy from diverging radically from that of its partners, especially when their support was sought for American-defined purposes.[28]

On the other hand, in some cases, when the United States has changed its policy because of its perception of the security situation, the result has often been to exacerbate relations with our partners. Changes in NATO strategy have tended to be American led and have not always been well received in

[28] William T. R. Fox and Annette B. Fox, *NATO and the Range of American Choice* (New York: Columbia University Press, 1967), p. 125.

Europe.[29] It is instructive of the costs of this type of regional military organization in a period of diminished external threat that former Secretary of Defense Robert McNamara's flexible defense doctrine of 1962 led to concern among Europeans who feared that it might weaken the nuclear deterrent. Ironically, this United States doctrine was not officially accepted by the NATO Council until 1968 after the departure of France had contributed to its obsolescence.

The prime benefit of the nonmilitary regional organization as an instrument of containment has been the prospect of diminishing the burden on the United States both economically and in terms of American domestic political costs. The theme has been prominent since the early debates on United States support for European regional organization as well as in the more recent Asian policy statements of the Johnson administration. There is the additional benefit that these economic and functional organizations may be the only means available for a containment policy in situations where local sentiment for nonalignment makes bilateral or regional military alliances with outside powers unpopular.[30]

The greatest cost of this policy is the risk of misperception of reality through the "telescoping of time"—a failure to take fully into account the length of the stages involved. The future image of a cohesive region capable of self-defense may be substituted for the divisive current reality, and the regional organization becomes a token or symbol that helps obscure a more accurate perception of reality. While it is true that political or cultural regional organizations may help establish a sense of regional identity, the type of integration or organizational structure that can be built on identity alone tends to be "token integration at the international level"—helpful but hardly sufficient as a basis for containment. It is also true that regional economic organizations can unleash a number

[29] See Robert E. Osgood, *Alliances and American Foreign Policy* (Baltimore, Md.: Johns Hopkins Press, 1968), p. 52.

[30] There may be some areas where local regional military alliances will be politically acceptable and might gain legitimacy through formation of a regional organization. See, for example, recent discussions between Australia, New Zealand, and Malaysia. (*The Economist,* March 1, 1969 [Vol. 230, No. 6549], p. 28.)

of dynamic forces which can bring about a "spillover" into a higher level of integration in an area. There are difficulties with this, however, as a basis for containment policy. Although we are still at an early stage in our knowledge in integration theory, there are both theoretical reasons and practical evidence to cause one to be wary about the extent of these forces outside of the Western European context.[31] Moreover, even in Europe the rate at which economic integration might lead to a level of political integration that would entail a common defense capability seems to be much slower than was expected in the 1950s.

In short, the failure to see how very long the short run really is may obscure a full realization of the problems involved in using nonmilitary regional organizations as more than a minor instrument in containment; and this may lead to underestimation of the costs of continuing a containment policy in the international system of the 1970s.

Economic Development

A third major foreign policy objective for which the United States has used regional organizations as an instrument has been economic development, first in the reconstruction and expansion of the Western European economies, later in the various parts of the less developed world.[32] There were two distinct aspects of United States support for regional economic organizations in Europe.

First, American support for regional economic organization in Europe was partly out of belief in the greater economic efficiency, including greater competition in larger-sized markets than those typical of European states. Its willingness,

[31] See Joseph S. Nye, "Comparative Regional Integration: Concept and Measurement," *International Organization,* Autumn 1968 (Vol. 22, No. 4), pp. 855–880; and Joseph S. Nye, (ed.), *International Regionalism* (Boston: Little, Brown, 1968).

[32] In general, development has been conceived of primarily in its economic dimensions. For some evidence that regional organization can have an effect on "political development" as well see J. S. Nye, "Regional Integration and Political Development," *International Development Review,* September 1967 (Vol. 9, No. 3), pp. 17–19.

however, to support regional protectionist abridgements of its universalist principle of most-favored-nation treatment in international trade and its readiness to suffer trade diversion were limited in Europe to "the Six" among which it was felt that the higher levels of economic integration would contribute toward political objectives as well.

The second aspect of United States support for regional economic organization in Europe had to do with the problems and tasks of allocating American economic aid. The desire to avoid being caught in the middle of constant disputes over allocation and a desire to avoid charges of domination were already reflected in the phrase in George Marshall's famous speech at Harvard University on June 5, 1947, that a unilateral plan would be "neither fitting nor efficacious." The result was the formation of the Organization for European Economic Cooperation charged with reaching agreements from a regional point of view on recommended distribution of American economic assistance.[33]

The United States was slow to extend this approach to less developed areas. Despite a rather beguiling remark by President Dwight D. Eisenhower that what was good for Europe might be good for Latin Americans, too, United States economic orthodoxy in the 1950s led to a cool reception for Latin American schemes for *Latin* regional economic organizations.[34] By the end of 1958, however, some United States leaders began to see the need to reappraise economic policy toward Latin America. (This perception was later enhanced

[33] For details see Ernst H. van der Beugel, *From Marshall Aid to Atlantic Partnership: European Integration as a Concern of American Foreign Policy* (Amsterdam: Elsevier Publishing Company, 1966).

[34] Eisenhower allegedly told a cabinet meeting in 1953,

> You know, we sit here and talk, all too rarely, about one commodity in one country, out of all the American republics. Yet when we speak of the affairs of Europe, we talk on a totally different level. Unity, unity, unity: we say it over and over. And we think back to Charlemagne. . . . But what is true for one continent should be just as true for another.

(Quoted in Emmet John Hughes, *The Ordeal of Power: A Political Memoir of the Eisenhower Years* [New York: Atheneum, 1963], p. 145.)

by Castro's revolution but actually antedated it.)[35] In addition, the United States was faced with a concrete opportunity to assist the Central American Common Market (CACM) which, after careful cultivation by the UN Economic Commission for Latin America (ECLA) throughout the 1950s, had signed its first major trade integration treaty in 1958. The decision to break with former economic orthodoxy was dramatized by the particularly obvious necessity for a larger market among such tiny states and the alternative prospect of unending instability in an area of primary United States security concern. Subsequently, the United States Agency for International Development (AID) established a unique Regional Office for Central America and Panama (ROCAP) and by 1967 had granted some $100 million in support of regional projects.[36]

Support for regional economic integration became accepted verbal policy after the 1961 Charter of Punta del Este that launched the Alliance for Progress. As Miguel S. Wionczek has argued, however, its peripheral priority before the 1967 Punta del Este summit conference at which the United States committed itself to support a Latin-American common market to be formed by 1985 meant that a variety of countervailing private and bureaucratic interests frequently prevailed in practice.[37]

In addition to support for Latin-American economic inte-

[35] See Robert Harrison Wagner, "Latin America and the Economic Policies of the United States" (Ph.D. dissertation, Harvard University, 1966), pp. 256–293.

[36] See Joseph S. Nye, Jr., "Central American Regional Integration," *International Conciliation,* March 1967 (No. 562), pp. 50–57. Three-fourths of United States aid to the area remained bilateral. See also James D. Cochrane, "United States Attitudes Toward Central American Economic Integration," *Inter-American Economic Affairs,* Autumn 1964 (Vol. 18, No. 2), pp. 73–91.

[37] Miguel S. Wionczek, "Latin American Integration and United States Economic Policies," in Robert W. Gregg (ed.), *International Organization in the Western Hemisphere* (Syracuse, N.Y.: Syracuse University Press, 1968), pp. 91–156. He cites United States resistance to regional shipping and payments schemes as examples. See also Christopher Mitchell, "Common Market—The Future of a Commitment: Punta del Este and After," *Inter-American Economic Affairs,* Winter 1967 (Vol. 21, No. 3), pp. 73–87.

gration the United States has experimented with and is a member of other forms of economic regional organization, such as: the Inter-American Development Bank (IDB) in which the staff is predominantly Latin American though the capital is North American; the Inter-American Committee on the Alliance for Progress (CIAP), based in part on the model of OEEC, which carries out multilateral studies of country programs designed (albeit somewhat imperfectly in practice) to be of assistance in the allocation of economic aid; and the Inter-American Economic and Social Council (IA-ECOSOC) which after the 1967 reforms of the OAS Charter which re-oriented the OAS toward economic questions was raised to coequal status with the political Council.

In United States policy toward Africa a convergence of congressional concern over the dangers of overcommitment which led to imposition of a legislated limit on the number of countries to which development assistance loans could be granted and a growing concern within the American adminis-tration with economic effects of the proliferation of tiny Af-rican states led to a redirection of the AID program toward promotion of regional economic organization. The catalyst for the change was the Korry Report,[38] commissioned and re-ceived by President Johnson in 1966, which will lead to some 40 per cent of United States aid to Africa for regional purposes.[39]

In Asia renewed emphasis on regional economic projects, in particular United States support since 1965 for the Asian Development Bank, was stimulated originally by the political difficulties that America encountered over its Vietnam pol-icy[40] (witness President Johnson's 1965 speech at Johns Hop-kins University, Baltimore, Maryland). Subsequently, how-

[38] Edward M. Korry, former Ambassador to Ethiopia, was com-missioned by President Johnson to recommend how AID could contribute more effectively to African development.

[39] See Anthony Astrachan, "AID Reslices the Pie," *Africa Re-port,* June 1967 (Vol. 12, No. 6), pp. 8–15. See also Robert S. Smith, "New AID Policies for Africa," *Foreign Service Journal,* February 1968 (Vol. 45, No. 2), pp. 16–19.

[40] Philip Geyelin, *Lyndon B. Johnson and the World* (New York: Frederick A. Praeger, 1966), pp. 276–278.

ever, the potential economic effects of the organization, as well as the prospect of getting Japan more involved in the region, have grown in importance.

A major benefit of supporting organizations involved in regional economic integration or regional services is simple economic efficiency. Some 90 less developed countries have populations under 15 million; 60 have markets under 5 million. At low levels of per capita income these population figures represent markets which can support only a limited range of efficient industry which the countries are bent on having for political reasons. Some such states are hard pressed to support a full panoply of services that go with sovereign status. The availability of this benefit is limited, of course, by the difficulty of promoting regional integration among less developed countries referred to above. In some cases at least, an outside catalyst or source of funds can increase the perception of regional economic cooperation as a nonzero sum game involving an expanding pie and thus may make a useful contribution.

A second benefit involves those regional economic organizations, including development banks, which are involved in the distribution of aid resources. As the giving of aid can sometimes appear demeaning and frequently involves considerable participation in domestic processes, the use of regional organizations may provide a means for recipient countries "to diminish their dependence and to increase the dignity of their position while accepting the international ties required."[41]

The potential costs of using regional economic organization for aid to economic development are the obverse of the benefits. Regional economic agreements may merely establish uneconomic industrial protection and only slightly reduce inefficiency; divert resources and attention away from other (e.g., agricultural) uses; and institutionalize the inefficiency in a way that may make it difficult to unscramble later. Thus far these costs are mainly hypothetical though there are some

[41] W. W. Rostow, "The Role of Emerging Nations in World Politics," Department of State *Bulletin*, April 5, 1965, p. 495. (Address made at the University of Freiburg, Freiburg, West Germany, March 15, 1965.)

signs of them in Central America.[42] The costs of using regional institutions in the allocation of aid may be a loss of efficiency by the donor as well as a diminution of leverage in return for gains in dignity and cooperation which prove to be only minimal, for, as John Montgomery remarks, in this field "it is doubtless easier to give than to receive."[43] The experience of CIAP thus far has not been wholly encouraging, and some African states have complained about United States regional aid policies.[44]

Whether the benefits of aiding economic development through regional organizations will exceed the costs will depend on levels of protection and capacity to cooperate in particular cases. Thus far the benefits seem far greater than the costs. Some difficulties may arise in the future, however, between the more protectionist Latin American vision and the generally liberal United States perception of a Latin American common market. On the other hand, the rationality of the policy in the 1970s will not be reduced if détente progresses and the need for political alignment leverage in the aid relationship decreases.

Conflict Prevention and Management

A fourth major foreign policy objective for which the United States has used regional organizations is the prevention and management of conflict. This policy includes two aspects: the use of regional organizations to promote "integrative solutions" in which parties are able to resolve an exist-

[42] See Roger Hansen, *Central American Regional Integration and Economic Development* (Studies in Development Progress, No. 1) (Washington: National Planning Association, 1967), Chapter V.

[43] John Montgomery, "Regionalism in U.S. Foreign Policy: The Case of Southeast Asia" (Paper prepared for the Wingspread Symposium on Southeast Asia, September 1965).

[44] See Raúl Sáez S., "The Nine Wise Men and the Alliance for Progress," *International Organization,* Winter 1968 (Vol. 22, No. 1), pp. 244–269. Also see *The New York Times,* May 14, 1967:
> The Guinean president made clear his opposition to multilateral or regional aid concepts. . . . He said this would subject him to economic neo-colonialism by the former colonial powers, particularly France.

ing dispute by agreeing on upgrading a third or common interest; and "peacekeeping" in which no "common interest" is found but pressure is put on the parties by outside conciliators, or intervening forces, to cease fighting. In regard to the latter type of capacity the OAS, the Organization of African Unity (OAU), and the Arab League were relatively successful in playing an independent role in dampening conflicts between their members in eleven out of twenty-one cases, not counting ones they did not try to handle. Two thirds of the successes, however, were achieved by the OAS where American leadership and logistic capacity played a crucial role.[45] Moreover, nearly all of the OAS cases concern the microstates of the Caribbean area rather than the larger states of South America, and there are grounds to believe that future OAS capacity in this role may be more limited than it was in the past.[46] Outside the Western Hemisphere American policy has employed UN peacekeeping procedures with the exception of a futile effort to use NATO in the Cyprus dispute. Although former Secretary of State Dean Rusk has applauded the performance of the OAU and testified to Congress that United States support for regional institutions in Africa "has to do with their ability to settle disputes among themselves,"[47] it is almost impossible to detect this concern as an operational criterion among AID officials involved in implementing the policy.

On the other hand, the United States has frequently turned to regional organization in hopes of providing "integrative solutions" to disputes in several areas. A strong and consistent motive for American support for "small Europe" of the Six has been the concern with "integrating" Germany and France and providing a context for successful resolution of traditional conflicts such as the Saar dispute settled in 1955. United States support of the Central American Common Market is

[45] For details see Joseph S. Nye, *International Regional Organizations* (Boston: Little, Brown, forthcoming).

[46] See Dreier, *International Organization*, Vol. 22, No. 2.

[47] U.S. Congress, House, Committee on Foreign Affairs, *Hearings, on H.R. 7099, Foreign Assistance Act of 1967*, 90th Congress, 1st Session, May 4, 1967, p. 855.

an example of another successful case.[48] On the other hand, attempts at promoting regional organizations as a means to an integrative solution of the Middle Eastern situation have been unsuccessful.[49] Similarly, President Johnson's 1965 announcement of support for the Asian Development Bank, a regional aid program, and the ensuing increased attention to the Committee for Coordination of Investigations of the Lower Mekong Basin seemed motivated in large part by the futile search for an integrative solution to the Vietnam imbroglio.

The benefits of a policy promoting either of the two types of use of regional organization for resolution of local conflicts are quite obvious. The more easily a dispute can be contained or resolved intraregionally, the less the likelihood of involving the superpowers and the less the burden on the United Nations system.

The costs are of several types. First, there is the possibility that a regional organization of which the United States is not a member might impose a solution intolerable to an American ally or in the case of the OAU or the Arab League might use any increments to its "peacekeeping capacity" for peacebreaking against what it considers intolerable regional enemies such as South Africa or Israel. Alternatively, the price of effective and acceptable regional peacekeeping action by the OAS may be a degree of United States initiative which may lead to resentment among Latin countries.

Second, the aid given to promote an integrative solution may have a cost in terms of interference with other criteria for giving aid such as economic efficiency or political alignment. If the probabilities of an integrative solution are very low, these costs may outweigh the benefits.

The prospect in the 1970s of achieving success in enhanc-

[48] Witness, for example, the 1968 resolution of the Honduras/ El Salvador border incident. See *Visión*, August 2, 1968.

[49] Although an ironic sequel to the United States proposal in 1957 of a Middle Eastern development bank was that the United States finally gave in on its resistance to creation of a similar instrument in this hemisphere. See John C. Dreier, *The Organization of American States* and the *Hemisphere Crisis* (New York: Harper & Row [for the Council on Foreign Relations], 1962).

ing the "peacekeeping" capacity of regional organizations, particularly outside the Western Hemisphere, might depend on continued détente and the capacity of the superpowers to agree to limit their involvement in the regions concerned. On the other hand, the rationality of a policy of promotion of regional integrative solution would be unlikely to be affected by changes in the international system, except perhaps if there should be a return to tight bipolarity in which case alignment might become an important criterion for aid.

PROJECTING THE FUTURE

As we enter the 1970s, there is a fifth major interest that the United States could pursue through regional organization that is of a different order of magnitude: encouragement of change in the structure of the international system in accord with a new vision of world order. One can claim to see hints of this in past policy. For instance, in some versions of the "Atlanticist" regional vision the creation of a unified Europe was desired as a means to change rather than preserve the bipolar structure of power.[50] More recently, there were signs that the Johnson administration was attempting to develop a doctrine of regionalism as a means of reconciling global involvement with a need to reduce "the burden that America has had to bear this generation."[51] This might be interpreted as a policy of creating regional balances of power from which the United States as the stronger superpower could stand back. Analogous to the United Kingdom's nineteenth-century European policy, the United States would intervene only occasionally to right the scales. Critics have pointed out that such a role is excluded in fact; for as long as containment in the ideological sense has priority, America could only intervene

[50] See Karl Kaiser, "The U.S. and the EEC in the Atlantic System: The Problem of Theory," *Journal of Common Market Studies,* June 1967 (Vol. 5, No. 3), p. 413; also George W. Ball, *The Discipline of Power: Essentials of a Modern World Structure* (Boston: Little, Brown, 1968), Chapter XV.

[51] President Johnson, "Four Fundamental Facts of our Foreign Policy," Department of State *Bulletin,* September 26, 1966 (Vol. 55, No. 1422), p. 453. (Address made at Lancaster, Ohio, September 5, 1966.)

on one side of the scales.[52] Many of the same critics, however, agree with the idea of supporting autonomous regional organization as a means of encouraging change in the international system.

Though the names and detailed descriptions of the current international system vary,[53] there seems to be general agreement that it is characterized by bipolarity in the basic structure of military power but by much looser structures in the various functional and geographic subsystems. A particularly interesting model that spells out the political characteristics of the current system is the one constructed by Stanley Hoffmann. In Hoffmann's view the consecration of the nation-state (with UN membership as a prime source of legitimacy) and the change in the role of force both because of the potential self-defeating costliness of an actual use of nuclear weapons and because of the cost of ruling mobilized alien populations have led to an "inflationary" type of international system in which the maneuvers of small powers in the dominant polycentric layer are divorced from the ultimate (but muscle-bound) realities of military nuclear power in the basic bipolar layer; and a possible multipolar layer has only begun to emerge. In such a system milieu goals (the environment of the international system) are more important than possession goals (direct territorial, economic, or other concrete interests); world politics becomes "internalized" as domestic problems are linked with international forces, and the sources and types of power become more diverse. "As the physics of power decline, the psychology of power rises."[54] Considerations of prestige, informal penetration, and capacity to communicate effectively take on added importance.

[52] Stanley Hoffmann, *Gulliver's Troubles, or the Setting of American Foreign Policy* (Atlantic Policy Studies) (New York: McGraw-Hill [for the Council on Foreign Relations], 1968), p. 67.
[53] See for example Wolfram F. Hanreider, "The International System: Bipolar or Multibloc?," *Journal of Conflict Resolution*, September 1965 (Vol. 9, No. 3), pp. 299–308; R. N. Rosecrance, "Bipolarity, Multipolarity, and the Future," *ibid.*, September 1966 (Vol. 10, No. 3), pp. 314–327; Oran R. Young, "Political Discontinuities in the International System," *World Politics*, April 1968 (Vol. 20, No. 3), pp. 369–392; Hoffmann.
[54] Hoffmann, p. 65.

In Hoffmann's view of the future of this system the possible proliferation of small, vulnerable, and thus unstable nuclear forces may present the superpowers with a choice between costly policing or a retreat that would let the world disintegrate into a series of jungles. The alleged benefits of certainty and control in a bipolar system[55] have already been greatly eroded by polycentrism and are likely to vanish completely if there should be creeping nuclear proliferation. As a Great Power the United States has an interest in preserving a degree of hierarchy in the system and in reducing the current separation between the capacity of states to participate in world politics and the responsibilities for world order which they are willing to undertake. The inflationary system that allows weak states more freedom of action to use their power than superpowers will likely lead to nuclear proliferation of the most dangerous kind. At the same time the United States has an interest in increasing diversity, particularly the emergence of China and the creation of an independent European power, for multipolarity would increase diplomatic flexibility and allow the Great Powers to devote more attention to each other rather than to policing their ideological "camps" and being drawn by bipolarity into marginal conflicts. To help keep the international system moderate and responsible the United States should encourage the creation of separate hierarchies in the various functional areas of international relations; the formation of an autonomous European power in world affairs; and the establishment of autonomous regional organizations of the types that would involve local regional powers in responsible leadership positions in economic, scientific, and peacekeeping tasks in the rest of the world—all under the ultimate nuclear umbrella of two or three superpowers and within the normative structure of the United Nations and the various global economic and functional agencies.

A possible objection to such a policy of support for regional organization as a means of changing the structure of the international system might be made on the ground that the setting of world politics of the 1970s will not be favorable

---

[55] See Kenneth Waltz, "The Stability of a Bipolar World," *Daedalus*, Summer 1964 (Vol. 93, No. 3), pp. 881–909.

to regionalism. In fact, one's vision of the future of the international system depends upon the means one chooses for projecting it. If we sketch the setting of the 1970s by projecting current technological trends and their effects on defense considerations and economic transactions, the setting may be uncongenial to regional organization. In Wohlstetter's view

> the revolution in transport and communications casts doubt not only on the new isolationism of a growing minority but also on the more respectable but rather mechanical regionalism that may frequently be found in both the Democratic and Republican establishments: the grand designs for Latin American common markets, Asian common markets, African unions, economic unities spanning the Middle East from Morocco to Afghanistan, and others.[56]

More generally, one could argue that as the tight bipolar system of the 1950s has loosened, some of the newly important subsystems have not had a regional basis. For example, the recently politically important monetary subsystem with its Group of Ten is nonregional, and the inclusion of Japan in the "Atlantic" Organization for Economic Cooperation and Development (OECD) in 1964 may be typical of the future. In a world of jumbo air freighters, giant supertankers, and large-scale data processing that facilitates capital movements and multinational corporations, geographically remote trading partners such as Japan and the United States should be able to increase mutual trade at least as rapidly as the regional European Economic Community (EEC). In the defense field nuclear and missile technology has already reduced the role of geographical distance in military security, and similar changes can be expected to result from satellite technology.[57] In the view of Thomas Schelling a new type of global geography may be taking over in which gravity, earth spin, and cloud cover may become as important in the world of satel-

[56] Wohlstetter, *Foreign Affairs,* Vol. 46, No. 2, p. 250.
[57] See *The Implications of Military Technology in the 1970's* (Adelphi Paper, No. 46) (London: Institute for Strategic Studies, March 1968).

lites as Suez or Gibraltar were for seapower.[58] In Wohlstetter's words, "the upshot of these considerations of technology in the 1970s is that basic interests in safety will extend further out than they ever have before."[59]

Thus one could conclude that a foreign policy for the 1970s that places heavy emphasis on the promotion of regional organizations will be mistaken because technological trends indicate that the most important international systems of interaction—whether economic or military—will not be regionally based. Such a conclusion would be somewhat premature, however, for the early 1970s. Despite falling transport costs geography will still have an impact on price. Despite missile and satellite technology local and conventional defense techniques will remain relevant. Moreover, some technological changes may encourage regional organization. Communications technology may make possible direct and inexpensive regional communications in areas like Latin America or Africa where intraregional communications now often have to go through New York, London, or Paris. In addition, inexpensive breeder reactors may lead to nuclear proliferation of a type that encourages disengagement by distant powers eager to minimize their risks, as Hoffmann argues.

If, instead of projecting the setting of the 1970s on the basis of technological effects on transactions and the geography of defense we predict the continuation of a number of the political features of the current system, we get a very different picture of the potential favorableness of the setting for regional organizations. We can extrapolate from Hoffmann's model of the current system a number of the political characteristics that could provide statesmen with incentives to turn to regional organizations as useful tools for a variety of purposes.

1) With the diversification of power the prestige of regional leadership can become a useful symbol of power as the foreign policies of France, Ethiopia, and the United Arab Republic indicate in the EEC, the OAU, and the Arab League.

2) With the increased importance of domestic populations

---

[58] Speech to Foreign Policy Association, New York, May 1968.
[59] Wohlstetter, *Foreign Affairs*, Vol. 46, No. 2, p. 252.

in world politics, yet the enhanced legitimacy of national sovereignty, regional organizations may provide an opportunity to appeal over the heads of governments to societal groups in other states (despite the sovereignty clauses often written in the charters) as the successful and unsuccessful efforts of the Ivory Coast and Ghana to influence their neighbors through the Conseil de l'Entente and the OAU demonstrate.

3) With the devaluation of military force traditional military alliances may be less attractive, but statesmen still feel the need to draw lines and introduce even a faint element of predictability into their search for security by political alliances under the guise of regional organization—witness ASPAC and the Association of Southeast Asian Nations.

4) With the predominance of milieu goals over possession goals regional organizations may be useful tools for shaping conditions beyond one's national boundaries, whether it be the creation of more favorable conditions for economic development aid, the establishment of regional balances of power, or a group's assertion on the world scene of its collective identity.

5) Finally, with the increased importance of communications and signals regional organizations may be useful as "no trespassing" signs or "firebreaks" that will help to avert confrontations in a refragmented world, either between the superpowers (e.g., the OAS and the Warsaw Pact) or between the weak (e.g., the OAU) and the superpowers.

In short, as long as the international system of the 1970s maintains certain features of the current structure, there will be a number of political incentives for the use of regional organizations despite an ambiguous balance in the long-run technological trends. Thus regional organization appears to be neither the "automatic" trend of the 1970s as some enthusiasts suggest nor a relic of the 1950s as the skeptics seem to imply. At best the projected setting is ambiguous and thus enhances the room for policy choices.

CHOICES ABOUT THE FUTURE

Simplified debates over "regional vs. global organization" are not very enlightening. Not only are these not the only alternatives (there is also bilateralism) but most of the policy goals outlined above require a mixture of approaches. Choices must be made, however, about the proper mixture, and occasionally decisions must be made between regional and global organization or between types of regional organization. We have already mentioned the choice of the OAS over the UN in the field of hemispheric security.

In the field of trade policy the United States allowed the meaning of Article 24 of the General Agreement on Tariffs and Trade (GATT) to be compromised in the 1950s because of its belief in the beneficial political effects of European regionalism.[60] Similar conflicts might arise in the trade policy field over a large but partial European trade agreement if that appeared to be the only way to associate the EFTA countries with the EEC and over the question of special hemispheric trade preferences for Latin America if the global United Nations Conference on Trade and Development (UNCTAD) scheme fails.[61]

In the security field conflicts may arise between the pursuit of détente and the maintenance of NATO or over the value of autonomous European organization, such as occurred in the recent dispute over whether the European Atomic Energy Community (EURATOM) or the International Atomic Energy Agency (IAEA) should be responsible for inspection in Europe under a nonproliferation treaty.

The outcome of such decisions will depend on the extent to which one decides to promote autonomous regional organizations as a part of a long-run vision of world order. This in turn depends on the probabilities involved in creating such an order. We have argued above that on the basis of technological and political projections the probabilities are ambiguous. In these circumstances a sense of timing becomes the crucial factor for policy. While it is useful to have a clear vision at a high level of abstraction, a policy of promoting

[60] See Gerard Curzon, *Multilateral Commercial Diplomacy: The General Agreement on Tariffs and Trade and Its Impact on National Commercial Policies and Techniques* (London: Michael Joseph, 1965), Chapter IX.

[61] For examples of the latter type of demand see J. W. Clark, *Economic Regionalism and the Americas* (New Orleans, La. Hauser Press, 1966).

autonomous regional organizations must not be applied in doctrinaire fashion to all regions at all times in the same way.

Even if the creation of autonomous regional organizations without United States membership or control is an appropriate goal for the end of the 1970s, too rapid an implementation (e.g., an early American withdrawal from NATO or the OAS) or too premature an implementation (e.g., "an Asian common market" modeled on the EEC) could have opposite effects from those intended. Future organizational potential must not be mistaken for current capacity. The important question is whether in the early 1970s the various types of autonomous regional organizations (with the possible exception of Western European organizations) can become sufficiently strong to bear the burden that is expected of them. As we have argued above, the peacekeeping record of organizations other than the OAS (in which the United States' membership seems to make what difference there is) has not been impressive to date. The capacity of less developed countries to cooperate successfully in economic regional organizations with a scope broad enough to make a significant difference to economic development or the promotion of integrative solutions has been limited thus far to two somewhat shaky cases, the East African Common Market and the Central American Common Market. The management of regional balances of power under conditions of proliferation of vulnerable nuclear forces (e.g., potentially the Middle East) involves a complexity of considerable and possibly dangerous dimension. In short, policy makers may wish to encourage regional organization in accord with a long-run vision when the costs are low but should not necessarily opt for the regional alternative when the costs in terms of other goals are high.

Not only must an American policy on regional organization in the 1970s take account of problems of timing; it should also be based on a clear perception of potential conflicts between goals. The five foreign policy goals examined above are not always complementary. Unless this problem is clearly perceived and priorities are deliberately chosen, one goal may have costs in terms of another that nullify its benefits. We have already noted the conflict between regionalism for ideological containment and regionalism for the creation of a series of autonomous balances of power. In some ways the regional organizations we have created in Asia seem designed to prevent a Chinese sphere of influence. Containment may also conflict with a policy of support for regional organization for economic development or for integrative solutions—witness the 1967 American *volte-face* on a Mekong Committee commitment after it was felt that Cambodia had become too close to Hanoi.[62] "Containment" in the ideological sense might also make it difficult for the United States to continue regional aid to an East African or Latin American common market if one of the members underwent a "Communist coup." A policy of regionalism for local peacekeeping might have costs in terms of regionalism for economic development if, for example, United States financial aid to the OAU or United States training of African army units for OAU peacekeeping led to an expensive guerrilla campaign against Portugal and South Africa.

In conclusion, the setting for regional organization in the 1970s will be neither as clearly favorable as the enthusiasts nor as unfavorable as the skeptics predict. There will be scope for choice in our policy. In such circumstances a long-run vision is important if we are to escape the mere perpetuation of past policies which are beginning to lose their relevance. It is mildly ironic that the vision of a more flexible and moderate international system toward which regional organization would contribute might make the debates of 1945 over Chapter VIII[63] of the UN Charter relevant again. The United States might well wish to "un-rewrite" the Charter and go back to a system of Security Council approval (and potential United States veto) of regional organization enforcement actions before the United States embarked on a policy of giving peacekeeping aid to the OAU or the Arab League. And the United States might be willing to pay the price that would have been unthinkable at the height of the Cold War, i.e., Security Council approval (and possible Soviet veto) of enforce-

---

[62] See John D. Montgomery, "The Political Decay of Foreign Aid," *Yale Review,* Autumn 1967 (Vol. 57, No. 1), pp. 1–15.

[63] Chapter VIII of the Charter is entitled "Regional Arrangements."

ment actions in the American sphere of influence in the Western Hemisphere.

Long-run visions, however, are not sufficient basis for short-run policy, and a doctrinaire support for certain types of regional organization that would ignore problems of timing and fail to make distinctions between different areas would be mistaken. We cannot, in the early 1970s at least, escape the frustrations and expense of attempting to provide leadership in organizations like NATO and the OAS until other security systems evolve for those areas. Similarly, though we may wish to promote autonomous regional organizations for economic development and conflict prevention and management, the promotion of effective organizations of which we are not a member is only in small part within our control. United States policy toward regional organization in the 1970s should be informed by a long-term vision of an improved world order, but we must be careful not to mistake organizational symbols and future hopes for current reality.

XVI   The Third World and American Politics

MICHAEL KENT O'LEARY

This exploratory essay will assess the nature of the two-way relationship existing between American domestic politics and American policy toward the third world, in order that we might make inferences about the effect which that relationship will have on the future course of American foreign policy in general. Primarily to give some finite boundaries to such a vast topic, discussion will focus on one major aspect of American policy, foreign aid, with largely illustrative reference to one other principal policy, American military involvement in Southeast Asia.

Two points should be stressed at the outset. In the first place, we shall view the relationship between domestic politics and foreign policy as a reciprocal process in which the impact of top-level policy decisions may well have a greater impact on national politics than politics upon policy. We shall, in other words, be concerned with the domestic consequences as well as the domestic sources of policy. Secondly, of concern to us will be the occasional comparative references that are made to American military involvement in Southeast Asia. On the surface this issue of American policy scarcely seems an appropriate conceptual cohort for American foreign-aid policy. Whereas the former is conducted with the utmost seriousness as befits a major war, the latter is a long-standing policy anticipating somewhat more positive results which are

The treatment of foreign aid in this essay is based on an updating of the discussion of the author's *The Politics of American Foreign Aid* (New York: Atherton Press, 1967).

more leisurely obtained. But it is just the apparent discrepancy of these two policy areas which makes them such attractive companion pieces. For we shall attempt to show that many of the same traits in the American political system are clearly at work with respect to both areas of policy, and that government-public relations in foreign aid and in the Southeast Asian war may profitably be viewed as subthemes of the same dominant trends in American thinking about foreign affairs.

We shall center our discussion around the two policy arenas by referring to three very general propositions about the politics of foreign policy making. The first of these is that the more a government becomes involved with the political and economic health of a foreign government, the more likely that relations with that government will be marked by political conflict. The second is that there is a fundamental, if partial, truth in the arguments of many critics of foreign policy when they say that policy must be judged in terms of domestic consequences within the United States. And the third is that strategies designed to generate favorable public opinion which prove successful in the short run may turn out, when continued, to have decidedly contrary effects.

We shall consider how these three points are related to an understanding of foreign aid, and then turn, somewhat more briefly, to their application with respect to the Southeast Asian war.

ECONOMIC POLICY AND POLITICAL CONFLICT

In dealing with the third world in the future, American foreign policy must take cognizance of the fact that economic growth in the less developed countries of the world is likely to generate changes in the nature of the international system in which the United States must live. American policy must recognize, for instance, the probable implications which worldwide economic development are likely to have for international politics. For even if a developing nation were able to achieve economic growth without dependence on external resources and assistance, the process of development still contains serious dangers of international conflict. Development almost always occurs unevenly within a society, and domestic conflict is a common by-product of development. In today's world, there are few internal conflicts which long remain isolated from international concerns. Hence, there exists a tendency for the internal conflict produced by the stresses of economic growth to eventually spill out into international conflict. Beyond this, there is a strong tendency for nations which have undergone development to become more insistent upon demands for status and deference within the international system. Nations frequently see their own demands as more legitimate than others do, and conflict is a likely consequence.

American foreign policy might also profitably pay attention to some other lessons which recent history teaches. It seems true that when, as in the case of bilateral economic aid, development is associated with expectations of political debt and obligation between donor and recipient, the chances for political conflict are even greater. Donor nations, especially the United States, have in the past tended to accompany their aid with a rich baggage of assumptions and expectations about the behavior of recipients. These have ranged from the relatively limited, such as the kinds of technical and administrative standards which should be used in administering aid, to extremely comprehensive expectations about the fundamental foreign policy stance of the recipient.

In principle, foreign aid should be able to serve as a useful medium in bargaining for desired domestic or external actions on the part of the recipient. Furthermore, it can potentially be used as either an inducement for future desired behavior or as a reward for previous behavior. In actual practice, however, aid does not appear to have served as the basis for any such acceptable bargains. Indeed, there seems to have been a direct correlation between the political content of relations between aid and donor and the amount of dissatisfaction with these relations. Not the least important indicator of this dissatisfaction is the attempt on the part of the underdeveloped countries to have more of their external resources supplied by trade, rather than aid. The unwillingness of donors to accept this position does not seem to have been related to any feelings of success which they felt as a result of their bilateral aid experience; it seems, rather, to have stemmed from the desire to maintain relations in which at least some semblance of influence remains, along with the fear of tackling the difficult economic and political questions involved in restructuring assistance policies to the benefit of the less developed nations.

THE CONSEQUENCES OF FOREIGN ECONOMIC POLICY

Throughout all the debate in the United States on policy toward the less developed nations, there is at least one characteristic which can be said to separate those who wish to do more from those who wish to do less in the form of aid. The former have stressed the humanitarian, ideological, strategic, and other desirable features overseas which they say will ensue from a healthy foreign-aid program. The latter, on the other hand, have decried the damage done to our domestic economy, political system and self-image through the long-standing foreign-aid program. While supporters of the program have occasionally addressed themselves to the impact of aid on domestic matters, and opponents have, somewhat more willingly, spoken of the external consequences, by far most of the discussion about internal consequences has been generated by the opponents of aid. We may well disagree with the argument of those who advocate reducing or ceasing what is already the most modest of programs. But there is, nonetheless, an implicit general truth in what the critics have been saying: economic policy, like all foreign policy, must ultimately be judged according to its consequences for the society engaging in the policy. The external effects of national policies are only, in the jargon of the statisticians, "intervening variables." To concentrate on them alone is to miss the fundamental purpose of foreign policy, which is to enable the nation to adapt successfully to its external environment in such a way that its own institutions and social processes will be protected and enhanced.

This is not to say, of course, that every external act must have an immediate payoff at home for it to be considered a success. Nor must we even expect that activity in one realm of policy, such as the economic, will have consequences in the same realm of domestic activity. In general, foreign trade does have observable domestic consequences in the various economic sectors; on the other hand, it definitely has much more impact upon the constitutional system (e.g. the role of Congress in foreign policy) than upon the domestic economy. The whole process—which begins with internal decisions, in turn affects external behavior, and ultimately ends with internal consequences—is a complex one which has been too little discussed, let alone systematically measured. But any thorough discussion of foreign policy must attempt to come to grips with this third part of the process, the "feedback" of external behavior to the domestic society. The critics of more liberal economic programs are certainly guilty of over-emphasizing this component and of assessing its impact with rather narrow and misanthropic criteria, but at least they have kept alive the debate on this aspect of policy making.

Their actions should be taken as a challenge by those who favor more expansive programs of assistance to provide more systematic consideration of the actual impact upon our institutions of aid programs, and of potential impacts of possible future aid and trade programs.

DOMESTIC VS. FOREIGN POLICY MAKING

The two problems mentioned above—conflict arising from bilateral participation in the development process and assessing the domestic consequences of economic relations with the third world—are closely associated with the third topic to which we shall devote more attention: the requirements of successful political leadership in domestic and foreign policy. We can conveniently classify the operations of American politics into two separate categories: the processing of domestic issues and the processing of international issues. In these two arenas of political activity the principal actors have often differed; when the actors are the same they have exhibited different relations to one another, and formal and informal political structures have differed markedly in their impact upon the total political process.

The domestic political process has been characterized by the slow speed with which issues have been defined, debated, and resolved. The political system has been marked by a high degree of decentralized power. Social and economic groups, party organizations, the states of the Union, and the separate institutions of the Federal government all interact to create a melange of power centers more frequently working to thwart one another than moving in coincident directions. It occurs naturally enough that the course from the first recognition of an issue to its more or less clear-cut resolution is erratic, uncertain, and unpredictable. It is thus almost impossible to establish consistent rankings of power and influence among even the most prominent actors. Today's winners may become tomorrow's losers. Even so powerful an official as the President must tread lightly in working for those domestic policies he favors.

Compromise, flexible goals, and a generally pragmatic outlook become the order of the day for those participating in the process. The uncertainty of the system elevates expediency and a concern with tactics to a particularly high plane; those most concerned with tactics often win out over those motivated by broad philosophical goals or strong ideological commitments.

By contrast, the political treatment of foreign policy issues has been notably different. Both formal constitutional dictum and informal precedent have rendered foreign policy making nearly a mirror-image of domestic politics. The President and his advisers have been given much greater leeway in arranging priorities for action and following through with the policies of their choice. Those institutions and informal power groupings which play such a large part in domestic issues are usually either inactive in or supportive of the Administration's course of action.

Partisanship, pluralism, and compromise are replaced by bipartisanship, coordinated action, and consensus. It is likewise the case that American foreign policy has been guided by rather clear-cut philosophical goals. The realism of these motivations is open to serious question, but it seems safe to say that they have been widely and firmly held within the nation. "The water's edge" has indeed been both the normative and actual boundary of American politics.

The reason for this sharp distinction between domestic and foreign policy making can be traced to the history of American participation in international affairs. Historically, American involvement has been episodic and marked by the need for rapid response. Typically, there has been an accompanying clarity with which the stimulus and goal have been defined in dealing with international problems. The incidence of crisis has tended to prompt citizens in and out of government to support the President and his immediate advisers; it has also tended to create the ideological consensus with which foreign involvement has been justified. But equally important has been the relative short-term nature of concern with any single foreign policy issue. Policy and judgments about policy could be fashioned as the occasion warranted, with relatively little concern for long-range implications.

This same characteristic of foreign policy making which has given the President short-run advantages in decision making has not been without its attendant dangers. It has become quite clear in the past few years that in giving up short-run freedom to the Executive on foreign policy questions, the American political system has also attached an implicit qualification: Support will be rendered only as long as progress is being made to solve the problem in the short run. If this does not occur the political system contains many opportunities for enforced retribution.

Events in our more immediate past have markedly differed from earlier experiences. But despite the substantial changes brought about since World War II, many of the problems we faced immediately after the war were of such a nature as to perpetuate the distinction between responses to foreign and domestic issues. In one sense, early postwar problems were different from the past principally because the episodes of involvement became somewhat longer in duration than before.

The first decade or so after World War II was an atypical period of international affairs because it was a period of great activity during which there was remarkably consistent alignment of allies and opponents. This feature of international politics had especially important consequences for the domestic response to foreign policy questions. The persistence of the same friends and enemies meant that a large portion of traditional political habits could continue to prevail despite the so-called "revolution in American foreign policy." American leaders, with the support of most citizens, could concentrate on opposing adversaries and assisting supporters. The magnitude and duration of the task were certainly unique as far as American peacetime history was concerned, but the political process could still respond to a notably constant set of signals from the friendly and unfriendly aspects of the international environment. We can even argue that the Marshall Plan—however innovative and dramatic—was at least as much a product of traditional American thought about foreign policy as it was the harbinger of future responses. Indeed, it may be that much of the difficulty associated with more recent foreign-aid activities stems from the tendency to see the Marshall Plan as the source and the model of what has been done since. It is true that people who ignore history are doomed to repeat the mistakes of the past, but it is likewise true that those who follow false historical precedents may be equally led astray.

The attempt to use American resources for explicit, instrumental foreign policy purposes is of course common to both the Marshall Plan and subsequent economic assistance activities. But we should not let this one important similarity mask an abundance of equally important differences. The Marshall Plan was a massive program to support a friendly coterie of nations against a feared powerful aggressive enemy. It was an enemy seemingly waiting impatiently to enlarge its territorial holdings in Europe through overt military action or through cooperation with subversive groups within the societies of Western Europe weakened by war. In addition, the area in the geographical scope of the Marshall Plan was clearly delimited. The Marshall Plan recipients were being assisted back to a level which they had previously enjoyed before the outbreak of war. Since they could achieve capability for self-sustained growth rather quickly, the temporal limits of our aid commitment were also well-defined. And given America's impatience with delayed success, this latter limitation may be one of the most important distinctions of all between the Marshall Plan and further aid developments. The major differences between this and other foreign-aid programs can be seen most clearly in the differences in the way the political processes have operated with respect to the two policies. Approval of the Marshall Plan resulted from a massive effort on the part of political leaders to mobilize Congress and the population, and the process by which the Marshall Plan was advocated and finally approved was a happy amalgam of the foreign and domestic political process. The goals featured such traditionally attractive objectives as helping those in trouble overseas and bolstering allies against a feared enemy, Communist Russia. In emphasizing these goals the Administration employed many of the tactics which are commonly used to obtain successful results in domestic policy, including the establishment of presidential study groups, informal lobbying with influential members of Congress, and the establishment of channels for reaching both the public and interested influential groups among the public.

In general, the executive branch has used modifications of these successful tactics appropriate for domestic policies to help effect the modest changes which have been achieved in trade policy. This has been because, for better or worse, trade policy has been defined as a domestic policy issue. Techniques have included constituency building, bargaining with congressmen, and liaison with selected interest groups. As a result, successive administrations have achieved at least marginal successes in their attempts to alter trade legislation. Appeals to foreign policy values have also been employed to the advantage of the Executive Branch, though they have been decidedly secondary to employment of domestic political techniques.

The political process surrounding foreign aid since the Marshall Plan is also a combination of external and domestic elements. In this case, however, the mixture has hardly reproduced the successful outcome of the Marshall Plan or of trade policy. In fact, a summary statement of the problem with current domestic politics and foreign aid is that the policy process involves an incompatible marriage between domestic and international patterns of American political behavior.

This is true in terms of the mixed public views of foreign aid which administrations have unsuccessfully tried to mobilize on behalf of the program, of ambiguous congressional feelings about foreign aid, and of the strategy employed by various administrations in attempting to achieve support for the program.

If we sort out available evidence about public opinion toward foreign aid we can come to at least one rather firm conclusion: Whatever we may say about the long-run consequences of "crying communism" by the Executive Branch, that very cry was certainly at the core of the most expedient and effective technique for obtaining short-run support for the program. American perceptions of and judgments about foreign aid are ambiguous and inconclusive, but the evidence we do have suggests that the most powerful attribute inducing support of foreign aid is a belief that aid can protect and even extend the American system of values abroad. There is also a somewhat weaker factor working for support of foreign aid which is a need recognized by the public to assist international allies. A credible argument that foreign aid helps stop the anathema—communism—or helps support those other nations which have joined us in the Cold War, is therefore that kind of argument most likely to receive support among the public. Foreign-aid programs which are seen as humanitarian gestures are likewise likely to be favorably received. The most successful appeals to the public include the arguments that foreign aid helps to project American values or practices abroad, furthers humanitarianism, avoids deep involvement in the affairs of other nations, and assists Cold War allies. These are the kinds of values to which credible appeals could be made in earlier years. But more recent applications of foreign aid have made it unrealistic to promise the fulfillment of such values.

In general, the linkages between opinion and decision making create a strange and paradoxical picture. On the one hand, we have the persistent results from opinion polls which show that on the average foreign aid is supported by at least half the population, with the remainder either uncertain or opposed. We likewise know that if we totaled the number of nongovernmental groups which supported foreign aid and compared them with those opposed, the former would easily outnumber the latter. On the other hand, it is the nearly unanimous consensus of congressmen and executive officials that such mail and other indicators of public opinion as they do receive is strongly opposed to foreign aid. Many congressional supporters of foreign aid admittedly work for goals directly in opposition to what they know about their constituents' opinions. Congressional opponents, on the other hand, are quick to cite what they claim are the demands of the voters for their opposing stands.

We may uncover part of the reason for this strange picture by considering the basic attitudes from which opinion is formed. While the sum total of these attitudes may result in approving aid as a general principle, there is, of course, no such thing as foreign aid "in general." What we have, on the contrary, are many alternatives for pursuing a whole range of specific goals in many disparate sections of the globe. Specific aid activities often fall far short of activating positive reactions; indeed, a good deal of a policy stimulates those very images creating hostile feelings among Americans. Aid to Communist countries, to less than friendly neutralists, and to nations in which the government exercises strong control over the economy all fail to measure up to the widely held standards needed for approval. Even military assistance to allies may provoke fears of dangerous and undesirable long-range commitments. The Peace Corps, which has benefited from its inexpensive, missionary halo, seems a clear exception proving the general rule.

The man in the street seems to evaluate foreign aid according to a variant of Churchill's aphorism that democracy is the worst form of government—except for all the others. As far as the public is concerned, foreign aid is a good policy, except for all the forms in which it has been applied.

The picture is equally complicated when we consider the relationships of pressure groups to support for foreign aid. To cite just one example, survey evidence shows that support for aid is quite low among workers, who are frequently union members. Yet it is the leaders of these very same unions who are among the most prominent nongovernmental supporters of aid. The divergence between official positions of leaders and the known position of followers in many groups stems from the fact that the leaders are often drawn from that small part of the population which is most favorable to foreign aid because of educational background, economic status, and more or less direct experience in observing or participating in the affairs of government. These are the individuals who write party platforms, formulate policy resolutions at conventions, and act as group spokesmen in Washington. Because these people are found in the two political parties and in a wide variety of other public organizations, their support for foreign aid helps give the appearance of widespread approval cutting across party and interest group divisions. Such approval is not found among the rank and file of most of these same organizations, but on the whole, members of these organizations demonstrate a rather passive antipathy. Leaders are free to differ from followers in supporting aid simply because the issue fails to provoke strong feelings among most citizens.

Taking widespread group support as an indicator of strong public support is quite illusory, for public support as measured by group activity is widespread, but not very intense. Indeed, support as measured by formal group pronouncements is quite ephemeral and contains strong ingredients of latent foreign-aid opposition. The more leaders attempt to move beyond mere verbalization through encouraging action by members of the group, or by lobbying in the support of foreign aid before congressmen, the more it becomes clear that these leaders are in fact speaking only for themselves and are unable to commit their group membership to anything like effective support for economic assistance policies.

The contrasting and contradictory views held by the public about what aid is and what it should be are also shared by members of Congress. Congressional opinion is expressed in ways much more directly pertinent to the operation of the program—through committee questioning of aid officials, speeches and private communications directed at the administration of the program, proposing and voting on amendments to foreign-aid legislation, and support given to passage of foreign-aid authorizations and appropriations. In general, congressmen seem to judge foreign aid according to

criteria based on a desire to spread Americanism, combined
with a fear of becoming overly involved in dangerous international situations; they are sensitive to the needs of Cold
War diplomatic strategy and they are concerned with the
cost in relation to other government spending.

Legislators are not presented with the relatively simple and
abstract questions used in opinion polling techniques. The
congressman, instead, must make complex choices: Will he
support increased funds for military assistance which will
give more aid to allies thereby upholding the desires of the
President, but at the same time increasing government spending, becoming more involved with other countries, and rejecting the recommendations of a congressional committee which
has carefully studied this question? Occasionally a program
such as the Peace Corps will present a much more clearly defined choice. Advertised as a means of stimulating American
patriotism and transmitting American values overseas via a
modestly paid cadre of volunteers, the Peace Corps has been
accepted on these terms and firmly endorsed. "To know
America is to love America," said one congressman by way
of explaining his enthusiasm for the Peace Corps.

Despite the general similarity of viewpoints, in at least
two respects Congress seems to differ from the public in its
reaction to foreign aid. In the first place, congressmen seem
more concerned than the public to make sure that foreign
aid is used in a thoroughly direct instrumental fashion. Evidence of this can be seen in the handling of amendments to
foreign-aid legislation. In one analysis of congressional responses to foreign aid, it was found that about one fifth of the
amendments proposed by members of the House and the
Senate were attempts to influence and control the behavior
and policies of other nations. These amendments included
attempts to control the rates of interest charged by foreign
governments, minimize governmental influence in the economy of recipient nations, induce nations not to trade with
Cuba, North Vietnam or other deadly enemies of the United
States, and induce "all nations" (i.e. Egypt) to permit unim-
peded navigation of international waterways. Over two thirds
of such amendments were approved on the floor of the House

and Senate, indicating they were by far the most popular class of congressionally initiated changes in the foreign-aid program.

The second most popular area of congressional initiative is one scarcely considered by the public at all. This is the effect of foreign aid on the manner in which power is shared by the legislative and executive branches. There seems to be a strong consensus in Congress—among both liberals and conservatives—that the legislature must maintain a constant alert to see that it does not lose out in its constitutional tug of war with the Executive Branch. Amendments to increase congressional control over foreign-aid administration were the second most frequently proposed; just under two thirds of such amendments were approved by the two houses in the period studied.

It is easy to build the indictment against the techniques used by the Executive Branch to win approval for foreign aid. Proponents of aid have, for the most part, accepted traditional American positions regarding foreign affairs and attempted to bend them into forms which will help secure support for economic assistance. In essence, the advocates of aid have asked: How can the benefits of free enterprise and other aspects of American society be transmitted abroad unless active steps are taken to facilitate this transmission? How can we maintain our alliance system unless we aid our allies to build their own soundly based defense establishments? How can we expect them to take our side in the Cold War unless we take their side in the struggle for development? Why should we be content with a defensive ring around our homeland when we have the opportunity to construct such a ring around our enemies? To critics questioning the feasibility of these objectives the proponents have answered that it takes time, and have occasionally attempted to delimit that time. The Kennedy administration's "Decade of Development" was a prime example of a traditionalist pro-aid answer to traditionalist anti-aid arguments. It has, of course, often happened that the instrumental effects promised by aid advocates have not been forthcoming. The decision to provide aid to Communist countries, for example, directly countermands one of the most powerful arguments previously used. It is not surprising, therefore, that the attempt to define the new program in traditional terms has not proved successful.

The same unfavorable judgment can be made about other attempts to increase effective approval of foreign aid. Presidents and their advisers have engaged in numerous public symbolic acts designed to increase the support of foreign-aid activities and to render them more acceptable to Congress and the public at large. Experienced foreign-aid officials have ranked presidential support near the top of the list of resources helpful in eliciting such favorable response as the program has received. Yet the overlay of bureaucracy and the high cost involved in carrying out the program have necessitated frequent reaffirmations of presidential support, often in terms of alleged emergency conditions. Occasionally the cry of emergency is persuasive and leads to relative success, as with the Marshall Plan, the special assistance to Latin America in 1960–61 (for which Congress appropriated the full Executive Branch requests), or the removal of specific restrictions from the aid legislation. More often critics can accuse the Executive Branch of crying "crisis" and "anticommunism" so often as to erode the credibility of such appeals. The effect of these appeals is further weakened by the fact that it is possible to make substantial decreases in funds and to add many far-reaching restrictions while still passing the program. Presidential determination of "vital security needs" cannot easily be seen to apply to actual percentages of funds requested.

But despite these critical remarks, one must, in all fairness, acknowledge the fact that there is probably no device which would avoid many of the problems involved in the politics of foreign-aid policy making. There is simply a tremendous gap between the kinds of problems with which foreign aid can deal and the inertia of habitual behavior motivating decision makers. There do not seem to be any simple or straightforward guidelines which the President and other officials can follow in using their relatively meager sources to build understanding and support for foreign aid. It is, in short, the fault of no one person or strategy that the foreign-aid policy process is in a kind of tenuous equilibrium. This equilibrium results not from consensus among the participants but from the inability of the Congress and the Executive either to avoid engaging in this particular policy conflict or to convince the other to accept its own preferences. The Executive must participate because it needs financial and other support for the program; Congress must participate because of its acknowledged responsibility to give at least some assent to serious, persistent requests by the President in the realm of foreign policy.

The policy-making system is probably not the "empty ritual" which some have called it, but it has clearly been an unsatisfying ritual from the standpoint of Congress and the Executive. Congressmen are constrained to approve annually a piece of major legislation whose goals are ambiguous, whose means are suspect, and the past application of which is characterized by well-publicized examples of alleged incompetency and dishonesty. Congressmen have little opportunity to find an acceptable middle ground between fears of tomorrow and the hopes of the day after tomorrow with which the Executive advocates its position, as opposed to the sweeping allegation of wrongdoings with which opponents urge the abandonment of foreign aid. Furthermore, congressional attempts to place philosophically satisfying restrictions on the program often lead to the very situations least desired by the legislature. In recent years Congress has made grand gestures against aid to Communists, countries which trade with Communist China or aid to nations who discriminate in international waterways. In each case, however, the gesture is accompanied by provisions permitting the President to waive the legislative restrictions. Congress thus formally delegates more discretion to the President while decrying the growth of Executive power at the expense of the legislature.

For its part the Executive has received the authority to conduct foreign aid. But it has received the authority only at the expense of great amounts of time, effort, and personal harassment. Its representatives must prepare lengthy documents for Congress, appear at hearings which may continue for weeks and last up to twelve hours a day, and respond daily to numerous congressional inquiries. The administration of aid is also complicated by the restrictions—changed almost annually—as to who may and may not receive money, the general criteria to be used in providing aid, and the precise details of allocating assistance.

Many of these same characteristics have appeared in the political processing of the conduct of the Southeast Asian war. If they have occurred in a somewhat shorter time period, they have nevertheless appeared in all the more intense and dramatic a form. Just as with the foreign-aid program, the early years of policy were characterized by high hopes of major achievement with relatively little cost. Just as with the case of foreign aid, the passage of time without notable successes has led to especially bitter counterreactions by the public. And just as with foreign aid, the Executive Branch has tried to reverse the negative tide of public opinion through the use of real or illusory changes in policy and dramatic gestures such as visits, speeches, and inspection trips. And, finally, just as with foreign aid, the effectiveness of these tactics has sharply diminished with the frequency of the repetition.

It is obvious that the Asian military conflict has had a great impact upon our own society. Indeed, despite the death and destruction we have inflicted on this sorry locale, there is some reason to believe that the most lasting effects of that policy may be within the United States. The war has energized and polarized many groups heretofore politically inert and has created youth as an identifiable and organized interest group. It has forced renewed consideration and sometimes reallocation of priorities of government and industry, and it has induced a searching evaluation of the actual and proper boundaries of American commitments in the contemporary world. No one can foresee the end result of these and related currents, but one can guess that they may still be at work in our own policy when the last American troops have left Indo-China and the peoples of that region return to their historic patterns of cooperation and conflict. They will, to be sure, exert a powerful influence on the course of future policy.

What is perhaps so disturbing about an overview of the

policy making process in economic and military relations with the third world is that there is so much to criticize in positions taken by both supporters and opponents of ongoing policies. We have already discussed this point with respect to foreign aid; it is no less true with respect to military policy. The policy has been sold on the basis of the most dubious historical images, selective presentation of evidence, and ambiguous charting of goals. The opponents have fared little better in their presentation of arguments. They have cited a morality which may be relevant for personal insight but of little use in evaluating public policy; they have frequently shown equal casualness about evaluation of evidence, and they have employed the flimsiest of logic to reach their conclusions. As a case in point it is noteworthy that one of the most common reasons for opposing the Vietnam war is that we have not yet achieved our objectives—a painfully familiar argument to anyone who has read the literature attacking foreign economic assistance.

It is highly questionable whether any segment of the political system, from the most central elites to the most undifferentiated mass groups, has come to terms with the inevitability that the United States exist in a world where there are few, if any, clear-cut friends or enemies, and where the friendly and unfriendly can change places in a relatively short period of time. Nor has there been adequate recognition of an equally important consideration—we live in a world in which there are very few clear-cut indicators of success and failure. Rather we find ourselves engaged in a constant process of seeking marginal advantages, modifying positions, and suffering marginal setbacks. As an attendant need, we must learn to accept the rather substantial time lag between cause and effect, which further complicates the evaluation of policies.

Until such time when a more balanced view of the limits and opportunities of American action is achieved, future American foreign policy seems destined to proceed much as it has: from one policy to another in an incremental, inefficient, and unsatisfying fashion, with the public following along behind a spasmodically moving leader, always lurching in some direction, but one is never quite sure where. It is easy enough to say that this behavior is the price we pay for democracy in policy making, but we must recall—perhaps as the most forceful argument that can be offered—that it is others who are paying the price for our system in hunger, ill health, deprivation, and violent death.

XVII   The American Economy After Vietnam

The only place from which an image of the future can come is from interpreting images of the past. Let us take a look at the American economy over the last forty years (Figures 1 and 2), for this period is long enough to give us considerable clues as to its possible behavior, as well as being a period over which we have reasonably full information, since National Income Statistics began in 1929. As we are considering a change in that segment of the economy which I call the "war industry," roughly equal to that portion of the economy allocated to the national defense budget, the implication of changes in that segment is particularly stressed.

The image of the economy can be divided into two parts: first, the change in the overall size of the economy, and second, perhaps more important, the change in its relative structure. For both of these we require a concept of the overall size itself, and this presents some difficulties. The Gross National Product, which is the usual measure of the size of the economy, is weak in that it fails to account for unemployment, which should properly be regarded as a "sector" of the economy, even though it does not contribute to the Gross Product. We have devised, therefore, a concept which can be called the Gross Capacity Product, which ideally is what the Gross National Product would be if there were no unemployment. Although this is rather difficult to measure and a number of other sophisticated measures exist, there are many advantages in taking a rather unsophisticated measure which is simply the Gross National Product adjusted

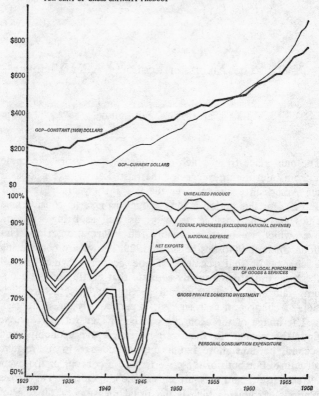

FIGURE 1. GROSS CAPACITY PRODUCT MEASURED IN CONSTANT AND CURRENT DOLLARS AND UNREALIZED PRODUCT AND MAJOR COMPONENTS OF GNP AS A PER CENT OF GROSS CAPACITY PRODUCT

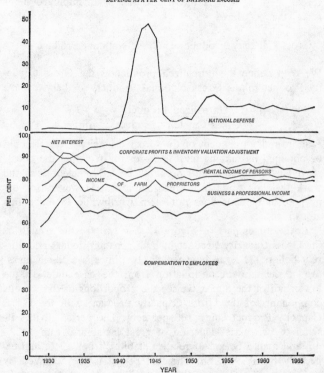

FIGURE 2. COMPONENTS OF NATIONAL INCOME AND NATIONAL
DEFENSE AS A PER CENT OF NATIONAL INCOME

upward according to the proportion of the unemployed labor force. That is, if u is the proportion of unemployed labor force, then we have

$$\text{Gross Capacity Product} = \text{Gross National Product} \; \frac{1}{1-u}$$

We then define the unrealized product as the Gross Capacity Product minus Gross National Product, so that we have

$$\frac{\text{Unrealized Product}}{\text{Gross Capacity Product}} = u$$

A more refined concept of the Gross Capacity Product could be obtained by making allowance for the fact that the unemployed labor force would probably be less efficient than the working labor force if it were employed. However, for the purpose at hand it does not seem worthwhile to make this adjustment.

In the upper part of Figure 1, then, we see the growth of the Gross Capacity Product in both constant dollars and current dollars. The gap between the two lines is a rough measure of the amount of inflation from the base date. In the lower half of the figure, we see the proportions of the various components of the Gross Capacity Product, with the Gross Capacity Product being 100 per cent. The period divides itself into two parts—a period of great instability from 1929–46, and then a period of relative stability from 1946, and especially from 1951, on. The first period is characterized by two major disturbances—the Great Depression, as we see it from 1929 to 1942, and then World War II, as we see it from about 1940 to 1946. At the depth of the Great Depression, unemployment was almost 25 per cent of the labor force. We see the relative failure of the New Deal, as unemployment declines a little, only to relapse in the Depression of '38. We see the Second World War getting us out of the Depression and that about half of the Second World War was financed out of previous unemployment and about half by squeezing the other components of the system—civilian government, Gross Private Domestic Investment, and Personal Consumption Expenditure. We see the great disarmament of 1945–46, when we transferred almost a third of the economy from the war industry into civilian uses without unemployment rising much above 3 per cent. We see the Korean war in 1953, the long, rather stable, Cold War period from 1955 to 1965, the proportion of National Defense slowly declining, and then the Vietnam expansion until 1968. The small relative size of the Vietnam expansion comes as quite a shock in the light of its enormous qualitative impact. We see what might be called the Eisenhower depressions in 1954 and 1958 and the Kennedy depression of 1961, and then the virtual disappearance of the business cycle in the sixties. We see from 1952 on, the proportion going to total government has been relatively stable, so that an expansion of national defense has generally squeezed civilian government and a contraction of national defense has permitted an expansion of civilian government. We see that Gross Private Domestic Investment has been relatively stable, except for the two Eisenhower business cycles, which are mainly inventory cycles. We see that Personal Consumption Expenditure has been remarkably stable. One striking feature is that the Kennedy-inspired tax cut of 1964 produces practically no impact on Personal Consumption, and all seems to be taken out in an expansion of state and local government. Net Exports, which I suppose is some measure of American economic imperialism, are negligible and declining. In the years from 1929 to 1969, what we see mainly is the expansion of national defense from about 0.6 per cent of the economy to about 9 per cent, some expansion of civilian government, and a corresponding decline in Personal Consumption. There is not much change in Gross Private Domestic Investment.

Figure 2 shows us for the same period the distribution of National Income among its various components. National Income is an unsatisfactory measure of the product which is to be distributed, just as the Gross National Product is an unsatisfactory measure of the total product. However, in this case, unfortunately, it is virtually impossible with the existing statistics to make the necessary adjustments. The main problem is that National Income is defined as the Gross National Product less a capital consumption allowance, that is, depreciation of fixed capital, which gives us approximately the net national product, less indirect business taxes with some minor adjustments. We do not deduct the direct taxes, which would be a much more sensible concept of what might be called Gross Disposable Income, but unfortunately we cannot allocate this among the parts. Hence, we have to do the best we can with this imperfect concept of National Income. In spite of this, however, the results are highly suggestive. The proportion of National Income in National Defense is put above the 100 per cent line for purposes of comparison. This shows very dramatically the structural change from the thirties, when National Defense was an almost negligible proportion of the total product, into the post-World War II long-term expansion.

Looking at the distribution of National Income, we see the Great Depression again dramatically expressed by the tremendous increase in Net Interest as a result of the deflation, suggesting that there was an astonishingly small repudiation of debt. We see the total disappearance of Corporate Profits, which became negative in 1932 and 1933, squeezed out by the rise in the proportional compensation of employees and Net Interest. All this, of course, reflects the deflation. We must recall that the total income was much less in 1932 and 1933 than it was in 1929, so that the rise in the proportion of National Income going to Employees also goes hand in hand with the decline of the absolute amount. Surprisingly, a rise in National Defense is associated on the whole with a fall in the short run in proportion of National Income going to Corporate Profits, as we see clearly in 1945 and again in 1953, and even in 1958. This certainly counters the belief that war is good for business; in proportional terms it is actually better for labor. This fact would certainly not be a full explanation as to why the labor movement is so hawkish, but it at least may reinforce the other explanatory factors.

The Rental Income of Persons is a small and highly heterogeneous category which is fairly stable, but its movements are not very significant. The decline of Income of Farm Proprietors can be seen as a result of the enormous decline in the proportion of agriculture in the Gross National Product, which in turn is a result of the almost fantastic technological improvements in agriculture from 1933 on. Business and Professional Income, again, is a rather heterogeneous item which includes the income of both unincorporated businesses and of professionals. It seems to have been declining slowly, which would perhaps reflect a decline in unincorporated business rather than in professional income. Unfortunately, it has not been possible to divide this item between Unincorporated Business and Professional Income. Then finally is the sharp rise of the Compensation of Employees in the Great Depression as a result of the elimination of profits. It has had a noticeable upward trend since 1929, but has been remarkably stable at about 70 per cent of National Income ever since the mid-fifties. One interesting fact that emerges is that a fall in unemployment generally seems to be absorbed more in profits than in wages, that is, the increase in total product as a result of a diminution of unemployment goes more to capital than it does to labor.

Figure 2 not only dispels the illusion that war is good for business, but also that capital is gobbling up labor. If we were to include Business and Professional Income and Income of Farm Proprietors under labor income, which is not quite legitimate, it would emerge as a remarkably stable proportion of the total, having been about 80 per cent from 1950 on. The 20 per cent of National Income which goes to capital does not seem an excessive price to pay for the flexibility and political liberty of a market-type society, so that the facts about the American economy do not seem to give much cheer to the radicals and certainly, of course, completely contradict the Marxist vision of a capitalist economy as one in which the proportion of the income going to capital continually increases.

Figures which give the proportion of the total economy devoted to different industrial sectors are not readily available for this whole period. We do, however, have a breakdown of Personal Consumption Expenditure which offers at least some indication of what the overall industrial composition of the economy might be, and it is shown in Figure 3. What is mainly noticeable here is what might be described as the Engle's Effect, with a decline in Food, Clothing and Shoes as a proportion of the total, and a certain increase in Miscellaneous Services. This is what we should expect with increasing real income. Apart from this, the picture again

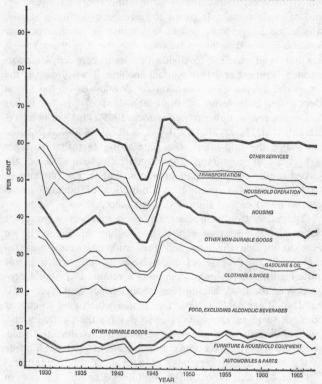

FIGURE 3. PERSONAL CONSUMPTION EXPENDITURE AS A PER CENT OF CAPACITY GROSS PRODUCT.

shows considerable stability, at least since 1950. It is striking, however, that one of the major sufferers from the Vietnam war has been Housing and Furniture and Household Equipment, both of which have declined very sharply since 1965. This may be partly due to the sharp decline in the number of births which, as having taken place since 1961, would certainly reduce demand for an expansion of housing. The stability of automobiles and parts from 1950 on is very striking, and considering all the hullabaloo that has been made about it, it is a remarkably small proportion of the total— about 4 per cent, with gasoline and oil adding about another

2 per cent. The illusion, incidentally, that the Second World War accompanied a reduction of the automobile industry is also dispelled, for though the automobile industry was reduced to very low levels, only about 2 per cent of the Gross Capacity Product was released by this. One problem here is that we have not allowed for changes in the relative price structure, which have been of some significance in this period. This would require a good deal of further work, however, and would probably not change the basic conclusions.

So much for the past—what now for the future? The great unknown, of course, is the international system itself, and even more important is the American image of it. On the whole, one could say that the proportion of the economy which goes to the war industry is determined by decisions outside the economy itself, decisions which are taken mainly as a result of the prevailing (government) image of the nature, and especially the future, of the international system. In other words, if we feel more threatened, we increase national defense; if we feel less threatened, we diminish it. Decisions about the war industry are taken with remarkably little consideration of their impact on the economy. It was only in the last few years that the Department of Defense has even had any apparatus for considering this in the small, much less in the large. The military budget must be regarded as the product partly of institutional arrangements and institutional inertia (the Department of Defense is an enormous pressure group in government with almost one lobbyist for every congressman), and partly as a result of the prevailing image, especially in Congress and in the Administration, and to a lesser extent in the public at large, of external threat. If we want to form an economic model of the war industry, the simplest one would assume that the war industry of every country is a function of the war industry of every other. This assumption gives us n equations and n unknowns, the unknowns being the size of the war industry in each country. If this set of equations has a solution, then there will be an equilibrium size for each war industry and we will have something like a balance of power or a balance of terror. It is quite easy, however, to postulate paramaters for this set of equations which gives no positive solution and in which the system is explosive with ever-increasing arms races until it finally disintegrates into war or some other kind of systems change.[1] Unfortunately these equations are always subject to sudden changes in their paramaters. Ever since 1954 we seem to have had a remarkable stability, at least in the proportion of the economy devoted to national defense, but there is no guarantee that this stability will persist into the future. About all we can do is to list either favorable or unfavorable elements of the situation, that is, those tending to produce a reduction and those tending to produce an increase in the size of the war industry.

On the favorable side, we might consider that the international system is not likely to have any sharp changes at least in the next fifty years in the "pecking order" or relative power position of the major nations. If we reckon the power index as measured by, say, the Gross National Product multiplied by some coefficient, which I have sometimes called the coefficient of disagreeability, we see that the major long-run changes here are in the Gross National Products of the various nations, although there are important changes from one generation to the next in the coefficients of disagreeability, with the Japanese, for instance, moving from high disagreeability to low, and the United States taking rather the reverse course in the last forty years. The major strains in the international system come at the point of "overtake" when one nation or power complex overtakes another in the power order. Overtakes occasionally are accomplished without any major war, as in the case of the overtake of Britain by the United States in the nineteenth century. But the three major wars of the last one hundred and fifty years were all accompanied by a complex system of overtakes. In the next fifty years the only candidate for overtaking anybody very much is Japan, and if Japan continues to have a low coefficient of disagreeability this will not cause any serious trouble. The Soviet Union is not going to overtake the United States. The only possibility would be a united Europe, which would then be

[1] K. E. Boulding, "The Parameters of Politics," University of Illinois Bulletin, July 15, 1966.

an economic power certainly comparable to the United States and much larger than the Soviet Union, but this seems rather unlikely at least in the next fifty years. It is not implausible, therefore, to suppose that the period ahead will be one of smaller strain on the international system than the preceding period. Whether the system breaks, of course, depends not only on the strain but also on its strength, and there is certainly no guarantee that the international system will not break down to create a major war in the next fifty years. But the existence of the international institutions (weak as they are—for altogether they are not much bigger than the Ford Foundation), plus the genuine fear of nuclear warfare on the part of the elite, certain increases in communication, and perhaps a lessening of general revolutionary disagreeability in the Socialist countries, all contribute to a modest optimism for the long-run picture.

In the poor countries, of course, the picture is much less favorable. The relative failure of development, the internal strains within these countries, and the continued competition of the two economic systems for their support make the possibility of minor breakdowns occurring a great one, any one of which could easily lead to a major one.

Another consideration which might lead to a modestly optimistic conclusion is the increasing internal pressure in virtually every country for a civilian government as opposed to national defense. We see this manifested in the United States in the last year or so in the form of the Committee on New Priorities, the Proxmire Committee, and so on. Perhaps this reflects the psychological end of the Great Depression: We have now had a whole generation without major unemployment, the number of people who were deeply traumatized by the Great Depression is diminishing every year, and the number of people who do not remember it at all is increasing all the time. This means that, until recently, we have passed from an essentially depression psychology to a full-employment psychology. Paradoxically, this reintroduces scarcity as a major political element. As long as we have a depression psychology, as do most labor leaders since almost all of them belonged to the depression-traumatized generation, we have the feeling that war is virtually costless because the alternative is simply unemployment. In other words, we can have guns and butter too. On the other hand, if we have full employment it becomes very clear that a dollar increase in the war industry is a dollar decrease from something and somebody else. What the history of the last twenty years suggests is that the "somebody else" is most likely to be civilian government, especially state and local government. Within state and local government, oddly enough, one of the relatively vulnerable areas is the police. Another is welfare, and while education is apparently less vulnerable, this is mainly because the education industry has been undergoing a period of enormous expansion, which has masked the fact that it stands to lose from an increase in the military.

Another consideration is that agriculture has now declined to the point where it is no longer a substantial labor force reserve for other occupations. The expansion of the war industry in this country has been made possible without any diminution in civilian disposable incomes, mainly because of the extraordinary technological change in agriculture, which has released millions of agricultural laborers into other occupations. Now only about 6 per cent of the labor force is in agriculture, so that even if agricultural productivity more than doubles in the next generation, as it did in the last, the most we can hope for is the release of some 3 per cent of the labor force from agriculture. The only great reserve of the labor force is now in the war industry, so that if we want to expand either civilian government or the private sector of the economy, we have nowhere else to turn except to the war industry as a source of released labor. Consequently, the feeling that the war industry is a burden and not an asset to the economy is likely to increase all the time, as the realization of its real cost becomes clearer. This happened perhaps a generation earlier in England, where the pressures of the claims on the economy from civilian government was an important factor in the abandonment of Britain's status as a great imperial power. The feeling of young people today in the United States that they are being "screwed" by the war industry is so strong that it would be very surprising if this feeling does not increase as these young people mature into voters.

On the pessimistic side are the potential instabilities of the international system which are still very great, although we might at the same time be encouraged by the further cooling of the Cold War. Recent developments in Germany are particularly encouraging on this score, and the possibility of stable peace in Europe certainly does not seem hopeless. The greatest danger at the moment is unquestionably the Middle East, where there is a disastrous effort being exerted to ally the United States with Israel and the Soviet Union with the Arabs. This seems to be almost the only thing on the horizon at the moment which could bring about a third World War, and an agreement among all the major powers to quarantine the Near East would seem to be absolutely essential for the future of mankind. It is most regrettable that President Nixon has not made moves in this direction, for the internal political situation would certainly have allowed him to do so.

A very important potential source of increased military expenditure anywhere is "irredenta," that is, the failure of political boundaries to coincide with cultural or community boundaries. Most existing boundaries have been established by some exercise of a threat system, and it takes a threat system to maintain them. On the other hand, where boundaries can be taken off everybody's agenda, the need for the use of threats very much diminishes, as we see for instance in North America and Scandinavia. As far as the world as a whole is concerned, we can detect both hopeful and pessimistic aspects of this situation. For almost the first time in European history national boundaries nearly coincide with cultural boundaries. All the Poles are in Poland, all the Germans are in one or other of the two Germanys, all the French are in France, and so on. There are one or two exceptions, like the German-speaking Italian Tyrole, and of course the very fact that there are two Germanys, but this situation is certainly much better than ever before.

In Africa, by contrast, the boundaries of the new nations are arbitrary, often meaningless, and in fact set up by some highly accidental decisions at the Treaty of Berlin in 1878. Nearly all the new African states are heterogeneous in regard to tribe and language, and furthermore many relatively homogeneous communities straddle the new national boundaries. The tragedy of Biafra is a tragedy of heterogeneity, but there are many other potential tragedies of this kind. There are also many places, notably the Somalia borders, where a relatively homogeneous society is divided by the new national boundaries. There are similar problems, especially of heterogeneity, in India and Thailand. The dispute between the Soviet Union and China is in large measure a matter of the accidental character of historical borders. In Latin America a slightly different problem exists—the division of a relatively homogeneous linguistic and cultural area into a number of different states, again with highly arbitrary historical borders. When borders are completely arbitrary and meaningless it may be easier to take them off everybody's agenda as we have done, for instance, between the states in the United States, though even here the heterogeneity of the society gave rise to a bloody civil war.

One cause for hope in this situation is that the most powerful countries have the least border problems. Hence, if the major powers could quarantine the unsettled parts of the world and leave these areas to work out their own problems without any intervention, we would have a much better chance of surviving the next hundred years.

It is virtually impossible to be anything but inconclusive about the future of the international system, simply because of its enormous sensitivity and unpredictability. But turning now to the internal scene in the United States, it may be possible to speculate on the role and legitimacy of the military and the nature of the national image. The Vietnam war has done a great deal to destroy the legitimacy of the military in the United States and even a certain amount to destroy the legitimacy of established government, as we see in the enormous volume of protest. The Mobilization of November 1969 was certainly unprecedented in the history of any modern nation. This is partly perhaps because of the cruel and unusual weapons used in the war, especially napalm and defoliation, and also the failure of the war itself to establish a satisfactory regime. The military derive legitimacy mainly from a sense that they present a "necessary evil." Their legitimacy rests on what might be called the "myth of defense," that they protect a society against the threats of external enemies. Like all myths, of course, this has some origin in the real world, but even at best it represents a grossly over-simplified view of the nature of the international system. When, however, the military are used as an instrument of positive policy rather than as a reaction to a clearly per-ceived threat, a divorce between the military and society easily takes place. This indeed has been the prime mistake of the intellectual hawks who have thought that one can use violence without being changed by it, and use the military as a delicate instrument of national policy.

The only way to answer this challenge to the legitimacy of the military is by a shift in the national image of the national interest. That the national interest is a variable in the system and not a constant is an extremely important notion, and one that may have a great impact on the international system. Certainly the United States has a wide range of choices in this matter, and a shift in the national image toward a more modest and noninterventionist posture is almost the only ra-tional response that a military establishment threatened with a decline in legitimacy can make. It would not be at all sur-prising to see a continual rise in internal pressure on the mili-tary in the United States and a continued attempt to cut the military budget, barring some unforeseen deterioration in the international system. This expectation rests both, as it were, on supply and on demand. What the military have to supply has become much less attractive and the alternative domestic costs of the military are rising sharply all the time. Under these circumstances it would certainly not be surprising to see the war industry decline to a considerably lower percentage of the Gross Product in the next ten years.

*   *   *   *

Recent events invite a further comment or two. The extraor-dinary intensity of the reaction in the universities to Presi-dent Nixon's invasion of Cambodia illustrates still further what might be called the "great paradox of Vietnam": the very small dimensions of the war from the point of view of the economy and the enormous internal reaction which it has produced in the field of legitimacy. It is hardly too much to say that the Vietnam war has produced an unprecented split between the academic community and the rest of society in the United States which could be potentially very dangerous for the internal welfare of the whole society. In military and economic terms the invasion of Cambodia seems almost trivial. It has been interpreted symbolically, however, especially by the student generation, as an action with a high chance of prolonging the war, even though the President seems to believe quite honestly that it was designed to shorten it. There has probably never been a period in the history of the United States when the prestige and the legitimacy of the military establishment and even the political establishment have been at such a low level in the academic community.

The particularly disturbing development of the sharp polarization between the academic community and the rest of society is the emerging of "hard hats" that represent perhaps the avant garde of the working class. There is something reminiscent here of the civil war in England between the Cavaliers, represented today by the long-haired, privileged, emancipated, loose-living student generation, and the Roundheads, as represented by the superpatriotic, religious, close-cropped, hardheaded working class. This polarization is fraught with potential danger both to the universities, who may find themselves under very severe financial pressure as a result, and for the society as a whole, which cannot readily afford to lose the legitimacy of its principal knowledge-transmitting and knowledge-expanding structures. If there is one lesson to be learned from the twentieth century, it is surely that the internal consequences of wars are likely to be much greater than their external consequences, win or lose. President Nixon seems to be in the unfortunate position of having taken on by virtue of the aura attached to his office the habits and attitudes of his predecessors who, however, lived in a totally different world. The lines are forming sharply indeed between those committed to the obsolete national image of winning wars, extending power, policing the world, and so on, and a "modest" national image, which is the only one capable of promoting national or even human survival as we move toward the twenty-first century. Fortunately, there are signs in Congress that the battle for a modern national image is not yet lost. In light of the fact, however, that our educational system is mainly designed to fit us into an anachronistic world, it is hard to be very optimistic.

XVIII   What We Should Learn from Vietnam

RICHARD A. FALK

The future of American policy in Asia will be shaped by the ways in which our leaders interpret the Vietnam experience of the last ten years. At present, three principal interpretations of America's long involvement in the Vietnam war are contending for dominant influence. The "lesson of Vietnam," as public officials understand it, will probably be a shifting composite of these three views. All three of them assume in differing degree that the United States should use its military strength to defeat and discourage revolutionary movements in Asian countries and to contain Chinese power.

I find this unfortunate, for each of the most common interpretations is so fundamentally misguided as to preclude enlightened changes in United States policy toward Asia in the seventies. I believe a fourth line of interpretation of American involvement in Vietnam, absent from the debate in Washington, provides a better basis for comprehending the past and planning for the future.

THREE INTERPRETATIONS

We still do not know how the Vietnam war will finally end, and thus we cannot know whether the outcome of the war will be generally understood as an American victory, a stalemate or compromise, an NLF victory, or indeed if there will be any consensus at all. It is already clear that the NLF and North Vietnam have scored an extraordinary success against overwhelming odds, although at a very high cost to themselves in blood and destruction. But it remains impossible to tell whether the war will eventually end because the Saigon regime collapses, because domestic dissent in America causes a rapid and total United States withdrawal, or, conversely, because the United States launches some desperate kind of re-escalation, or even because a negotiated compromise is worked out in Paris at some point. Future American policy in Asia will depend heavily on how the final outcome in Vietnam is actually perceived by policy makers. At this point, however, it seems fair to suppose an inconclusive ending to the war with enough ambiguity to support a number of differing interpretations on who won and who lost what. We can also suppose that regardless of the outcome, a consensus will emerge around the conclusion that American involvement in Vietnam was too costly to serve as a model for future United States foreign policy.

Despite these imponderables, three different interpretations dominate the Vietnam debate at the present time: that the war has been

Position 1: A qualified success;
Position 2: A failure of proportion;
Position 3: A qualified failure of tactics.

Position 1—that the war has been a qualified success—is the view of most professional military men and the American Right. They see American involvement in Vietnam as a proper exercise of military power, but feel that our effort has been compromised by presidential insistence on pursuing limited ends by limited means. They criticize Washington for seeking "settlement" rather than "victory," and join the Left in condemning President Johnson for his failure to declare war on North Vietnam. They argue that our armed forces have had to fight the war with one hand tied behind their backs, pointing to the refusal to authorize bombing the dikes in North Vietnam, restrictions on targets in Hanoi and Haiphong, and the failure to impose a blockade on shipping to North Vietnam.

Even though victory has not been sought by all means at our disposal, this view does not regard the Vietnam war as a failure. In a characteristic statement, Colonel William C.

Moore of Bolling Air Force Base, writing in the *Air University Review,* argues: "There is reason to believe that Ho Chi Minh would never have initiated action in Vietnam had he vaguely suspected that United States determination would escalate the war to its current magnitude. There is also reason to believe that this lesson has not been lost on other would-be aggressors." Such an interpretation of the lesson of Vietnam relies on two assumptions: first, that the Vietnam war was similar to the Korean war in which the United States may also have shrunk back from the complete execution of its mission, but in which it at least displayed a willingness to defend a non-Communist country against attack by a Communist aggressor. Position 1 sees the Vietnam war as a war of conquest by one country against another, the NLF as a mere agent of Hanoi whose role is to pretend that the war is a civil war and thereby discourage an effective response. In short, Position 1 accepts fully the view presented during the Johnson presidency by Dean Rusk and Walt Rostow. The implication for the future is that the United States is not about to be fooled into treating Communist-led insurgencies any differently from outright Communist aggression against a friendly state.

The second assumption of Colonel Moore's assessment has an even greater implication for the future because it views Vietnam as demonstrating that deterrence works in a counter-insurgency setting as well as it has worked in the nuclear setting. In Colonel Moore's words: "This willingness to escalate is the key to deterring future aggressions at the lower end of the spectrum of war. This, I think, is why history will be kind to President Johnson and Secretary of State Rusk, because if we continue to stand firm in Vietnam as they advocate, then the world will have made incalculable progress toward eliminating war as the curse of mankind."[1] Thus, the key to the future is American willingness to escalate the conflict to high levels of destructivity—so high, in fact, that no prudent revolutionary would ever initiate a war if confronted by such a prospect. Position 1 is critical of Johnson's war diplomacy

[1] Colonel William C. Moore, "History, Vietnam, and the Concept of Deterrence," *Air University Review,* XX (September–October 1969), pp. 58–63.

only insofar as it failed to carry the logic of escalation to higher levels on the battlefield and at home.

This interpretation also claims that the American decision to fight in Vietnam gained time for other anti-Communist regimes in Asia to build up their capacities for internal security and national defense, assuming that the American effort in Vietnam created a shield that held back the flow of revolutionary forces across the continent of Asia. More extravagant exponents of this line of interpretation even contend, on the most slender evidence, that the Indonesian generals would not have reacted so boldly and successfully to the Communist bid for power in Djakarta in October 1965 had not the American presence in Vietnam stiffened their resolve.

Advocates of Position 1 tend to admire the Dominican intervention of 1965, where massive force was used and results quickly achieved with little loss of life. The domestic furor over the Dominican intervention disappeared quickly, mainly as a consequence of its success and brevity. Sophisticated adherents to Position 1 admire the Soviet intervention of August 1968 in Czechoslovakia for similar reasons. This model of overwhelming capability (rather than the slow escalation of capability as in Vietnam) is likely to influence the doctrine and future proposals of those who favor interventionary diplomacy.

The second position—that the war is a failure of proportion —is widely held by American liberals. They feel that the Vietnam war was a mistake from the moment President Johnson decided in 1965 to bomb North Vietnam and to introduce large numbers of American ground combat forces. Position 2 also, by and large, rejects the notion that the war was caused by the aggression of one state against another, but views Vietnam instead as an international civil war in which both sides have received considerable outside support. One of the most revealing formulations of this position is found in Townsend Hoopes's book, *The Limits of Intervention*. Mr. Hoopes, who served in the Pentagon from January 1965 to February 1969, first as Deputy Assistant Secretary of Defense for International Security Affairs and then as Under Secretary of the Air Force, explains the failure of Vietnam as the result of a loss of a sense of proportion by decision makers at the top. He

builds a convincing insider's case that Johnson and his principal advisers were locked into a rigidly doctrinaire view of
the war and hence were unable to moderate their objectives
to conform with the costs in blood, dollars, and domestic cohesion. Writing of the situation prevailing in Washington late
in 1967, just a few months before Johnson's withdrawal
speech of March 31, 1968, Hoopes says: "The incredible disparity between the outpouring of national blood and treasure
and the intrinsic United States interests at stake in Vietnam
was by this time widely understood and deplored at levels
just below the top of the government. But the President and
the tight group of advisers around him gave no sign of having achieved a sense of proportion." Such a view of the lesson
of Vietnam had no quarrel with our initial objective to defend
Saigon and defeat the NLF, but urged that our effort to do so
be abandoned if it could not be made to succeed within a
reasonable time and at a reasonable cost. Many members of
government during the Kennedy period who originally supported America's role in Vietnam later came to hold similar
views, concluding either that the war was weakening our
ability to uphold more significant interests in Europe and the
Middle East, or that the disproportionate costs of the Vietnam
war deprived the country of energies and resources that were
desperately needed to solve domestic problems.

Former Ambassador Edwin Reischauer, respected among
liberals, has carried this kind of analysis to a more general
level of interpretation: "The 'central lesson' of Vietnam—at
least as the American public perceives it—is already quite obvious . . . the limited ability of the United States to control at
a reasonable cost the course of events in a nationally aroused
less developed nation. . . . I believe," Reischauer adds,
"that we are moving away from the application to Asia of the
'balance of power' and 'power vacuum' concepts of the Cold
War, and in the process we no doubt will greatly downgrade
our strategic interest in most of the less developed world."[2]
According to Reischauer, the means used in Vietnam were
disproportionate to the end pursued, and, in general, a country

---

[2] Richard N. Pfeffer (ed.), *No More Vietnams?* (New York:
Harper & Row, 1968), pp. 267–68.

like the United States cannot effectively use its military power to control the outcome of Vietnam-type struggles.

David Mozingo takes this argument one step further, recognizing the need for a perspective on Asia that is suited to the special historical and political conditions prevailing there, a perspective that might even suggest the end of a rigid policy of containment of China. "Since the Korean war," he argues, "United States policy in Asia has been modeled after the containment doctrine so successfully applied in Europe after 1947. . . . Washington has seen the problem of Chinese power in Asia in much the same light as that posed by Soviet power in Europe and has behaved as if both threats could be contained by basically the same kind of responses. In Asia," Mozingo continues, "the containment doctrine has been applied in an area where a nation-state system is only beginning to emerge amidst unpredictable upheavals of a kind that characterized Europe three centuries earlier. . . . The kinds of American technical and economic power that could help restore the historic vitality of the European system would seem at best to have only partial relevance to the Asian situation."[3] Such a view of the Vietnam experience supports a policy that emphasizes a more specific, less abstract appreciation of how to relate American economic, military, and political power to a series of particular struggles for control going on in various Asian countries.

Among the lessons drawn from Vietnam is the futility of aiding a foreign regime that lacks the capacity to govern its society and the conclusion that certain types of intervention, if carried too far, help produce results that are the opposite of the goals of the intervener. The American failure in Vietnam is partly laid to ignorance about Vietnamese realities and partly to exaggerated confidence in the ability of massive military intervention to fulfill political objectives. This is essentially the view of Stanley Hoffmann.[4] Again, as with Hoopes, the search is for an effective foreign policy, combined with a sense of proportion and an awareness of the inherent limits

[3] David P. Mozingo, *The United States in Asia: Evolution and Containment* (New York: Council on Religion and International Affairs, 1967), pp. 7–8.

[4] See esp. Hoffmann in Pfeffer (ed.), *op. cit.*, pp. 193–203.

imposed on American policy. But, like Colonel Moore's interpretation, this liberal critique does not repudiate American objectives in Vietnam. The main lesson for the future, according to Professor Samuel Huntington, who served as head of Hubert Humphrey's Vietnam task force during the 1968 presidential campaign, is to keep Vietnam-type involvements in the future "reasonably limited, discreet, and covert."[5]

The third, and now dominant interpretation of the Vietnam war—that it is a qualified failure of tactics—is the one favored by President Nixon and such important foreign policy advisers as Henry Kissinger, William Rogers, and Melvin Laird. The Nixon doctrine, announced at Guam on July 25, 1969, is an explicit effort to avoid repeating the mistakes of Vietnam, as these leaders understand them, without altering the basic mission of American policy in Asia. The Nixon administration is critical of the Vietnam effort to the extent that it believes the same ends could have been achieved at lesser cost in American blood and treasure, and, as a result, with less strain on American society. In his November 3, 1969 address on Vietnam, President Nixon explained the Nixon doctrine as embodying "three principles as guidelines for future American policy toward Asia": "First, the United States will keep all of its treaty commitments. Secondly, we shall provide a shield if a nuclear power threatens the freedom of a nation allied with us or of a nation whose survival we consider vital to our security. Third, in cases involving other types of aggression, we shall furnish military and economic assistance when requested in accordance with our treaty commitments. But we shall look to the nation directly threatened to assume the primary responsibility of providing the manpower for its defense." The "central thesis" of the doctrine, according to the President, is ". . . that the United States will participate in the defense and development of allies and friends, but that America cannot—and will not—conceive *all* the plans, design *all* the programs, execute *all* the decisions and undertake *all* the defense of the free nations of the world. We will help where it makes a real difference and is considered in our interest."

Thus, the Nixon doctrine backs a step away from the

[5] *Ibid.,* p. 255.

world order absolutism of Johnsonian diplomacy and instead advocates specific assessments of each potential interventionary situation in terms of its strategic importance to the United States and the ability of America to control the outcome. It is difficult, however, to extract much sense of concrete policy from the rhetoric of the State of the World message to Congress February 18, 1970: "The fostering of self-reliance is the new purpose and direction of American involvement in Asia."

In practical terms, such a position seems midway between those of Colonel Moore and Mr. Hoopes: Uphold *all* treaty commitments, give *all* allied regimes our help and advice, but get fully involved in a direct military way only when vital interests are at stake and when the military instrument can be used effectively, which means successfully, quickly and without losing too many American lives. "Vietnamization," as one expression of the Nixon doctrine, leaves the main burden of ground combat to Saigon's armed forces, without any reduction in logistic support, B-52 air strikes and long-distance artillery support. Ambassador Ellsworth Bunker is reported to have said that the policy of Vietnamization involves only changing the color of the bodies. Another expression of the Nixon doctrine seems to be an escalation of American involvement in Laos, increasing our covert role in training and financing government forces and staging saturation bombing raids on contested areas, thereby causing a new flow of refugees and seeking to deprive the Pathet Lao of its rural population base.

A CRITIQUE

These three positions identify the present boundaries of serious political debate in the United States. It is likely that the early seventies will witness a struggle for ascendancy between the advocates of the liberal view (Position 2) and the advocates of the Nixon doctrine (Position 3). Extending the doctrine of deterrence to counterinsurgency situations (Position 1) could gain support if the political forces behind George Wallace or Barry Goldwater gained greater influence as "a third force" in American politics or significantly increased their already strong influence within the Agnew-Mitchell wing of the Nixon administration.

Position 1 accepts "victory" as the proper goal of the American involvement in Vietnam and regards the means used as appropriate to the end of defeating the insurgency in South Vietnam, whether that insurgency is viewed as a species of civil war or as an agency of North Vietnamese aggression. In contrast, Position 2 shifted away from victory as a goal and moved toward the advocacy of some kind of mutual withdrawal of foreign forces and toward some effort to reach a settlement by nonmilitary means once it became evident that the means required for the more ambitious goal were so costly in lives, dollars, and domestic support. Position 3 specifies the goal of the involvement as obtaining conditions of self-determination for South Vietnam and its present governing regime, a position that seems to imply an outcome of the war that is close to total victory; however, there is a certain ambiguity as to whether the real goals are not more modest than the proclaimed goals. In any event, Position 3 regards the means used to have been unnecessarily costly, given the goals of the involvement, and accepts, at least in theory, the desirability of a nonmilitary outcome through a negotiated settlement of the war.

Position 1 seems to interpret Vietnam as a qualified success and to favor, if anything, a less constrained military effort in the future to defeat any Communist-led insurgencies that may erupt on the Asian mainland in the 1970s. As with strategic doctrine, the deterrence of insurgent challenges rests on the possession of a credible capability and on a willingness to respond with overwhelming military force to any relevant challenge.

Position 2, which is much less tied to an overall doctrine, views the post-Kennedy phases of the Vietnam involvement as a clear mistake and argues for a much greater emphasis on nonmilitary responses to insurgent challenges. This position also seeks to limit overt intervention to situations in which its impact can be swift and effective. Position 2, therefore, depends on having a fairly secure regime in power in the country that is the scene of the struggle. It also emphasizes keeping a sense of proportion throughout such an involvement, either by way of a ceiling on the magnitude of the commitment or by way of a willingness to liquidate an unsuccessful commitment.

Position 3 is midway between the first two positions in tone and apparent emphasis. It develops a more globalist strategy, emphasizing that the United States has far-flung treaty relations with Asian countries and that it is important to our overall preeminence in world affairs and the continuing need to resist Communist pressures that these commitments be honored. The merits of the particular case are thus tied to a global strategy, but there is an effort to shift more of the burdens of response to the local government. What this means in those cases where the government cannot meet these burdens, as was surely the case in Vietnam all along, is very unclear. What happens under Position 3 when self-reliance fails? The prevailing response to this question may well determine the central line of American foreign policy in Asia throughout the 1970s.

Both Positions 2 and 3 look toward Japan as a more active partner in the development of a common Asian policy. President Nixon's decision to return Okinawa to Japan by 1972 arises out of this hope for sharing the geopolitical burdens of the region with Japan in the mid and late seventies.

What is most surprising about these three positions is the extent to which they accept the premise of an American counterrevolutionary posture toward political conflict in Asia. To be clear, however, this espousal of counterrevolutionary doctrine is applicable only in situations that appear to be revolutionary. Where there is no formidable radical challenge on the domestic scene, as in India or Japan, the American preference is clearly for moderate democracy, indeed the kind of political orientation that the United States imposed upon Japan during the military occupation after World War II. However, where an Asian society is beset by struggle between a rightist incumbent regime and a leftist insurgent challenger, then American policy throws its support, sometimes strongly, to the counterrevolutionary side. As a result, there has been virtually no disposition to question the American decision to support the repressive and reactionary Saigon regime provided that support could have led to victory in Vietnam at a reasonable cost. In fact, the last four American Presidents have been in agreement on the political wisdom of the decision to help Saigon prevail in its effort to create a strong anti-Communist state in South Vietnam, thereby defying both the military results of the first Indochina war and the explicit provisions on the reunification of Vietnam embodied in the Geneva Accords of 1954. Positions 1 and 3 share an acceptance, although to varying degrees, of the basic postulates of "the domino theory." Position 2 is least inclined to endorse the image of falling dominoes, and some of its adherents (such as Donald Zagoria in *China in Crisis*) indeed argue that the prospects for communism need to be assessed on a country-by-country basis, and the success or failure of communism in Vietnam or Laos will not necessarily have much impact upon the prospect for revolution in other Asian countries.

McGeorge Bundy, a belated convert to Position 2 (after an earlier allegiance to the moderate form of Position 1), gave up on the war because its burden was too great on American society. Nevertheless, he took pains to reaffirm the wisdom of the original undertaking: "I remind you also, if you stand on the other side, that my argument against escalation and against an indefinite continuation of our present course has been based not on moral outrage or political hostility to the objective, but rather on the simple and practical ground that escalation will not work and that a continuation of our present course is unacceptable."[6] Arthur Schlesinger, Jr., has said: "The tragedy of Vietnam is the tragedy of the overextension and misapplication of valid principles. The original insights of collective security and liberal evangelism were generous and wise."[7] Actually, adherents of Position 2, while sharply dissenting from the Vietnam policies of both Johnson and Nixon, still maintain the spirit of an earlier statement by McGeorge Bundy, made at a time when he was rallying support for Johnson's air war against North Vietnam: "There are wild

[6] McGeorge Bundy, "De Pauw Address" in Falk (ed.), *The Vietnam War and International Law, II* (1969).

[7] Arthur Schlesinger, Jr., "Vietnam and the End of the Age of Superpowers," *Harper's* (March 1969), pp. 41–49.

men in the wings, but on the main stage even the argument on Vietnam turns on tactics, not fundamentals."[8]

Unfortunately, from my perspective, these so-called wild men still remain in the wings, if anything, further removed than ever from the center of the political stage, for positions 1, 2, and 3 all affirm the continuing wisdom of two American objectives in Asia: first, to prevent Chinese expansion, if necessary by military means, and second, to prevent any anti-Communist regime, however repressive, reactionary, or isolated from popular support, from being toppled by internal revolutionary forces, whether or not abetted by outside help.

THE EXCLUDED FOURTH POSITION

There is another interpretation which has been largely excluded from the public dialogue thus far. It repudiates our present objectives in Vietnam on political and moral grounds. It holds, *first,* there is no reason to believe that China has expansive military aims in Asia; *second,* even if China were militarily expansive, it would not be desirable or necessary for the United States to defend China's victims; and *third,* there is neither occasion nor justification for aiding repressive governments merely because they follow anti-Communist policies. I favor this fourth position for several good reasons. There is no evidence that China needs containing by an American military presence in Asia. Of course, countries in the shadow of a dominant state tend to fall under the influence of that state whenever it is effectively governed. This process is universal and has deep historical roots in Asia. But there are important countervailing forces.

First, China is preoccupied with its own domestic politics and with principal foreign struggles against the Soviet Union and Formosa. Second, many of the countries surrounding China have struggled at great sacrifice to achieve independence, and their search for domestic autonomy is much stronger than any common ideological sentiment that might tempt Asian Communist regimes to subordinate their independence

[8] McGeorge Bundy, "The End of Either/Or," *Foreign Affairs,* XLV, pp. 189–201.

to Peking. Third, China's foreign policy may often have
been crude and ill-conceived, but it has rarely exhibited any
intention to rely on military force to expand its influence beyond its boundaries; its uses of force against India, Tibet,
and the Soviet Union have been to support its claims to dis-
puted territory, and its entry into the Korean war seemed motivated mainly by a reasonable concern about danger to its
industrial heartland.

The evidence thus suggests that the American effort to contain China in Asia is a determination to contend with a paper
tiger.

More significantly, the multifaceted conflicts in Asia cannot
be comprehended in abstract or ideological terms. Asia is undergoing a two-phase revolution that began as a struggle
against colonialism during World War II and will continue for
at least another decade. The first phase represented the struggle to reacquire national control over the apparatus of government by defeating foreign rule. This struggle is largely com-
pleted. In most parts of Asia the colonial system has collapsed
and foreigners have been removed from power. But in several
Asian countries, including South Vietnam, the native groups
allied with the colonial system have clung to political power,
stifling social progress and economic reform. Thailand, although never formally a colony, continues to be governed
by a traditional elite that is ill-inclined to initiate the reforms
needed to build a society devoted to the welfare of its population as a whole.

After formal independence is won, the second phase of
Asian national revolutions involves continuing struggle against
the residues of the colonial system, including the more informal patterns of domination that result from American donations of military equipment, foreign aid, and political and
economic advice. Most governments in Asia today are composed of conservative forces that hold onto their positions of
power and privilege with the aid of such donations and advice, usually at the expense of their own people. Therefore,
the second phase of the revolutionary struggle involves wrest-
ing political control from traditional ruling classes and in-
stituting a mass-based program of land reform, education,

public hygiene, and economic development. In most of Asia, aside from India, the United States is allied with regimes that are trying to hold back this second surge of the revolutionary impulse that has swept across the Third World to crush the colonial system.

Position 4 accepts this analysis of political conflict in Asia and would adjust American policy accordingly. First of all, it seeks accommodation with China through a flexible compromise of outstanding issues, including the future of Formosa. What is implied here is the removal of the American military presence from the area, especially the withdrawal of the Seventh Fleet and the elimination of our military bases on Formosa. Such a course would leave the outcome of the Chinese civil war, which has not yet been fully resolved, to the contending forces on both sides. It would encourage the possibility of negotiations between Peking and Taipei as to the governance of Formosa, perhaps allowing for semiautonomous status within the Chinese People's Republic, with guarantees of a measure of economic and political independence for the island.

An American accommodation with China would help the United States handle an increasingly competitive economic relationship with Japan in the 1970s and give Washington more bargaining power in relation to the Soviet Union. More importantly, accommodation with China could make it possible to proceed more rapidly with arms control and disarmament, to denuclearize world politics, and to resist pressures to proliferate weapons of mass destruction to additional countries.

Position 4 favors as well a total abandonment of America's counterrevolutionary foreign policy. This would mean renouncing all treaty relations with governments that are repressing their own populations and holding back the forces of self-determination. Clearly such a revision of policy would require the renunciation of American treaty obligations to promote the security of the regimes now governing South Vietnam, Cambodia, Laos, South Korea, Formosa, Thailand, and the Philippines. The only commitment that should be reaffirmed is our obligation under the U.N. Charter to resist overt military aggression of the Korea type. Position 4 would imply an end to large-scale military assistance and covert interference in the affairs of Asian countries. Civil strife is likely to occur in several Asian countries and dislodge present governments, but to the extent that it tends to reflect the true balance of political forces within these national societies, it would be beneficial for the welfare of the population and for the stability of each country and the region. At present, several regimes are being maintained in power only through a combination of domestic oppression and American support.

There seems virtually no prospect for the adoption, or even the discussion, of Position 4 during the 1970s unless major shifts in American political life occur. Only extraordinary domestic pressure, fueled perhaps by economic troubles at home and foreign policy setbacks abroad, are likely to produce a change of leadership and a change of world outlook in America.

Yet in historic retrospect, it is important to appreciate that Position 4 once was close to being our foreign policy. Its rejection by today's American leaders is not an inevitable outcome of United States policy in Asia after World War II. Franklin Roosevelt was opposed to restoring the French colonial administration in Indochina at the end of the war. If Indochina had been allowed to become independent after the Japanese left, Ho Chi Minh would clearly have emerged as the leader of a united Vietnam, and perhaps of a united Indochina. In his initial Proclamation of Independence of September 25, 1945, Ho Chi Minh explicitly referred to the French and American revolutions as the main sources of inspiration for the Vietnamese struggle for national independence. The Communist response was not altogether enthusiastic —the Soviet Union initially withheld recognition from Ho Chi Minh's Republic of Vietnam, and in 1947, Maurice Thorez, the Communist Vice-Premier of France, actually countersigned the order for French military action against the newly proclaimed Republic. As O. E. Clubb points out: "In 1945 and 1946 the Ho Chi Minh government looked mainly to the United States and Nationalist China for foreign political support."[9] In the period since World War II anti-colonialism probably would have been a better guideline for American foreign policy in Asia than anti-communism. And even now it would make better sense. It would work better because it accords more closely with historic trends in Asia, with the dynamics of national self-determination in most non-Communist Asian countries, and because it flows more naturally out of America's own best heritage and proudest tradition.

[9] Oliver E. Clubb, Jr., *The United States and the Sino-Soviet Bloc in Southeast Asia* (Washington: The Brookings Institution, 1962), p. 15.

Contributors

GRAHAM T. ALLISON is Assistant Professor of Government at the Kennedy Institute of Politics, Harvard University. A former special assistant to Deputy Assistant Secretary of Defense for Arms Control, he is the author of *Bureaucracy and Policy: Conceptual Models and the Cuban Missile Crisis*.

JOHN S. BADEAU is Professor of Middle Eastern Studies at the Edmund A. Walsh School of Foreign Service, Georgetown University. Formerly director of the Middle East Institute at Columbia University and Ambassador from the United States to the United Arab Republic, he is the author of *The American Approach to the Arab World*.

GEORGE W. BALL has served the United States as Undersecretary of State and as Ambassador to the United Nations. His most recent publication is *The Discipline of Power*. He is now an investment banker.

RICHARD J. BARNET is codirector of the Institute for Policy Studies, Washington, D.C., and was formerly a member of United States Arms Control and Disarmament Agency and adviser to President Kennedy. He has authored *Intervention and Revolution* and *The Economy of Death*, and has coauthored (with Marcus Raskin) *After 20 Years: The Decline of NATO and the Search for a New Policy in Europe*.

KENNETH E. BOULDING is Professor of Economics and is director of the Program of Research on General Social and

Economic Dynamics, Institute of Behavioral Sciences, at the University of Colorado. A former president of the American Economics Association, he numbers among his many publications *Conflict and Defense, Disarmament and the Economy, The Meaning of the Twentieth Century,* and *Beyond Economics.*

INIS L. CLAUDE, JR., is Professor of Government and Foreign Affairs at the University of Virginia, and serves as consultant to the State Department. He is the author of *Swords into Plowshares, Power and International Relation,* and *The Changing United Nations.*

WILLIAM D. COPLIN is Associate Professor of Political Science at the Maxwell School, Syracuse University, where he is currently director of the International Relations Program. He has authored *The Functions of International Law* and *Introduction to International Politics,* and has edited *Simulation in the Study of Politics.*

RICHARD A. FALK is Albert G. Milbank Professor of International Law and Practice at Princeton University. He serves on the World Law Fund and has authored, among others, *Law, Morality and War in the Contemporary World; The Role of Domestic Courts in the International Legal Order;* and co-edited *The Strategy of World Order* and *International Law and Organization.*

MORTON A. KAPLAN is Professor of Political Science and chairman of the Committee on International Relations at the University of Chicago. Among his publications are *System and Process in International Politics, The Political Foundations of International Law* (with Nicholas Katzenbach), and *Great Issues of International Politics.*

LESLIE M. LIPSON is Professor of Political Science at the University of California at Berkeley. Among his many books are *The Democratic Civilization, The Great Issues of Politics,* and *The Politics of Equality.*

ERNEST R. MAY is Professor of History at Harvard University and Dean of Harvard College. He is the author of *The American Image, American Imperialism,* and *The World War and American Isolation.*

MARTIN C. NEEDLER is Professor of Political Science and director of the Division of Inter-American Affairs at the University of New Mexico. He has written *Understanding Foreign Policy* and *Latin American Politics in Perspective,* and has edited *Dimensions of American Foreign Policy.*

JOSEPH S. NYE, JR., is Associate Professor of Government and program director, Center for International Affairs, Harvard University. He is the author of *Pan-Africanism and East African Integration* and has edited *International Regionalism.*

MICHAEL K. O'LEARY is Associate Professor of Political Science at the Maxwell School, Syracuse University. He has authored *The Politics of American Foreign Aid* and coauthored *Congress in Crisis,* and has contributed chapters to a number of other books.

RICHARD L. PARK is Professor of Political Science at the University of Michigan, where he is an associate of the Center for South and Southeast Asian Studies. He has coauthored *Leadership and Political Institutions in India* and *U. S. Foreign Policy: Asia.*

MARSHALL D. SHULMAN is Professor of Political Science and director of the Russian Institute at Columbia University. Formerly president of the American Association for the Advancement of Slavic Studies and a special assistant to the State Department, he is the author of *Beyond the Cold War* and *Stalin's Foreign Policy Reappraised.*

MAX SINGER is president of the Hudson Institute, which he helped found, as well as a member of the Bar of New York State and the District of Columbia. He is a specialist in national security policy and arms control.

IMMANUEL WALLERSTEIN is Professor of Sociology and chairman of the Seminar on Africa at Columbia University. He is the author of *Africa: The Politics of Independence, Social Change: The Colonial Situation,* and *Africa: The Politics of Unity.*

AARON WILDAVSKY is Professor of Political Science and chairman of the Department at the University of California, Berkeley. Among his publications are *Presidential Elections* (with Nelson Polsby), *The Politics of the Budgetary Process,* and *Dixon-Yates: A Study in Power Politics.*

ADAM YARMOLINSKY is Professor of Law at Harvard University. He was formerly special assistant to the Secretary of Defense and Deputy Assistant Secretary of Defense for International Security Affairs. He recently authored *The Military Establishment: Its Impacts on American Society.*

ANCHOR BOOKS

GOVERNMENT AND POLITICAL SCIENCE